ISRAEL AND THE ASSYRIANS

Society of Biblical Literature

Ancient Near East Monographs

Number 8
ISRAEL AND THE ASSYRIANS
Deuteronomy, the Succession Treaty of Esarhaddon,
and the Nature of Subversion

ISRAEL AND THE ASSYRIANS
Deuteronomy, the Succession Treaty of Esarhaddon, and the Nature of Subversion

C. L. Crouch

SBL Press
Atlanta

The Ancient Near East Monographs/Monografi as Sobre El Antiguo Cercano Oriente series is published jointly by SBL Press and the Universidad Católica Argentina Facultad de Ciencias Sociales, Políticas y de la Comunicación, Centro de Estudios de Historia del Antiguo Oriente.

For further information, see:
http://www.sbl-site.org/publications/Books_ANEmonographs.aspx
http://www.uca.edu.ar/cehao

Library of Congress Cataloging-in-Publication Data

Crouch, Carly L. (Carly Lorraine), 1982-
  Israel and the Assyrians : Deuteronomy, the succession treaty of Esarhaddon, and the nature of subversion / by C. L. Crouch.
    pages cm. — (Society of Biblical Literature ancient Near East monographs ; volume 8)
  Includes bibliographical references and index.
  Summary: "This volume investigates Deuteronomy's subversive intent within its social context, and reconsiders the relationship between Deuteronomy and Assyria, its relationship to ancient Near Eastern and biblical treaty and loyalty oath traditions, and the relevance of its treaty affinities to discussions of its date"—Provided by publisher.
    ISBN 978-1-62837-025-6 (paper binding : alk. paper) — ISBN 978-1-62837-026-3 (electronic format) — ISBN 978-1-62837-027-0 (hardcover binding : alk. paper)
  1. Assyro-Babylonian literature—Relation to the Old Testament. 2. Bible. Deuteronomy—Criticism, interpretation, etc. 3. Assyria—Religion. 4. Esarhaddon, King of Assyria, -669 B.C. I. Title.
  BS1184.C76 2014
  222'.15067—dc23
                        2014036419

for roo roo

I tell you, Captain, if you look in the maps of the world, I warrant you shall find, in the comparisons between Macedon and Monmouth, that the situations, look you, is both alike. There is a river in Macedon, and there is also moreover a river at Monmouth. It is called Wye at Monmouth; but it is out of my [b]rains what is the name of the other river; but 'tis all one, 'tis alike as my fingers is to my fingers, and there is salmons in both.

Henry V (IV.vii.22-31)

CONTENTS

ACKNOWLEDGEMENTS

Many people have helped to bring this book into existence. Early versions of the material were read at the biblical studies seminars at Durham, Sheffield, and Edinburgh; thanks are due to the chairs—Walter Moberly, Hugh Pyper, and Alison Jack—for their kind invitations as well as to the membership of those seminars for their critical feedback and suggestions, which both encouraged me in my pursuit of the subject and improved my thinking in a number of its particulars. A version was aired in a special session of the Assyriology and the Bible unit at the 2012 SBL in Chicago and I am grateful to my fellow presenters, the chairs, and the audience of that session for making this a useful process. My colleagues at the University of Nottingham deserve mention for supporting my arrival and integration into the department in a manner which allowed me to continue writing alongside my new teaching and administrative responsibilities.

Jonathan Stökl and Casey Strine, despite their divergent chronological opinions on Deuteronomy, have served as vital sounding boards on the nature of subversive activities from the early stages of the project. Jeremy Hutton deserves credit and thanks for making me think more carefully about the nature of translation and for the introduction to Toury, while Seth Sanders has been an appreciated conversation partner on text production and performance. Together these have been collegial interrogators of the ideas put forth here, though they are hardly to blame for any lingering shortcomings. Others have leapt into the bibliographic breach with resources not immediately available to me, and far too many to name have lent their support in other ways. The manuscript itself has gone through iterations too numerous to count and several colleagues have read it in whole or in part at one time or another: the aforementioned, as well as Jacob Lauinger, Daniel Block, Joshua Berman, and the anonymous reviewers.

My mother remains, despite her protestations, the font of all wisdom. My husband has endured a house overrun by books, notebooks, and papers, as well as the myriad other trials which come with proximity to an academic. My father was privy to the early stages of the book while in hospital in February 2012; he did not live to see it in print but his support was ever-present in the months that it took to transform the manuscript from those rough beginnings into its final form. My sister introduced me to Hutcheon and Sanders and lent a modern perspective in our numerous discussions of adaptation and subversion, as well as editing the final manuscript. This one is for her: a once little book for an always little sister.

C. L. Crouch
Nottingham
August 2014

ABBREVIATIONS

AB	Anchor Bible
AHR	*American Historical Review*
AnBib	Analecta biblica
ARA	*Annual Review of Anthropology*
ATD	Das Alte Testament Deutsch
BA	*Biblical Archaeologist*
BASOR	*Bulletin of the American Schools of Oriental Research*
BBR	*Bulletin for Biblical Research*
BBVO	Berliner Beiträge zum Vorderen Orient
BEATAJ	Beiträge zur Erforschung des Alten Testaments und des Antiken Judentum
Bib	*Biblica*
BibOr	Biblica et orientalia
BN	*Biblische Notizen*
BO	*Bibliotheca orientalis*
BSac	*Bibliotheca Sacra*
BZABR	Beihefte zur Zeitschrift für altorientalische und biblische Rechtsgeschichte
BZAW	Beihefte zur Zeitschrift für die alttestamentliche Wissenschaft
CA	*Cultural Anthropology*
CAD	M. T. Roth, ed. *The Assyrian Dictionary*. 21 vols. Chicago, Ill.: The Oriental Institute of the University of Chicago, 1956–2010.
CBQ	*Catholic Biblical Quarterly*
CDOG	Colloquien der Deutschen Orient-Gesellschaft
CHANE	Culture and History of the Ancient Near East

COS   W. W. Hallo and K. L. Younger, Jr., eds. *Context of Scripture*. 3
            vols. Leiden: Brill, 1997–.
DCH   D. J. A. Clines, ed. *The Dictionary of Classical Hebrew*. 9 vols.
            Sheffield: Sheffield Phoenix, 1993–2014.
EdF   Erträge der Forschung
FAT   Forschungen zum Alten Testament
FOTL   Forms of Old Testament Literature
FRLANT   Forschungen zur Religion und Literatur des Alten und Neuen
            Testaments
Ges¹⁸   U. Rüterswörden, R. Meyer, and H. Donner, eds. *Wilhelm
            Gesenius' Hebräisches und aramäisches Handwörterbuch über das
            Alte Testament*. 7 vols. 18th ed. London: Springer, 1987–2012.
HALOT   L. Koehler and W. Baumgartner, eds. *The Hebrew and Aramaic
            Lexicon of the Old Testament*. Translated by M. E. J. Richardson.
            5 vols. Leiden: Brill, 1994–2000.
HAT   Handbuch zum Alten Testament
HBM   Hebrew Bible Monographs
HBS   Herders Biblische Studien
HBT   *Horizons in Biblical Theology*
HTR   *Harvard Theological Review*
HUCA   *Hebrew Union College Annual*
JAA   *Journal of Anthropological Archaeology*
JAJ   *Journal of Ancient Judaism*
JAS   *Journal of Archaeological Science*
JAOS   *Journal of the American Oriental Society*
JBL   *Journal of Biblical Literature*
JCS   *Journal of Cuneiform Studies*
JCSMS   *Journal of the Canadian Society for Mesopotamian Studies*
JEA   *Journal of Egyptian Archaeology*
JHI   *Journal of the History of Ideas*
JNES   *Journal of Near Eastern Studies*
JR   *The Journal of Religion*
JSOT   *Journal for the Study of the Old Testament*
JSOTSup   Journal for the Study of the Old Testament: Supplement
            Series
JSS   *Journal of Semitic Studies*
KTU   M. Dietrich, O. Loretz, and J. Sanmartín. *Die keilalphabetischen
            Texte aus Ugarit, Ras Ibn Hani und anderen Orten (Dritte,
            erweiterte Auflage) / The Cuneiform Alphabetic Texts from Ugarit,
            Ras Ibn Hani and Other Places (KTU: Third, Enlarged Edition)*.
            Münster: Ugarit-Verlag, 2013.
LHBOTS   Library of Hebrew Bible/Old Testament Studies

MQR	*Michigan Quarterly Review*
NCB	New Century Bible
NEchtB	Neue Echter Bibel
OBO	Orbis biblicus et orientalis
OBT	Overtures to Biblical Theology
Or	*Orientalia* (New Series)
OTL	Old Testament Library
OTM	Oxford Theological Monographs
OTS	*Old Testament Studies*
PEQ	*Palestine Exploration Quarterly*
RHR	*Revue de l'histoire des religions*
RINAP	The Royal Inscriptions of the Neo-Assyrian Period
SAA	State Archives of Assyria
SBLABS	Society of Biblical Literature Archaeology and Biblical Studies
SBLMS	Society of Biblical Literature Monograph Series
SBLWAW	Society of Biblical Literature Writings from the Ancient World
SBT	Studies in Biblical Theology
SBTS	Sources for Biblical and Theological Study
Sem	*Semeia*
SSI	*Social Science Information*
TA	*Tel Aviv*
TF	Theologie und Frieden
TSAJ	Texts and Studies in Ancient Judaism
UF	*Ugarit-Forschungen*
VT	*Vetus Testamentum*
VTSup	Supplements to Vetus Testamentum
WO	*Die Welt des Orients*
WUANT	Wissenschaftliche Untersuchungen zum Alten und Neuen Testament
ZABR	*Zeitschrift für altorientalische und biblische Rechtsgeschichte*
ZAW	*Zeitschrift für die alttestamentliche Wissenschaft*
ZDPV	*Zeitschrift des deutschen Palästina-Vereins*

INTRODUCTION

The origins and purpose of the book of Deuteronomy remain, despite significant progress in the two centuries since de Wette, two of the most contested points in biblical scholarship. A prominent feature of attempts to ground the deuteronomic text in a historical context over the last half century has been the observation of certain affinities between Deuteronomy and ancient Near Eastern vassal treaties and loyalty oaths. More specifically, it has been suggested that the book of Deuteronomy, in some more or less original form, constituted a subversive appropriation of Neo-Assyrian imperial ideology in favor of a Yahwistic theocentricity: a text deliberately designed to undermine the authority of the Assyrian king by planting YHWH in his stead. The prevalence of this assertion has its roots in the widespread recognition of similarities between elements of Deuteronomy, especially chapters 13 and 28, and Assyrian vassal treaties and loyalty oaths, with a particular focus on the Succession Treaty of Esarhaddon, commonly referred to as VTE.[1] The

---

[1] This developed out of an older interpretive strand that saw the nearest links to the deuteronomic material in the Hittite treaties. Recent attempts to reassert the connection to the Hittite material include J. Berman, "CTH 133 and the Hittite Provenance of Deuteronomy 13," *JBL* 131 (2011): 25–44 and, more broadly, A. Taggar-Cohen, "Biblical *Covenant* and Hittite *išḫiul* Reexamined," *VT* 61 (2011): 461–88. These attempts have proved controversial; note especially the debate between Berman, Levinson, and Stackert in B. M. Levinson and J. Stackert, "Between the Covenant Code and Esarhaddon's Succession Treaty: Deuteronomy 13 and the Composition of Deuteronomy," *JAJ* 3 (2012): 133–136; J. Berman, "Historicism and Its Limits: A Response to Bernard M. Levinson and Jeffrey Stackert," *JAJ* 4 (2013): 297–309; B. M.

idea that there are extensive allusions to VTE in Deuteronomy has become a persistent element in discussions regarding the origins and purpose of the book.

Although there have been some recent efforts to question the relationship between Deuteronomy and VTE—Koch, Zehnder, and Pakkala most notable among these—the idea that Deuteronomy relies on Assyrian forms and Assyrian ideology in formulating a subversive agenda remains prominent, especially in English-speaking scholarship. The following aims to go beyond the doubt cast on the nature of Deuteronomy's relationship with VTE to question the nature of its relationship with Assyrian ideology more widely and, as a consequence, to challenge the interpretation of the book in subversive terms.

For those already persuaded of the exilic origins of these texts, what follows will be of interest for its methodological implications for the study of subversion elsewhere in the Hebrew Bible. To the extent that arguments for the book's exilic origins have been entwined with arguments regarding the extraction of these subversive chapters from a deuteronomic whole, the critical implications of what follows will need to be absorbed and carried forward. Consideration of the ongoing interpretation and use of the book in the exilic and post-exilic periods will also be affected by the rejection of any subversive intent *vis-à-vis* the Assyrian empire.

It remains the reality of much scholarship on Deuteronomy, however, that the possibility of a pre-exilic date for some form of this text continues to be entertained. Further, there is a very strong correlation between these discussions and discussions of Judah's relationship with the Assyrian empire, of Josiah's relationship with the same, and of Deuteronomy's own relationship with both VTE in particular and Assyrian ideas more generally. It is to this thrust of the scholarly discussion that the current argument is primarily oriented, observing the numerous recent challenges to the traditional reconstructions of the Assyrian period in Judah and taking this as an

---

Levinson and J. Stackert, "The Limitations of »Resonance«: A Response to Joshua Berman on Historical and Comparative Method," *JAJ* 4 (2013): 310–33.

The *editio princeps* for VTE is D. J. Wiseman, "The Vassal Treaties of Esarhaddon," *Iraq* 20 (1958): 1–99; the edition used here is the standard edition of S. Parpola and K. Watanabe, *Neo-Assyrian Treaties and Loyalty Oaths* (SAA 2; Helsinki: Helsinki University Press, 1988). On VTE as a loyalty oath rather than vassal treaty, see I. J. Gelb, Review of D. J. Wiseman, "The Vassal Treaties of Esarhaddon," *BO* 19 (1962): 159–62; M. Weinfeld, "The Loyalty Oath in the Ancient Near East," *UF* 8 (1976): 379–414; see also M. Liverani, "The Medes at Esarhaddon's Court," *JCS* 47 (1995): 57–58, with further references.

opportunity to interrogate one of the most entrenched elements of such reconstructions—that Deuteronomy represents a profoundly anti-Assyrian project—for those who continue to imagine some pre-exilic form of this book.

RECENT SCHOLARSHIP

Scholarship on the relationship of Deuteronomy to VTE and its relatives is divisible into various subcategories. One major focus concerns Deuteronomy's date: those who see the similarities to VTE as constitutive of the book's origin in the Assyrian period, as opposed to those who prefer a later, exilic date for the parts of Deuteronomy which incorporate these treaty and loyalty oath elements.[2] In the former

---

[2] Among the former are included M. Weinfeld, "Traces of Assyrian Treaty Formulae in Deuteronomy," *Bib* 46 (1965): 417–27; idem, "Loyalty Oath"; R. Frankena, "The Vassal-Treaties of Esarhaddon and the Dating of Deuteronomy," *OTS* 14 (1965): 122–54; P. E. Dion, "Deuteronomy 13: The Suppression of Alien Religious Propaganda in Israel during the Late Monarchical Era," in *Law and Ideology in Monarchic Israel* (ed. B. Halpern and D. W. Hobson; JSOTSup 124; Sheffield: JSOT, 1991), 147–216; B. Halpern, "Jerusalem and the Lineages in the Seventh Century BCE: Kinship and the Rise of Individual Moral Liability," in *Law and Ideology in Monarchic Israel* (ed. B. Halpern and D. W. Hobson; JSOTSup 124; Sheffield: JSOT, 1991), 28 n. 20; H. U. Steymans, "Eine assyrische Vorlage für Deuteronomium 28:20–44," in *Bundesdokument und Gesetz: Studien zum Deuteronomium* (ed. G. Braulik; HBS 4; Freiburg: Herder, 1995), 119–41; idem, *Deuteronomium 28 und die adê zur Thronfolgeregelung Asarhaddons: Segen und Fluch im Alten Orient und in Israel* (OBO 145; Göttingen: Vandenhoeck & Ruprecht, 1995); E. Otto, "Treueid und Gesetz: Die Ursprünge des Deuteronomiums im Horizont neuassyrischen Vertragsrechts," *ZABR* 2 (1996): 1–52; idem, *Das Deuteronomium: Politische Theologie und Rechtsreform in Juda und Assyrien* (BZAW 284; Berlin: de Gruyter, 1999); R. D. Nelson, *Deuteronomy* (OTL; London: Westminster John Knox, 2004); B. M. Levinson, "Esarhaddon's Succession Treaty as the Source for the Canon Formula in Deuteronomy 13:1," *JAOS* 130 (2010): 337–48; idem, *"The Right Chorale": Studies in Biblical Law and Interpretation* (Winona Lake, Ind.: Eisenbrauns, 2011), 112–94. Among the latter are A. D. H. Mayes, *Deuteronomy* (NCB; London: Marshall, Morgan & Scott, 1981); T. Veijola, *Das 5. Buch Mose: Deuteronomium. Kapitel 1,1–16,17* (ATD 8,1; Göttingen: Vandenhoeck & Ruprecht, 2004); J. Pakkala, "Der literar- und religionsgeschichtliche Ort von Deuteronomium 13," in *Die deuteronomistischen Geschichtswerke: redaktions- und religionsgeschichtliche Perspektiven zur "Deuteronomismus"-Diskussion in Tora und Vorderen Propheten* (ed. M. Witte, et al.; BZAW 365; Berlin: de Gruyter, 2006), 125–37; C. Koch, *Vertrag, Treueid und Bund: Studien zur Rezeption des altorientalischen Vertragsrechts im Deuteronomium und zur*

category are scholars from the earliest days of research through to more recent studies by Dion, Halpern, Steymans, Otto, and Levinson. Among the earliest to pursue the chronological implications of the similarities between VTE and Deuteronomy was Frankena, who explicitly applied himself to the question of when and how a Judahite scribe might have become familiar with VTE, arguing that such vassal treaties would have been pronounced orally in the presence of vassals assembled in Assyria. He points specifically to reports of an assembly (of Assyrians) in 672 B.C.E. in connection with the installation of Assurbanipal as crown prince as well as lists of western vassal kings, including Manasseh of Judah, that indicate their presence in Assyria for tribute purposes and that, according to Frankena, support the suggestion that they would have been present at the ceremony in 672.[3] More recently, Dion has argued that "the closer to 672 BC one places the composition of Deuteronomy 13, the easier to understand are its precise contacts with the vassal treaties of Esarhaddon," while also contending that the majority of Deuteronomy 13 is a deuteronomistic expansion from the reign of Josiah; he sees the similarities between Deuteronomy and VTE as reflecting the use of VTE by Deuteronomy, at the moment of Assyria's collapse, to articulate non-Yahwistic worship in terms of sedition.[4] Similarly, Levinson's several studies on the relationship between VTE and Deuteronomy suggest a deuteronomic text originating in the Josianic period and using VTE to articulate the concerns of the "historical crisis" of that period.[5] Drawing on some of the same texts as Frankena, Steymans has argued that Manasseh was bound by VTE and thereby the Judahite author(s) of Deuteronomy would have been familiar with it; elsewhere he argues that the elements of Deuteronomy that he traces to VTE should be identified as originating between the proclamation of

---

Ausbildung der Bundestheologie im alten Testament (BZAW 383; Berlin: de Gruyter, 2008), 108–70.

[3] Frankena, "Vassal-Treaties," 124, 139, 150–51. The vassal lists are Esarhaddon 1 v 55 and Esarhaddon 5 vi 7′ and the references to the succession of Assurbanipal are Esarhaddon 77 64B and Esarhaddon 93 40, as enumerated in E. Leichty, *The Royal Inscriptions of Esarhaddon, King of Assyria (680–669 BC)* (RINAP 4; Winona Lake, Ind.: Eisenbrauns, 2011).

[4] Dion, "Deuteronomy 13," 196–205, with the quotation from 204–205; he maintains that "the imitation of long-familiar Assyrian models remained as natural an option as under the empire" (198–99).

[5] Levinson, "Esarhaddon's Succession Treaty," 342; cf. idem, "'But You Shall Surely Kill Him!': The Text-Critical and Neo-Assyrian Evidence for MT Deuteronomy 13:10," in *Bundesdokument und Gesetz: Studien zum Deuteronomium* (ed. G. Braulik; HBS 4; Freiburg: Herder, 1995), 37–63.

VTE in 672 and Josiah's reform in 622.[6] A similar case for a Josianic origin for Deuteronomy's treaty affinities has also been made by Otto, relying heavily on the work done by Steymans, though Otto contends that the material derived from VTE was combined with the rest of the deuteronomic text at a later date.[7] In the commentaries one may readily see the acceptance of variations of these arguments; thus, for example, the similarity between VTE and Deuteronomy "offers nearly conclusive evidence that a form of Deuteronomy that included most of ch. 28 emerged in the period of Assyrian ascendancy over Judah."[8]

---

[6] H. U. Steymans, "Die literarische und historische Bedeutung der Thronfolgevereidigungen Asarhaddons," in *Die deuteronomistischen Geschichtswerke: redaktions- und religionsgeschichtliche Perspektiven zur "Deuteronomismus"-Diskussion in Tora und Vorderen Propheten* (ed. M. Witte, et al.; BZAW 365; Berlin: de Gruyter, 2006), 331–49; idem, *Deuteronomium 28*, 380. Elsewhere he allows the possibility of a date as late as 597 (idem, "Eine assyrische Vorlage," 140–41).

[7] Otto, "Treueid und Gesetz."

[8] Nelson, *Deuteronomy*, 326 n. 1. As the work of several of these makes obvious, there has been a particular focus on the reign of Josiah as the most historically appropriate context for this adaptive project. This conception of Josiah's reign and his reforms bears the profound influence of scholars such as McKay and Spieckermann, whose depictions of Assyrian religious imperialism provided the background for an interpretation of Josiah as regent over an era of new-found Judahite nationalist fervor, with both the reform as recounted in 2 Kings and the book of the law, identified as Deuteronomy, understood as expressions of this fervor (J. W. McKay, *Religion in Judah under the Assyrians, 732–609 B.C.* [SBT 26; London: SCM, 1973]; H. Spieckermann, *Juda unter Assur in der Sargonidenzeit* [FRLANT 129; Göttingen: Vandenhoeck & Ruprecht, 1982]). The historiographical issues of Kings are too numerous to recount in detail and, in any event, have been capably addressed by others (E. Ben Zvi, "Prelude to a Reconstruction of Historical Manassic Judah," *BN* 81 [1996]: 31–44; F. Stavrakopoulou, *King Manasseh and Child Sacrifice: Biblical Distortions of Historical Realities* [BZAW 338; Berlin: de Gruyter, 2004]; E. A. Knauf, "The Glorious Days of Manasseh," in *Good Kings and Bad Kings: The Kingdom of Judah in the Seventh Century B.C.E.* [ed. L. L. Grabbe; LHBOTS 393; London: T&T Clark, 2005], 164–88), while the idea of Assyrian religious imperialism has been thoroughly refuted (S. W. Holloway, *Aššur is King! Aššur is King!: Religion in the Exercise of Power in the Neo-Assyrian Empire* [CHANE 10; Leiden: Brill, 2001]; D. R. Miller, "The Shadow of the Overlord: Revisiting the Question of Neo-Assyrian Imposition on the Judaean Cult during the Eighth-Seventh Centuries BCE," in *From Babel to Babylon: Essays on Biblical History and Literature in Honor of Brian Peckham* [ed. J. R. Wood, J. E. Harvey, and M. Leuchter; LHBOTS 455; London: T&T Clark, 2006], 146–68; A. Berlejung, "The Assyrians in the West: Assyrianization, Colonialism, Indifference, or Development Policy?," in *Congress Volume Helsinki 2010* [ed. M. Nissinen; VTSup 148; Leiden: Brill, 2012], 21–60; idem, "Shared Fates: Gaza and Ekron as Examples for the Assyrian Religious Policy in the

Despite the certainty among a large number of scholars that Deuteronomy's connections to VTE indicate the origins of Deuteronomy in the pre-exilic period, this does not hold the status of consensus. Rejections of this point are usually connected to arguments against the exclusivity of the VTE-Deuteronomy relationship and are sometimes also linked to arguments against the originality of Deut 13 and 28 to the deuteronomic text. Pakkala is characteristic of both of these trends; he contends that Deut 13 is alien to the deuteronomic material of Deut 12; 14–16 and proposes that it constitutes a late addition to the book, characterized by language he associates with a deuteronomistic redaction after 586. He then goes on to argue that, in any case, the relationship between Deut 13 and VTE is illusory; because of the large number of treaties and loyalty oaths in circulation in the ancient Near East in antiquity it is implausible to require VTE to be Deuteronomy's specific *Vorbild*. He concludes, therefore, that Deut 13 surely draws upon a treaty tradition other than VTE and that it therefore need not be directly tied to the chronological parameters of VTE—coinciding with his contention that Deut 13 is in any case exilic.[9] Similarly, Koch locates the form and function of Deut 13 and 28 in the exilic period, focusing especially on Deuteronomy's articulation of covenant theology as a response to the exilic experience. In order to enable this focus, Koch is obliged to extract Deuteronomy from the chronological framework of VTE; he achieves this by identifying a "mixed" tradition behind the chapters, comprised of discrete West Semitic and Assyrian elements, and

---

West," in *Iconoclasm and Text Destruction in the Ancient Near East and Beyond* [ed. N. N. May; Oriental Institute Seminars 8; Chicago, Ill.: The Oriental Institute of the University of Chicago, 2012], 151–74; A. M. Bagg, "Palestine under Assyrian Rule: A New Look at the Assyrian Imperial Policy in the West," *JAOS* 133 [2013]: 119–44; following in the footsteps of M. D. Cogan, *Imperialism and Religion: Assyria, Judah and Israel in the Eighth and Seventh Centuries B.C.E.* [SBLMS 19; Missoula, Mont.: Scholars Press, 1974]; idem, "Judah under Assyrian Hegemony: A Reexamination of Imperialism and Religion," *JBL* 112 [1993]: 403–14). I have discussed both the geopolitical realities of this period and the problems associated with using the language of nationalism in this context in C. L. Crouch, *The Making of Israel: Cultural Diversity in the Southern Levant and the Formation of Ethnic Identity in Deuteronomy* (VTSup 162; Leiden: Brill, 2014), 90–93, 107–12, and point the interested reader to the much fuller analysis there. Here it must suffice to emphasize that the historical premises of this association between the reign of Josiah and a subversive Deuteronomy are deeply flawed.

[9] Pakkala, "Deuteronomium 13," 125–37. His arguments regarding the date of Deuteronomy more generally may be found in idem, "The Date of the Oldest Edition of Deuteronomy," *ZAW* 121 (2009): 388–401 and idem, "The Dating of Deuteronomy: A Response to Nathan MacDonald," *ZAW* 123 (2011): 431–36.

concludes that this disallows the possibility that the Deuteronomy material could be based on a single treaty or loyalty oath text. Of particular interest, in light of the present focus, is his identification of Deut 28:25–34* as a palindromic reflection of the Assyrian deity hierarchy.[10]

As some of this hints, another focus concerns the technical classification of the perceived literary relationship between Deuteronomy and VTE; nearly fifty years of scholarship on the subject has produced assertions ranging from claims that Deuteronomy directly translated large sections of VTE to arguments that the similarities between these texts derive from a common tradition and have been subject to excessive attention merely because of the particular familiarity

---

[10] The core of the technical work on Deut 13 and 28 is at Koch, *Vertrag*, 106–247; the historical reconstruction is at 315–23. Unfortunately, Koch's identification of discrete West Semitic and Assyrian components—especially prominent in his analysis of Deut 28—does not favor his interpretation of these components as part of a diffused cultural milieu on which the exilic scribes were drawing. Indeed, the depiction of Deut 28:25–36 as a palindromic manipulation of the Assyrian deity hierarchy rather suggests a deliberate engagement with the very Assyrian source material that Koch needs to deny in order to escape the seventh century. The identification of the major locus of the West Semitic material in Deut 28:1–6*, 15–19 also leaves him subject to debates regarding the origins of this section of the chapter that, whatever its exact redactional relationship to Deut 28:20–44 (and beyond), is widely agreed to stem from a different hand than the latter (note especially the common view that the syntax of these verses indicate their origins in a liturgical rather than political background, rendering their relationship to the objectives of the subsequent curses problematic). In identifying discrete West Semitic and Assyrian components to the treaty, loyalty oath, and curse tradition employed by Deuteronomy, Koch thus undermines his overall argument, which relies on the general "acculturation" of these materials into the Judahite scribal repertoire in the eighth and seventh centuries B.C.E., such that they were available for exilic scribes' use in the articulation of a post-monarchic covenant theology. The precision of the analysis also poses the question of why, in the scenario Koch envisions, an author living in Babylonian exile would have chosen an Assyrian textual form to express his purposes (on the basis of the deity hierarchy involved Koch insists that it is Assyrian, not Babylonian) and how that author would have been familiar with this material. With regard to the former Koch makes no answer (and no real attempt to account for how or why such material might have been rendered in Hebrew in such a form); with regard to the latter, Koch is obliged to suggest—on the basis of evidence that the writers of the Assyrian royal correspondence were familiar with the *adê* tradition— that Deuteronomy's *Vorbild* was a Judahite loyalty oath whose contents were preserved by the Judahite scribal elites who were also responsible for the articulation of Deuteronomy's covenant theology.

of VTE within modern scholarship.[11] Unsurprisingly, conclusions on this
point are often related to conclusions about the importance of the VTE-
Deuteronomy relationship to the matter of Deuteronomy's date.

The contention that there is a very close textual and literary
relationship between these texts may be traced directly to the earliest
observers of their similarities. Frankena speaks of an "Assyrian
'Vorlage'" followed by the author of Deut 28, familiarity with which he
attributes to the author's presence at a vassal ceremony in Assyria in
connection with the appointment of Assurbanipal as Assyrian crown
prince in 672, and to which the author appears also to have had written
access.[12] Weinfeld suggests that the similarities between the texts arose as
a result of parts of Deuteronomy having been "literally transcribed from
a Mesopotamian treaty copy to the book of Deuteronomy"; while he
does not demand that this text is VTE itself—he was at the time
unwilling to make such a claim in light of the small number of treaty
exemplars to which Deuteronomy could then be compared—he is very
clear in his assertion of a Judahite scribe in possession of one or more
Assyrian treaty documents from which he "transposed an entire and
consecutive series of maledictions."[13] The diffusion of this research
continues to be felt; thus "the deuteronomic editor, it seems, has simply
compiled his collection of curses according to the model of the treaty text
from the city or temple archive in Jerusalem."[14]

---

[11] In favor of a direct relationship are Weinfeld, "Traces"; Frankena, "Vassal-
Treaties"; Steymans, *Deuteronomium 28*; idem, "Eine assyrische Vorlage"; Otto,
"Treueid und Gesetz"; B. M. Levinson, "Textual Criticism, Assyriology, and the
History of Interpretation: Deuteronomy 13:7a as a Test Case in Method," *JBL* 120
(2001): 236–41; idem, "The Neo-Assyrian Origins of the Canon Formula in
Deuteronomy 13:1," in *Scriptural Exegesis: The Shapes of Culture and the Religious
Imagination: Essays in Honour of Michael Fishbane* (ed. D. A. Green and L. S. Lieber;
Oxford: Oxford University Press, 2009), 25–45; idem, "Esarhaddon's Succession
Treaty"; idem, "'But You Shall Surely Kill Him!'" In favor of a more general
relationship are Pakkala, "Deuteronomium 13"; Koch, *Vertrag*; K. Radner, "Assyrische
ṭuppi adê als Vorbild für Deuteronomium 28,20–44?," *Die deuteronomistischen
Geschichtswerke: redaktions- und religionsgeschichtliche Perspektiven zur
"Deuteronomismus"-Diskussion in Tora und Vorderen Propheten* (ed. M. Witte, et al.;
BZAW 365; Berlin: de Gruyter, 2006), 351–78.

[12] Frankena, "Vassal-Treaties," especially 145, 150–51.

[13] Weinfeld, "Traces," 422–23.

[14] E. Nielsen, *Deuteronomium* (HAT I/6; Tübingen: Mohr Siebeck, 1995), 256 ("Die
dt Redaktion hat, so scheint es, einfach ihre Kompilation von Verfluchungen nach
dem Modell von Vertragstexten aus dem damaligen Stadt- oder Tempelarchiv
Jerusalems zusammengestellt").

Subsequent discussions of the particularities of this relationship have attempted to nuance these early reconstructions somewhat. Both Dion and Levinson, for example, have acknowledged that the texts in Deuteronomy do not seem to be quite the simple translations which Frankena and Weinfeld imagined. Thus Dion allows that Deut 13 is not a mechanical calque of VTE, while nevertheless observing "precise contacts with the vassal treaties of Esarhaddon"; Levinson acknowledges that a direct translation is beyond the evidence and suggests instead a process of "selective adaptation and creative transformation."[15] Both, however, remain clear about envisioning the possession of a copy of an Assyrian treaty text by the deuteronomic author, to which the latter makes deliberate reference; Levinson describes Deuteronomy's use of VTE as "citation," albeit creative, and suggests that specific terminology in Deuteronomy derives from VTE.[16] More recently, Steymans and Otto have produced arguments for the specific and extensive literary citation and revision of significant portions of VTE, with the former in particular arguing for the complex literary usage of VTE §56 to structure Deut 28.[17]

Recently, however, there have also been voices arguing against the traditional conclusion that Deuteronomy reflects some kind of "citation" or "creative transformation" of VTE, often picking up on the uncertainty—already noted by Weinfeld—as to whether VTE itself constituted the specific source for Deuteronomy. Koch, for example, makes an extended case that, while Deut 13 and 28 reflect knowledge of Assyrian treaty rhetoric, this is not necessarily the same as evidence of knowledge of VTE specifically; he suggests that there is not a single text behind Deuteronomy but rather a shared scribal culture across the ancient Near East, comprised in turn of West Semitic and Assyrian treaty and loyalty oath traditions.[18] Pakkala argues that "literary dependence between Deut 13 and VTE is improbable" and suggests that it might be based on another, unknown treaty; one of the reasons he cites as contrary to the connection between Deuteronomy and VTE in particular is the

---

[15] Dion, "Deuteronomy 13," 196, 205; Levinson, "Esarhaddon's Succession Treaty," 341.

[16] Levinson, "Esarhaddon's Succession Treaty," 343; cf. idem, "'But You Shall Surely Kill Him!'," 60–61; idem, "Textual Criticism," 236–41.

[17] Steymans, "Eine assyrische Vorlage," 119–141; idem, *Deuteronomium 28*, especially 129–49, 221–383; Otto, "Treueid und Gesetz," 44; idem, *Das Deuteronomium*, 57–88.

[18] Koch, *Vertrag*, 106–247, 284–86.

number of such treaties in existence in the ancient Near East.[19] Similar reservations have been voiced by Radner, who observes that most examples of treaties and loyalty oaths from the ancient Near East have been poorly preserved and that these are likely only a few of those originally extant. She concludes that "I would certainly be very cautious about regarding a specific oath—or even only its curse section—as *the* prototype for passages in the book of Deuteronomy."[20] As noted above, some of these arguments (on both sides) are related to contentions regarding the appropriate dating of the relevant deuteronomic texts, particularly with regard to their pre-exilic or exilic origins: scholars arguing against Deuteronomy's direct citation of VTE have tended to have an interest in Deuteronomy's origins in the exilic or post-exilic period.

Regardless of the technical literary conclusions of these various interpretations, scholars have consistently identified the book's ideological intent as an attempt to subvert Mesopotamian imperial power. Smith, for example, is able to take this for granted in his analysis of the development of Israelite monotheism, asserting that "[i]f the core of Deuteronomy is any indication, it may be said that Judean monotheism also served as an expression of religious resistance against this empire power"; he links this explicitly to the connections between Deuteronomy and Assyrian treaty materials and concludes that these suggest "a form of literary resistance to Assyria."[21] Parpola unpacks this by suggesting that "*in the mind of the writer of Deuteronomy 13, the God of Israel has taken the place previously occupied in the collective mind of the nation by the feared, almighty king of Assyria,*" calling on an underlying logic common to such assertions that, if VTE constitutes an Assyrian loyalty oath, then the use of VTE in the deuteronomic discussion of Israelite loyalty to YHWH constitutes the subversion of Assyrian royal authority.[22]

---

[19] Pakkala, "Deuteronomium 13," 129, 133–34 ("die literarische Abhängigkeit zwischen Dtn 13 und VTE unwahrscheinlich [ist]").

[20] Radner, "Assyrische *ṭuppi adê*," 375 ("Ich wäre allerdings doch sehr vorsichtig, wenn es darum geht, eine bestimmte Vereidigung—oder eigentlich ja nur deren Fluchsektion—als *das* Vorbild für Passagen im Buch Deuteronomium anzusehen").

[21] M. S. Smith, *God in Translation: Deities in Cross-Cultural Discourse in the Biblical World* (Grand Rapids, Mich.: Eerdmans, 2010), 160.

[22] S. Parpola, "Assyria's Expansion in the 8th and 7th Centuries and Its Long-Term Repercussions in the West," in *Symbiosis, Symbolism, and the Power of the Past: Canaan, Ancient Israel, and Their Neighbors—From the Late Bronze Age through Roman Palaestina* (ed. W. G. Dever and S. Gitin; Winona Lake, Ind.: Eisenbrauns, 2003), 99–111, here 105 (italics original); cf. Dion, "Deuteronomy 13," 197; Weinfeld, "Loyalty Oath," 383–87. On the relationship of the entity that Deuteronomy describes as

This logic is made more explicit by Otto, who writes: "Not only is the genre of the Neo-Assyrian loyalty oath used to express a comparable loyalty to YHWH, the Judean God, but, through the direct transference of the Neo-Assyrian texts, the Assyrian Great King's claims to loyalty are reassigned to YHWH."[23] Though naturally more prominent in the pre-exilic discussions, this understanding of Deuteronomy's relationship with the treaty and loyalty oath tradition is apparent on both sides of the dating divide and on both sides of the argument over the literary nature of these texts' relationship. Pakkala describes Deuteronomy as the modification of a Mesopotamian political document for theological purposes, while Schmid calls it "a subversive reception of Neo-Assyrian vassal-treaty theology"; Levinson declares that Deuteronomy "subverted its source" and that "[t]he instrument of Neo-Assyrian imperialism, as transformed by the Judean authors of Deuteronomy, thereby supported an attempt at liberation from imperial rule; the literary reworking came in the service of a bid for political and cultural autonomy."[24]

"Israel" to the population of Judah, see chapter six and Crouch, *The Making of Israel*, 4–7 *et passim*.

[23] Otto, "Treueid und Gesetz," 45 ("Wird nicht nur die Gattung des neuassyrischen Loyalitätseides genutzt, um die Loyalität JHWH, dem judäischen Gott, gegenüber auszudrücken, sondern geschieht dies durch direkte Übertragung des neuassyrischen Textes, so wird damit dem assyrischen Großkönig der Anspruch auf Loyalität ab-, JHWH aber zugesprochen"). He speaks elsewhere in slightly more generalized terms of Deuteronomy as part of *"the revolt against Assyrian sovereign and royal ideology"* and as containing *"covenant theology formed ... in opposition to hegemonic Neo-Assyrian power"* (idem, *Das Deuteronomium*, 86 [*"die Revolte gegen die assyrische Herrschafts- und Königsideologie"*], 88 [*"Die Bundestheologie formiert ... im Gegenwurf gegen die neuassyrische Hegemonialmacht"*] [italics original]).

[24] Pakkala, "Deuteronomium 13," 135; K. Schmid, *The Old Testament: A Literary History* (transl. L. M. Maloney; Minneapolis, Minn.: Fortress, 2012), 101; Levinson, "Esarhaddon's Succession Treaty," 342 (though note that he has recently retreated from this view, in B. M. Levinson and J. Stackert, "Between the Covenant Code and Esarhaddon's Succession Treaty: Deuteronomy 13 and the Composition of Deuteronomy," *JAJ* 3 [2012]: 123–40, especially 137); note too the presuppositions of, among others, P. Altmann, *Festive Meals in Ancient Israel: Deuteronomy's Identity Politics in Their Ancient Near Eastern Context* (BZAW 424; Berlin: de Gruyter, 2011), 5–36; M. W. Hamilton, "The Past as Destiny: Historical Visions in Sam'al and Judah under Assyrian Hegemony," *HTR* 91 (1998): 215–50. A rare exception is Koch, but this is a matter of omission rather than opposition; he is focused on the presentation of Deuteronomy's covenantal theology as exilic and does not explore Deuteronomy's rationale in using the treaty, loyalty oath, and curse material.

THE WAY FORWARD

The current study aims to consider the question of Deuteronomy's relationship to the treaty and loyalty oath traditions from a different perspective. Rather than another contribution to the argument over the extent of the textual relationship between Deuteronomy and VTE, it focuses on Deuteronomy's supposedly subversive intent, asking what would be required in order for Deuteronomy to successfully subvert either a specific Assyrian source or Assyrian ideology more generally. By investigating the nature and requirements of subversion, and by considering Deuteronomy's ability to fulfil those requirements, it tests the theory of Deuteronomy's subversive intent against the social context in which it would have functioned. By extension, it reconsiders the nature of the relationship between Deuteronomy and Assyria; its relationship to ancient Near Eastern and biblical treaty and loyalty oath traditions; and the relevance of its treaty affinities to discussions of its date.

Chapter one addresses the nature and requirements of subversion, drawing on discussions of adaptation in contemporary literary and film studies and allusion in biblical studies. It argues that successful subversion requires an audience to recognize the relationship between the subversive text and the source which it intends to subvert. If the audience is either unaware of the source or unable to recognize the new text's use of the source, the subversive efforts will fail.

Chapters two and three take these criteria under consideration with respect to Deuteronomy. Chapter two addresses the proposed subversion of VTE specifically by assessing whether Deuteronomy uses material that is recognizable as specific to that text and that is distinguishable from the wider Assyrian treaty, loyalty oath, and curse tradition. It argues that neither Deut 13 nor 28 use words or phrases from VTE with the precision necessary to render such a relationship recognizable. The claim that the Deuteronomy text is alluding to VTE as part of an adaptation imbued with subversive intent is therefore impossible to justify.

Chapter three asks whether Deuteronomy may nevertheless be understood to be subverting Assyrian ideology, referring to the Assyrian treaty, loyalty oath, and curse tradition as a whole by using ideas and concepts that distinguish the Assyrian form of this tradition from other ancient Near Eastern variants. The chapter considers Deuteronomy against the background of known treaties, loyalty oaths, and curses from the ancient Near East. It argues, first, that this tradition is not exclusive to Assyria and, second, that Deuteronomy's use of this tradition is not specific or distinctive enough to indicate a relationship with the Assyrian version of it. There is therefore no basis for interpreting Deuteronomy's use of treaty and loyalty oath traditions as intending to subvert the Assyrian empire.

Bearing in mind, however, that audience knowledge (or lack thereof) will have affected the way in which Deuteronomy's use of treaty, loyalty oath, or curse traditions was interpreted, chapters four and five consider Deuteronomy's subversive potential from the perspective of audience knowledge. Chapter four does this with regard to the specific text of Deut 13 and 28, using the wider biblical tradition to imagine the linguistic and conceptual framework in which interpretation of this material would have occurred. It concludes that there is little, if anything, that would have stood out against the background of a native tradition of treaties, expressions of loyalty, and curses, and that might have suggested to its audience that Deuteronomy intended to signal to an Assyrian context for its interpretation.

Chapter five then asks whether—if some aspect of these chapters did pique audience interest—Deuteronomy's audience would have had the knowledge necessary to recognize an Assyrian source for such material. Recalling the caveat, noted in chapter one, that an adaptation that succeeds in signaling a relationship with a particular source will nevertheless fail to be read as an adaptation if the audience is unfamiliar with the source, the chapter considers the social function of ancient Near Eastern treaty and loyalty oath texts and the social and linguistic capacities of Deuteronomy's audience, concluding that the evidence weighs heavily against Deuteronomy's audience having had the knowledge necessary to recognize use of an Assyrian treaty and loyalty oath tradition.

Finally, chapter six addresses the relationship of Deut 13 and 28 to the deuteronomic text overall. It observes that a non-subversive interpretation of these chapters is consistent with the interests and focus of the rest of the deuteronomic material, in which a negative, subversive attitude toward Assyria is similarly absent.

1
THE NATURE OF SUBVERSION

Given the current study's intention to approach the relationship of Deuteronomy to VTE and to Assyria through an examination of the requirements of subversion, it is necessary to begin with a discussion of subversion itself: what it is, where the concept originated, and how it might be achieved.

THE DEFINITION OF SUBVERSION

Although the *Oxford English Dictionary* offers several current uses for the verb "to subvert," common to the majority—as well as the root's noun and adjectival forms—is the negative effects or intentions of the activity described. Thus subversion may be used to refer to the overthrow of a nation, government, ruler, or other (ostensibly) more powerful force; similarly, it may refer to efforts to overturn an existing practice, belief, or rule. More abstractly, it may constitute an attempt to undermine an established authority, system, or institution without necessarily bringing it down. The description of such attempts as subversive may especially indicate that they are undertaken covertly—although the allowance of covertness is with respect to the entity that is being subverted, not with respect to the audience of the subversive activity. Emphasizing the phenomenon's transformative aspect, the terminology may be used to specify an intention to change, alter, distort, or corrupt an existing entity. The term's use in literary criticism—relevant to the current question for obvious reasons—concretizes such intentions into efforts "to challenge and undermine (a conventional idea, form, genre, etc.), esp. by using or presenting it in a new or unorthodox way."[1]

As this makes clear, the description of an act as subversive establishes the action as reactive, responding to an entity—personal, social, political, textual, *et cetera*—that already exists. Whether the specific intention is to overthrow, overturn, undermine, or challenge this entity, transformational change is central to the concept. In concrete terms, therefore, subversion entails the existence of (at least) two entities, one old and one new, in which the meaning and purpose of the new, subversive entity is inextricably connected to its relationship to its predecessor. Although the rejection of the older entity is not an absolute requirement, this meaning dominates usage: observe how the definitions focus on the negative effects of subversion on the entity subverted, using words like "undermine," "overthrow," and "corrupt," with neutral or positive connotations exceptional and requiring special notation. This is also, explicitly or implicitly, the meaning with which this idea is used in relation to Deuteronomy and VTE or other Assyrian treaty and loyalty oath material. Thus Levinson describes Deuteronomy as "an attempt at liberation from imperial rule," Smith as "an expression of religious resistance against this empire power," and Otto as *"revolt against Assyrian sovereign and royal ideology."*[2]

THE MOTIVATION FOR SUBVERSION

As these suggest, the attractive feature of subversion for most scholars' discussions of Deuteronomy is its association with efforts to undermine a rejected political power and, in particular, with attempts to do so in relation to a specific written expression of that power. This social and political function of subversion, however, is worth closer attention: in anthropological and political discourse, acts of subversion are closely connected to the perceived necessity of rebellion against hegemony. That

---

[1] "Subvert, *v.*," *OED Online* (Oxford University Press, 2014). Cited 10 October 2012. Online: http://www.oed.com/view/Entry/193262. Cf. "subversion, *n.*" and "subversive, *adj.*" Definitions that *OED* deems "rare" or "obsolete" have been excluded.

[2] B. M. Levinson, "Esarhaddon's Succession Treaty as the Source for the Canon Formula in Deuteronomy 13:1," *JAOS* 130 (2010): 342; M. S. Smith, *God in Translation: Deities in Cross-Cultural Discourse in the Biblical World* (Grand Rapids, Mich.: Eerdmans, 2010), 160; E. Otto, *Das Deuteronomium: Politische Theologie und Rechtsreform in Juda und Assyrien* (BZAW 284; Berlin: de Gruyter, 1999), 86 (*"die Revolte gegen die assyrische Herrschafts- und Königsideologie"* [italics original]).

is: subversive acts are the attempts of the dominated to resist domination by a hegemonic power.[3] In the context of the discussion of Deuteronomy, this has been used to articulate an ancient Near Eastern context in which Judah was subordinate to a hegemonic Assyrian power, in terms which strongly imply, if not effectively demand, that the subordinate Judah must have been resisting that power. Especially critical to this anthropological framework is the idea that subordinate groups are, by submitting to a hegemonic power, acting against their own interests, which would be better served by their independence.[4] In the case of Judah and Assyria, the implicit assumption is that Judah's vassal status vis-à-vis Assyria was socially, politically, economically, and therefore ideologically intolerable, and that Judah must therefore have resisted this status. Judah's reason(s) for submitting to Assyrian hegemony, at least superficially, require explanation, while at the same time indications of its real-but-disguised resistance to Assyria must be uncovered.

Both the concept of hegemony and the resistance thereof known as subversion developed in the twentieth century, deriving specifically from a Marxist need to explain the lack of revolutionary response among subordinate economic classes in Western capitalist states.[5] The idea that power imbalance implies inevitable resistance to the dominant power by the dominated is thus closely connected to twentieth century ideas about class conflict, rather than the expression of and responses to power which might be found in the first millennium ancient Near East. While this is not to say that the concept of hegemony and its attempts to articulate various struggles over the assertion of and responses to power cannot be helpful in articulating the relations between dominating and dominated groups, its presuppositions about the social, economic, and historical circumstances of these groups should be held in mind in discussions of ancient phenomena. The political and military sprawl of the Assyrian empire during the late Iron Age in the southern Levant,

---

[3] T. J. J. Lears, "The Concept of Cultural Hegemony: Problems and Possibilities," *AHR* 90 (1985): 567–93; S. Gal, "Language and the 'Arts of Resistance'," *CA* 10 (1995): 407–24.

[4] This is complicated also for the modern context by S. Gal, "Diversity and Contestation in Linguistic Ideologies: German Speakers in Hungary," *Language in Society* 22 (1993): 337–59.

[5] On the origins of the idea of a hegemonic culture with Gramsci and early twentieth century Italian history, see T. R. Bates, "Gramsci and the Theory of Hegemony," *JHI* 36 (1975): 351–66; Lears, "The Concept of Cultural Hegemony," 567–74.

especially toward its outer borders, is not quite akin to the single dominating hegemon envisioned by most discussions of hegemony and subversion. In the case of Judah it should be reiterated that Judah was always a vassal state, semi-autonomous and on the periphery of the imperial system; it was never a fully-integrated provincial territory. The implications of this distinction for Judah's relationship with and experience of the Assyrian empire should not be underestimated; studies of the expression of Assyria's cultural and political powers in its provincial territories and vassal states have revealed notable differences in the degree of active involvement in different types of territories.[6] Indeed, the mechanics of the Assyrian empire were hardly designed for direct control over all its vassals' internal activities; provided that a vassal produced the requisite tribute and did not provoke trouble among its neighbors, the level of direct involvement from Assyria remained relatively low.[7] For the entirety of its experience of the Assyrian empire, Judah functioned as a vassal state, rather than a province under direct Assyrian rule, thereby preserving at least a certain degree of autonomy, especially in its internal affairs.[8] Meanwhile, the general atmosphere of

---

[6] For an accessible overview of Assyrian imperial policies, see M. Van De Mieroop, *A History of the Ancient Near East: ca. 3000–323 BC* (2d ed.; Oxford: Blackwell, 2007), 248–52, 258–60; also J. N. Postgate, "The Land of Assur and the Yoke of Assur," *World Archaeology* 23 (1992): 247–63; F. M. Fales, "On Pax Assyriaca in the Eighth-Seventh Centuries BCE and Its Implications," in *Swords into Plowshares: Isaiah's Vision of Peace in Biblical and Modern International Relations* (ed. R. Cohen and R. Westbrook; Basingstoke: Palgrave Macmillan, 2008), 17–35; B. J. Parker, "At the Edge of Empire: Conceptualizing Assyria's Anatolian Frontier ca. 700 BC," *JAA* 21 (2002): 371–95.

[7] On Assyrian policy in its western territories see A. M. Bagg, "Palestine under Assyrian Rule: A New Look at the Assyrian Imperial Policy in the West," *JAOS* 133 (2013): 119–44; A. Berlejung, "The Assyrians in the West: Assyrianization, Colonialism, Indifference, or Development Policy?," in *Congress Volume Helsinki 2010* (ed. M. Nissinen; VTSup 148; Leiden: Brill, 2012), 21–60; idem, "Shared Fates: Gaza and Ekron as Examples for the Assyrian Religious Policy in the West," in *Iconoclasm and Text Destruction in the Ancient Near East and Beyond* (ed. N. N. May; Oriental Institute Seminars 8; Chicago, Ill.: The Oriental Institute of the University of Chicago, 2012), 151–74; N. Na'aman, "Province System and Settlement Pattern in Southern Syria and Palestine in the Neo-Assyrian Period," in *Neo-Assyrian Geography* (ed. M. Liverani; Quaderni di geografia storica 5; Rome: University of Rome, 1995), 103–15; A. Zertal, "The Province of Samaria (Assyrian *Samerina*) in the Late Iron Age (Iron Age III)," in *Judah and the Judeans in the Neo-Babylonian Period* (ed. O. Lipschits and J. Blenkinsopp; Winona Lake, Ind.: Eisenbrauns, 2003), 377–412.

[8] In the current context the lack of Assyrian interest in local religious affairs is especially pertinent; see Bagg, "Palestine under Assyrian Rule," 125–26; Berlejung, "Shared Fates"; idem, "The Assyrians in the West"; S. W. Holloway, *Aššur is King!*

pax Assyriaca in the southern Levant minimized the necessity of (and opportunities for) external conflict. That Assyrians, at least in small numbers, were present in Judah is likely—probably a *qīpu* and his entourage who, if the recent excavators of Ramat Rahel are correct, perhaps resided just outside the capital—but there is far less evidence than is commonly assumed to suggest that these left a direct impression of Assyria on this small vassal state.[9]

Contributing to the reconsideration of Judah's relationship with the Assyrian empire is that many of the advantages of Judah's integration into the economic system of the southern Levant would have accrued to

---

Aššur is King!: Religion in the Exercise of Power in the Neo-Assyrian Empire (CHANE 10; Leiden: Brill, 2001); D. R. Miller, "The Shadow of the Overlord: Revisiting the Question of Neo-Assyrian Imposition on the Judaean Cult during the Eighth-Seventh Centuries BCE," in *From Babel to Babylon: Essays on Biblical History and Literature in Honor of Brian Peckham* (ed. J. R. Wood, J. E. Harvey, and M. Leuchter; LHBOTS 455; London: T&T Clark, 2006), 146–68, following in the footsteps of M. D. Cogan, *Imperialism and Religion: Assyria, Judah and Israel in the Eighth and Seventh Centuries B.C.E.* (SBLMS 19; Missoula, Mont.: Scholars Press, 1974); idem, "Judah under Assyrian Hegemony: A Reexamination of Imperialism and Religion," *JBL* 112 (1993): 403–14 (and contra J. W. McKay, *Religion in Judah under the Assyrians, 732–609 B.C.* [SBT 26; London: SCM, 1973]; H. Spieckermann, *Juda unter Assur in der Sargonidenzeit* [FRLANT 129; Göttingen: Vandenhoeck & Ruprecht, 1982]; R. J. Thompson, *Terror of the Radiance: Aššur Covenant to YHWH Covenant* [OBO 258; Göttingen: Vandenhoeck & Ruprecht, 2013]).

[9] Berlejung argues compellingly that there was no policy of "assyrianization" in vassal states and that when assimilation of Assyrian culture did occur it was both voluntary and less extensive than generally supposed (Berlejung, "The Assyrians in the West," 23, 32; idem, "Shared Fates," 162–66). A number of scholars also argue that exposure to Assyrian material culture was through second- and third-hand (and beyond) contacts rather than original Assyrian materials (P. Bienkowski and E. Van der Steen, "Tribes, Trade, and Towns: A New Framework for the Late Iron Age in Southern Jordan and the Negev," *BASOR* 323 [2001]: 21–47; L. Singer-Avitz, "Beersheba: A Gateway Community in Southern Arabian Long-Distance Trade in the Eighth Century B.C.E.," *TA* 26 [1999]: 3–75; idem, "On Pottery in Assyrian Style: A Rejoinder," *TA* 34 [2007]: 182–203; N. Na'aman and Y. Thareani-Sussely, "Dating the Appearance of Imitations of Assyrian Ware in Southern Palestine," *TA* 33 [2006]: 61–82). The majority of the evidence for Judah's exposure to outsiders during the Assyrian period concerns its immediate neighbors: the Philistine coast and the Transjordan (see C. L. Crouch, *The Making of Israel: Cultural Diversity in the Southern Levant and the Formation of Ethnic Identity in Deuteronomy* [VTSup 162; Leiden: Brill, 2014], 8–82; also Bagg, "Palestine under Assyrian Rule," 128: "the archaeological material is often overrated as evidence for the assumed Assyrianization"; cf. Berlejung, "The Assyrians in the West," 38, 50).

the elites, among whom the majority of Judah's literate population would have been included.[10] The identification of such elites as subordinates oppressed by a hegemonic Assyrian power and therefore impelled to resist that power as detrimental to their interests is, in other words, more problematic than a straightforward application of hegemony and subversion theory to the myriad players of the Assyrian empire might at first suggest.

The point here is that, despite the wider context of Assyria's political and economic power in the ancient Near East in general and the southern Levant in particular, Judah remained a distinguishable and semi-independent southern Levantine state, part of but not subsumed by the Assyrian empire and, indeed, benefitting from it in significant ways. While Assyria and its exertions of power surely did impinge upon

---

[10] On the economic development of the southern Levant during the Assyrian period and Judah's integration into this regional economy see, among others, Bienkowski and van der Steen, "Tribes, Trade, and Towns"; A. Faust and E. Weiss, "Judah, Philistia, and the Mediterranean World: Reconstructing the Economic System of the Seventh Century BCE," *BASOR* 338 (2005): 71–92; I. Finkelstein, "Ḥorvat Qitmīt and the Southern Trade in the Late Iron Age II," *ZDPV* 108 (1992): 156–70; idem, "The Archaeology of the Days of Manasseh," in *Scripture and Other Artifacts: Essays on the Bible and Archaeology in Honor of Philip J. King* (ed. M. D. Coogan, J. C. Exum, and L. E. Stager; Louisville, Ky.: Westminster John Knox, 1994), 169–87; I. Finkelstein and N. Na'aman, "The Judahite Shephelah in the Late 8th and Early 7th Centuries BCE," *TA* 31 (2004): 60–79; D. Master, "Trade and Politics: Ashkelon's Balancing Act in the Seventh Century B.C.E.," *BASOR* 330 (2003): 47–64; E. Weiss and M. E. Kislev, "Plant Remains as Indicators of Economic Activity: A Case Study from Iron Age Ashkelon," *JAS* 31 (2004): 1–13. Luxury trading is witnessed by, among other things, the presence of fish bones (H. Lernau and O. Lernau, "Fish Bone Remains," in *Excavations in the South of the Temple Mount: The Ophel of Biblical Jerusalem* [ed. E. Mazar and B. Mazar; Qedem 29; Jerusalem: Institute of Archaeology, Hebrew University of Jerusalem, 1989], 155–61; idem, "Fish Remains," in *Stratigraphical, Environmental, and Other Reports* [vol. 3 of *Excavations at the City of David 1978–1985 Directed by Yigal Shiloh*; ed. A. De Groot and D. T. Ariel; Qedem 33; Jerusalem: Hebrew University of Jerusalem, 1992], 131–48; cf. H. K. Mienes, "Molluscs," in *Stratigraphical, Environmental, and Other Reports* [vol. 3 of *Excavations at the City of David 1978–1985 Directed by Yigal Shiloh*; ed. A. De Groot and D. T. Ariel; Qedem 33; Jerusalem: Hebrew University of Jerusalem, 1992], 122–30). On the involvement of central Judahite administration in these activities, see Y. Thareani-Sussely, "The 'Archaeology of the Days of Manasseh' Reconsidered in the Light of Evidence from the Beersheba Valley," *PEQ* 139 (2007): 69–77; cf. F. Stavrakopoulou, *King Manasseh and Child Sacrifice: Biblical Distortions of Historical Realities* (BZAW 338; Berlin: de Gruyter, 2004), 73–120. As Na'aman points out, "the flourishing and economic success of its vassal states was in Assyria's interest, since rich countries were able to pay heavier tributes" (N. Na'aman, "Ekron under the Assyrian and Egyptian Empires," *BASOR* 332 [2003]: 87).

Judah's consciousness in the seventh century, the assumption that the mere existence of a broadly Assyrian-designed stage upon which Judah was obliged to play its small part would have been sufficient to provoke major literary efforts to subvert this imperial "hegemony" may be more problematic than commonly supposed.

THE MECHANICS OF SUBVERSION

The attempt to define subversion concluded that subversion is a phenomenon that entails a relationship, with the subversive act, text, or entity fundamentally linked to a previous one. In grammatical terms, subversion requires an object: a text cannot simply *subvert*, but must subvert *something*. The relational quality of subversion, however, is not merely abstracted, involving the author's inner awareness of a relationship between two entities. As transformative action, a successful act of subversion requires an audience: those whose minds are to be changed, ideas transformed, and opinions undermined. If subversion leads to action, it is the audience that, thus affected, undertakes to overthrow governments and overturn institutions. Without an audience, subversion has no effect.

The implication of this understanding of subversion is that subversion, to succeed, must operate in two directions. First, it must relate to the entity it intends to subvert. Second, it must relate to its audience, whose relationship with that entity is altered through its encounter with the subversive entity. A subversive endeavor must therefore establish its relationship with the entity it intends to subvert; more specifically, however, it must do so in such a way that its audience is able to recognize this relationship, in order that the audience's own relationship with the subverted entity may be altered. The success of a subversive endeavor thus relies upon, first, its success in signaling its relationship with its predecessor and, second, the audience's ability to recognize this signal and interpret the subversive act in light of this relationship.

The audience must be able to recognize the relationship between the adapted and adapting works. Significantly, this means the audience must be aware of the work being adapted. If the audience does not know the source, it will not recognize the relationship between the old text and the new text, and it will not recognize the new work's intention to subvert the old one. Even the clearest signals will fail in the face of an ignorant audience.

In sum: if an audience does not or cannot recognize the subversive text's relationship with its source text—either because the new text fails to make its relationship with the source clear or because the audience is unaware of the source text—the new text's subversive potential will not be realized.

SUBVERSION AND THE SOURCE

If a text must make its audience aware of its source text in order for its subversive intent to be understood, how might it go about identifying its source? Especially when encountered in a literary context, as is the potential situation with Deuteronomy, subversive endeavors are prone to clearly signaling a relationship through the explicit citation of source material within the new work. The narrower textual manifestation of this type of phenomenon within biblical texts in particular, commonly called inner-biblical allusion or exegesis, will be discussed below. First, however, it will be useful to consider recent research on adaptation more generally, insofar as this consists of the use, manipulation, and adaptation of a source for an author's own particular purpose.

Hutcheon describes adaptation as "an announced and extensive transposition of a particular work or works," requiring an "overt relationship to another work or works" in order to succeed.[11] By clearly signaling its relationship with another work, the successful adaptation establishes a framework in which its intention and meaning are to be understood: informing the audience that the new work is to be interpreted in light of another, older one. When Hutcheon characterizes adaptation as "repetition, but repetition without replication," it is the adaptation's successful signaling to the audience and the audience's recognition of the two works' relationship that renders the exact replication of the older material unnecessary.[12] Having announced the relationship, the new work is able to adapt its source material, secure in the knowledge that the audience will recognize and appreciate the adaptation as adaptation, rather than as a work produced *de novo*.[13]

---

[11] L. Hutcheon, *A Theory of Adaptation* (New York, N.Y.: Routledge, 2006), 7, 6; cf. the discussion of allusion in similar terms—as requiring the recognition by the audience in order to actualize—in J. M. Hutton, "Isaiah 51:9–11 and the Rhetorical Appropriation and Subversion of Hostile Theologies," *JBL* 126 (2007): 271–303, especially 276–78, and in more detail below. On terminology see J. Sanders, *Adaptation and Appropriation* (The New Critical Idiom; Abingdon: Routledge, 2006), 17–41.

[12] Hutcheon, *Theory of Adaptation*, 7; cf. Sanders, *Adaptation and Appropriation*, 22.

[13] On the effect of audience knowledge on the recognition of an adaptation as adaptation, see below.

The way in which the work signals its relationship with its source depends on the nature of the source, its relation to other potential sources, and how specific the author intends to be in identifying the source. The more complex the relationship between the source and other potential sources, and the more specific the author intends to be in identifying the source, the more specific the signal needs to be: precision in the face of complexity demands a signal capable of singling out the intended source among a number of alternatives. For example, if an adaptation of the fairy story "Cinderella" wishes to be read not just as a generic fairytale type story but as an adaptation of the "Cinderella" story, it might signal its relationship with that tradition by using a plot device involving a lost slipper and the search for its owner by the romantic hero: a combination of features that characterize that specific story. (If it intends to be subversive, it might turn the slipper into a boot and have its owner sought by the heroine, but the subversive effect only works if the adaptation succeeds in signaling its intention to be interpreted in relation to the original.) If however, the author intends the adaptation to be read in relation to the animated 1950 Disney film *Cinderella*, the signal will need to be more specific, as it needs to be able to specify its relationship with the Disney film in particular. In both cases, the signal needs to be specific enough to be able to distinguish the source with which the adaptation has a relationship from other possible interpretive contexts (the fairy tale genre, as opposed to the "Cinderella" tradition, as opposed to *Cinderella*), with the more specific source requiring a correspondingly more specific signal.[14] Given the nature of our ultimate question—does Deuteronomy signal a (subversive) relationship with a specific source and, if so, what kind of source is it—it is worthwhile to examine the mechanics of these kinds of signals in more detail.

At one end of the spectrum, an adaptation of a single source is obliged to signal its use of this specific source by using a correspondingly unique signal: one which precisely identifies the individual source that the new work adapts. At the most extreme such a signal may comprise an explicit declaration of the new work's relationship to the older work: in contemporary media, an announcement in the opening credits that a film or television show is "based on," "adapted from," or "inspired by" a source text, as with Gatiss and Moffat's *Sherlock* as "based on the works of Sir Arthur Conan

---

[14] *Cinderella* (dir. C. Geronimi, W. Jackson, and H. Luske; Walt Disney Productions, 1950).

Doyle," or the use of an explicit title, as with Luhrmann's 1996 film, *William Shakespeare's Romeo + Juliet*.[15] In these overt cases, in which the announcement opens or closes the new work, the subsequent material may (although is not obliged to) take a great deal of liberty with regard to its source, as the relationship between the two works is immediately and unambiguously established and therefore dictates the audiences' interpretation of the entirety of what follows.

If the relationship between an adaptation and its source is not explicitly announced at the beginning of the adaptive work, however, the material that follows bears the responsibility of communicating this relationship to its audience. Here matters become more complex. In cases in which the source is closely related to other works—cases in which the source is also part of a wider tradition—the connection between the adaptation and its source will need to be more specific. In the Cinderella example, an adaptation might signal its relationship with the Disney *Cinderella* rather than the general "Cinderella" tradition by using one or more of the film's songs or preserving the names of the other characters as they appear in that specific version of the story. For *Romeo and Juliet*, the retention of the language of Shakespeare's play helps signal that Luhrmann's film intends to be interpreted as an adaptation of the older play, rather than (or in addition to) an adaptation of the star-crossed lovers "Romeo and Juliet" type story (on which the Shakespeare play is itself based) or in the context of other adaptations of Shakespeare's *Romeo and Juliet*. Although an adaptation desirous of this degree of specificity in the identification of its source may choose not to identify the source through titles or other explicit equivalent (or may be unable to do so due to other considerations), the demands of this level of specificity tend, as these examples suggest, to produce signals which involve precision closely akin to the use of titles and opening announcements: the use of specific and distinctive names, words, and phrases. Depending on the nature of the source and the complexity of its relationship to other possible sources, the signaling may extend to extensive quotation.

If, however, the source to which the new work intends to signal a relationship is not a single work but a more general tradition, the signal does not require such an acute degree of precision. In the cinematic context, this type of signal might rely on a plot element or combination of plots and props that are distinctive to the tradition but not precise

---

[15] *Sherlock* (dir. M. Gatiss and S. Moffat; Hartswood Films and BBC Wales, 2010–); *William Shakespeare's Romeo + Juliet* (dir. B. Luhrmann; Bazmark Films and Twentieth Century Fox, 1996).

enough to signal a specific version; in a textual adaptation this type of signal is likely to involve ideas or concepts characteristic of the source tradition but not exclusive to any particular form of it. To return to the Cinderella example: an adaptation of Disney's *Cinderella* requires a signal specific to that film, such as a song or distinctive names; an adaptation of the fairytale tradition of Cinderella more generally only requires a signal specific to the tradition, such as the trope of the lost slipper and its pursuit by the romantic hero. Similarly, a man on a cross may be used to signal that a new work should be understood in relation to the gospel tradition of Jesus' crucifixion. However, because the crucifixion is not exclusive to any one of the four gospels (or indeed, even to the canonical gospels), this only works as a signal to the general tradition; something more specific would be required to signal that the new work should be read in relation to the crucifixion tradition in John, for example, while— given the even greater similarities of the synoptic gospels—something quite specific indeed would be necessary to differentiate Matthew, Mark, or Luke as the single source of the adaptation. Such an adaptation might well choose to quote extensively in order to achieve this point.

The type of signal that an author chooses to use thus reflects the nature of the source, the extent to which that source needs to be distinguished from a wider tradition, and the intention of the author with respect to the spectrum of adaptive possibilities. An adaptation may use very precise signals, such as quotation or distinctive terminology, if it is meant to be interpreted in relation to a very specific text; it may use more generalized signals, such as a characteristic combination of tropes or ideas, if it is meant to be interpreted in relation to a general tradition. (Or a work might not use any signals at all, if it is not intended to be interpreted as an adaptation.) The nature of the source, whether a specific, single source or a more general tradition, but also the purpose of the adaptation itself, determines the kind of signals that the author must use to ensure that the source is recognizable to the audience.

SIGNALING THROUGH ALLUSION

The most precise way for an adaptation to announce its relationship with a source, especially when that source is related to a wider tradition from which it must be distinguished, is the use of distinctive words and phrases, extending even to the use of extensive quotation. Such words and phrases serve to signal that it is *that* particular source in relation to which the new work should be understood. Before examining

Deuteronomy and its relationship to VTE and to the Assyrian treaty and loyalty oath tradition, it is worth considering a few specifically biblical examples of this phenomenon in order to observe how biblical texts in particular might undertake such a task.

In biblical studies the use of distinctive words and phrases or the use of extensive quotation to signal a relationship with a source is generally referred to as allusion, and there has been extensive discussion on the nature of this phenomenon in the biblical literature. The godfather of the subject is surely Fishbane, whose early work on "inner-biblical exegesis" provided the impetus for numerous subsequent discussions of biblical texts' relationships to each other.[16] Among the most prominent of these is Sommer's *A Prophet Reads Scripture*, although his methodology for discerning cases of allusion is more explicit in an earlier article; for the present purposes, Sommer's and Leonard's discussions regarding the identification of different types of relationships among biblical texts are particularly useful.[17]

Sommer deliberately distinguishes among a number of kinds of relationships among texts, including intertextuality, influence, and allusion. In intertextuality, the focus is on relationships among multiple texts within their wider linguistic and cultural system, without a great deal of regard for chronological considerations. In influence and allusion, the focus is more narrowly on the diachronic relationship between specific texts. All three attend to the way the audience will interpret these textual relationships; studies of influence and allusion also consider authorial intent.[18] Differentiating a deliberate allusion from a more general influence is allusion's focus on the conscious intent of the author in using an earlier text in the composition of a new work.[19]

As he investigates the nature and purpose of allusion, however, Sommer pays particular attention to the importance of the audience's or reader's recognition of an allusion as a necessary component of the actualization of its allusive, interpretive potential.[20] Like Hutcheon and Sanders, he realizes that "it is precisely when one juxtaposes two works

---

[16] M. Fishbane, *Biblical Interpretation in Ancient Israel* (Oxford: Oxford University Press, 1985).

[17] B. D. Sommer, *A Prophet Reads Scripture: Allusion in Isaiah 40–66* (Contraversions; Stanford, Ca.: Stanford University Press, 1998); idem, "Exegesis, Allusion and Intertextuality in the Hebrew Bible: A Response to Lyle Eslinger," *VT* 46 (1996): 479–89; J. Leonard, "Identifying Inner-Biblical Allusions: Psalm 78 as a Test Case," *JBL* 127 (2008): 241–365.

[18] Sommer, *A Prophet Reads Scripture*, 6–13.

[19] Ibid., 10–15.

[20] Ibid., 10–12.

(as one is forced to do by allusion) that one notices their differences."[21] Drawing especially on Ben-Porat, Sommer breaks the process of audience recognition down into the recognition of "an identifiable element or pattern in one text belonging to another independent text"; the identification of the specific text that is evoked by this element or pattern; and "the modification of the interpretation of the sign in the alluding text."[22] In other words, the audience must recognize an element of the text as originating outside the text; be able to identify its origins; and then juxtapose the original and secondary uses so that their differences are appreciated and the interpretation of the latter is affected accordingly.

The reasons for contrasting two texts in this fashion are manifold. While the juxtaposition of a new work against an older one may be intended by the alluding text simply to explain the meaning of an older text ("exegesis"), the juxtaposition may also be revisionary or polemical, intended to alter, develop, or replace the older text's message with the new.[23] Texts of this latter kind thus "attempt to take the place of the texts against which they argue."[24] Critically, however, such

> polemic depends on the older text even while rejecting it. When the reader recognizes the marked vocabulary and identifies the source, he or she takes particular note of the disagreement with the source. The juxtaposition of the texts calls the new idea into sharper focus than would have been possible if the new text had merely asserted an idea without stressing the departure from the older text.[25]

A subversive text is inherently Janus-like in its relationship with the text it subverts: the source text is at once denigrated, by virtue of being the target of the subversive efforts, yet also perversely honored, by virtue of having been deemed significant enough to merit them.[26] The very act of adaptation, in fact, contains an innate subversive potential, insofar as

---

[21] Ibid., 19.

[22] Ibid., 11–12, drawing on Z. Ben-Porat, "The Poetics of Literary Allusion," *PTL: A Journal for Descriptive Poetics and Theory of Literature* 1 (1976): 105–28. It is also possible, though not necessary, that this process may activate the evoked text as a whole, with the interpretation of the alluding text altered as a result (Sommer, *A Prophet Reads Scripture*, 12–13).

[23] Sommer, *A Prophet Reads Scripture*, 22–31.

[24] Ibid., 28–29.

[25] Ibid., 29.

[26] Cf. Sanders, *Adaptation and Appropriation*, 105 *et passim*.

adaptation implies at least the possible inadequacy of the source. The development of the adaptation as not merely an extension of or addition to the interpretive possibilities of the original, but as actually incompatible with them, renders this subversive potential a reality.

As suggested in the discussion of adaptation, the audience's ability to recognize a relationship between two texts is especially critical when the relationship between the texts is meant by the author to be antagonistic, because it is the *contrast* between the two texts that highlights this aspect of the newer text. If the audience does not recognize that the new text is positioning itself in relation to an older text, it may gain some meaning from the new text, but not the full, polemical meaning intended by the author. It cannot, to use the terminology of this investigation, recognize that the new text intends to subvert the older one. As Hutton observes,

> The study of allusion assumes that the author of the marking text used the literary device in order to provide the reader/intended audience with a fuller appreciation of the allusive text's significance, without explicitly divulging that significance. While the marking text may be read and understood without the reader's recognition of the marker, the actualization of the allusion provides a depth not otherwise present in the marking text alone by creating a dialectic relationship between the two texts.[27]

From the perspective of literary textual relations, then, the same issue arises: if the intention of an author is to reject the message of his or her source, it is critical that the audience be able to (and actually does) recognize the new work's allusions to the older source, so that it is able to appropriately modify its interpretation.

How might a new text allude to its source? Affirming the classification of allusion as a literary form of adaptation, the means of signaling the use of older material in this context parallel quite closely the mechanisms observed above: explicit citation, in which the new work's reliance on the older material is overtly stated; the much more common—and much more difficult to identify—implicit reference, in which markers such as borrowed vocabulary or imagery point the reader to the older text; and the large-scale inclusion of the older material in the new work, with the new work's intent signaled by "small but highly significant changes" in the reused material.[28] The first and last of these— like the use of explicit titling or extensive quotation—are usually

---

[27] Hutton, "Isaiah 51:9–11," 277.
[28] Sommer, *A Prophet Reads Scripture*, 20–22.

relatively easy to identify. The middle category, implicit reference, is subject to substantial interpretive license.

Recognizing this difficulty, Sommer's work attempts to develop criteria for recognizing allusions in the Hebrew Bible. He draws especially on the work of Hays on the letters of Paul, who suggests that in determining the likelihood of allusion the scholar ought to consider several factors: the availability of the alleged source to the author; the volume or extent of the new work's explicit repetition of the source material's words or syntax; whether knowledge of the source is affirmed by its repetitive use; whether the use of the allusion is thematically coherent with the rest of the work; whether such an allusion is historically plausible, both from the perspective of the author and the perspective of the audience; whether others have noticed the allusion; and whether the proposed allusion makes satisfactory sense.[29] Sommer himself focuses on criteria that might aid in distinguishing "between cases in which texts share vocabulary by coincidence or by their independent use of a literary tradition, on the one hand, and cases in which one author borrows vocabulary from an older text, on the other."[30] He especially emphasizes the importance of the distinctiveness of the shared vocabulary, observing that if the shared items are themselves common, or if a cluster of shared vocabulary comprises terms which are often found together, then the fact that two texts share these terms most likely reflects their frequent use in ordinary speech or in speech pertaining to the subject in question rather than a deliberate attempt to link two texts. Distinctive vocabulary, on the other hand, especially if it is complemented by a perceivable coherence in the use or alteration of the borrowed vocabulary, provides a stronger case for allusive intent.[31] The logic is similar to the analysis of adaptation: the more specific and more distinctive the shared material, the more likely that it is intended as a deliberate signal of a specific relationship.

More recently, Leonard has proposed eight principles for evaluating evidence of textual connections.[32] The first of these is the presence of shared language in the two texts in question: though efforts to identify allusions through use of thematic similarities have also been attempted, Leonard is wary of the subjectivity of identifying such similarities, which

---

[29] R. B. Hays, *Echoes of Scripture in the Letters of Paul* (New Haven, Conn.: Yale University Press, 1989).

[30] Sommer, "Exegesis," 483–84.

[31] Ibid., 485; Sommer, *A Prophet Reads Scripture*, 32–35.

[32] Leonard, "Identifying Inner-Biblical Allusions," 247–57.

makes them difficult to evaluate. Specific lexical parallels, therefore, "provide the most objective and verifiable criteria for identifying these allusions."[33] Like Sommer, Leonard emphasizes that shared vocabulary that is otherwise rare or distinctive constitutes stronger evidence for the deliberate use of an earlier text than does the sharing of ordinary language; he adds that shared phrases are even better evidence than individual shared terms. An accumulation of shared material also increases the likelihood of a connection, although he allows that the presence of language that is not shared by the two texts does not, in itself, undermine the possibility of a connection between the texts: "unique or idiosyncratic language may be a reflection of the creativity or writing style of a given author."[34] In a polemical context, such points of divergence serve to indicate the focus of the new text's disagreements with the older. Application of this criterion thus requires critical nuance: "if the features in question are unexceptional, or if we observe just a handful of similarities distributed over large expanses of text, an argument in favor of allusion will most often fall short."[35] On the other hand, "an especially dense cluster of similarities might prove decisive even where each of them, taken individually, could otherwise have been seen as coincidental: the larger the number of moderately suggestive parallels, the more compelling they become when considered together."[36] Even more subtle is Leonard's suggestion that "shared language in similar contexts" bodes well as an indicator of a connection; he gives the example of two relatively common words, אש and שמע, which are used in Ps 78:21 and Num 11:1 in identical contexts, namely, describing the divine response to complaints about food.[37] Such contextual similarities

---

[33] Ibid., 247.

[34] Ibid., 249–55.

[35] Y. Berger, "Ruth and Inner-Biblical Allusion: The Case of 1 Samuel 25," *JBL* 128 (2009): 254; cf. P. R. Noble, "Esau, Tamar, and Joseph: Criteria for Identifying Inner-Biblical Allusions," *VT* 52 (2002): 219–52.

[36] Berger, "Ruth," 254.

[37] Leonard, "Identifying Inner-Biblical Allusions," 255. Note that the application of this criteria must still account for the use of certain complexes of common terminology in relation to particular contexts; Sommer, for example, points out that Isa 44:22–26 and Isa 1:10–18 share a great deal of vocabulary but that almost the entirety of this relates to sacrifice: "hence they fail to show that one text is based on the other, since any author discussing the topic at hand might use the terms in question" (Sommer, "Exegesis," 484 n. 10; cf. idem, *A Prophet Reads Scripture*, 32–35). A shared context may, therefore, contribute to the likelihood that two texts are related, but the criterion of distinctiveness has an important role to play in evaluating the likelihood that this is so.

are naturally even stronger if the vocabulary is also unusual. Finally, he notes that texts are not obliged to share ideological or formal similarities in order to be related. Focusing on Leonard's positive criteria, the evaluation of proposed allusions is based, first and foremost, on the presence of shared language; the suggestion that this sharing is intentional is strengthened if the language is distinctive, if it is extensive, if it involves whole phrases rather than or in addition to individual words, and if the shared words are used in similar contexts.

A few examples of the application of these criteria within the Hebrew Bible are useful. Sommer, focusing especially on the relationship between Isa 40–66 and Jeremiah, notes that there is an abundance of shared language and imagery between these books; most of this may be chalked up to their common Israelite predecessors and their common use of ancient Near Eastern traditions. The sheer frequency of terms appearing in both texts, therefore, does not create an effective case for the use of material from Jeremiah in Deutero-Isaiah.[38] Sommer bases this more specific case on the consistency of the patterns into which the common material falls: with respect to interpretive patterns, these include the reversal of the earlier prophetic utterances, the re-prediction of earlier statements, and the fulfilment of earlier prophecies. Stylistically they include sound play, word play, identical word order, and what Sommer calls the "split-up" pattern.[39] Leonard's work takes as its test case the relationship between Ps 78 and the sources of the Pentateuch, especially the JE account of the exodus. The majority of the allusive material he identifies is straightforward, comprising significant lexical overlap in the recitation of the plagues, the use of distinctive language in both texts' descriptions of the parting of the sea, and the use of similar phrases in both texts, especially in similar contexts, in addition to the sharing of individual terms; the extent of the cumulative case for the psalm's relationship to the pentateuchal material is also significant.[40] Similarly attesting to the importance of both frequency and distinctiveness in the identification of allusion is Berger's case that the

---

[38] Sommer, *A Prophet Reads Scripture*, 32–35.

[39] Ibid., 32–72. By "split-up pattern" Sommer means the division of a phrase from the source into two parts, separated by several words or even verses (ibid., 68). Note that the further apart the two parts, and the less familiar the hearer with the source, the greater the risk that the allusion will not be recognized.

[40] Leonard, "Identifying Inner-Biblical Allusions," 246–48, 251–55.

book of Ruth alludes to the story of Abigail in 1 Sam 25; similarities include structural elements as well as similar phrases and terms.[41]

Deuteronomy's relationship with the Covenant Code provides its own wealth of material for the analysis of allusive relationships between biblical texts; two examples will suffice for the present purposes. The first is the asylum legislation in Deut 19:1–13, recently the focus of an analysis specifically dedicated to determining the passage's relationship to Exod 21:12–14.[42] Because Stackert is focused on countermanding an argument by Barmash that the Deuteronomy text does not derive from the Exodus material, he is particularly attentive to the criteria by which Deuteronomy's reuse of another text may be identified. Echoing the discussions of allusion, he argues that "dependence is evidenced by several significant conceptual, lexical, and sequential ties ... as well as by correspondences in their legal formulation."[43] He devotes significant space to identifying "several simple, exact verbal correspondences" between the texts as well as cataloguing Deuteronomy's various repetitions of variants of the borrowed phrases; he also identifies aspects of the asylum situation that are articulated similarly in both texts, supporting in more general terms the specific correspondences already noted.[44] His ultimate conclusion is that the deuteronomic author uses specific Exodus text units in order to subvert the Exodus altar asylum law through a process of direct borrowing and revision. Perceiving that "the continuity between Exod 21:12–13 and Deut 19:1–13 is but a guise, masking the considerable innovation of the Deuteronomic author," Stackert observes that the deuteronomic text's "specific polemic against sanctuary asylum" is recognizable only because the degree of precision in these texts' relationship allows both the identification of Deuteronomy's reliance on the Exodus text as well as the detection of the precise points at which the deuteronomic text deviates from its predecessor. Again, recognition of the source material is a prerequisite for the audience's ability to fully appreciate the significance of the new text.

Similar observations regarding Deuteronomy's use of Covenant Code source material have been made by Levinson, especially with regard to centralization, the festivals of Passover and Unleavened Bread

---

[41] Berger, "Ruth and Inner-Biblical Allusion."

[42] J. Stackert, "Why Does Deuteronomy Legislate Cities of Refuge? Asylum in the Covenant Collection (Exodus 21:12–14) and Deuteronomy (19:1–13)," *JBL* 125 (2006): 23–49.

[43] Ibid., 24.

[44] Ibid., 32.

and judicial authority.[45] Here, too, the antagonistic relationship and subversive intention of Deuteronomy with respect to the Covenant Code text is visible to the audience precisely insofar as it is able to recognize Deuteronomy's use of and allusions to the source text. Though Deuteronomy's relationship with the Covenant Code is often complex and its exact nature not universally agreed, the extent and the precision of the correspondences between the texts lead most scholars to understand Deuteronomy to have been using substantial, specific material from the Covenant Code with the intention of altering its priorities and its theology, achieved through the adaptation of the source material in minor but meaningful ways to reflect Deuteronomy's own interests. This relationship might reasonably be described as subversive: Deuteronomy presents familiar, recognizable material from the Covenant Code in a new, unorthodox fashion, thereby challenging—and effectively undermining—the authority of the original.[46]

Last but not least: as the proposed relationship between Deuteronomy and VTE or the Assyrian treaty and loyalty oath tradition constitutes a case of allusion in which the source is non-biblical, a couple of attempts to establish an allusive relationship between biblical and non-biblical texts are worth mention. Early in the explorations of biblical allusion, O'Connell argued that Isa 14 used elements of Gilgamesh XI, echoing the Mesopotamian epic "so as to mortify a Mesopotamian

---

[45] B. M. Levinson, *Deuteronomy and the Hermeneutics of Legal Innovation* (Oxford: Oxford University Press, 1997).

[46] Ibid., 150 is explicit: "Deuteronomy's use of precedent subverts it." The future of the Covenant Code in light of this intention is not entirely clear; Morrow contends that "[i]t does not follow ... even if Deuteronomy was meant to supersede and replace the Covenant Code as Israel's working legal reference, that there was no further place for study or transmission of the Covenant Code in its scribal culture" (W. S. Morrow, "Mesopotamian Scribal Techniques and Deuteronomic Composition: Notes on Deuteronomy and the Hermeneutics of Legal Innovation," *ZABR* 6 [2000]: 312), while Levinson speaks of "planned obsolescence" (Levinson, *Deuteronomy and the Hermeneutics of Legal Innovation*, 46). Although it is perhaps possible to conceive of the author of Deuteronomy as producing a simple alternative to the Covenant Code, it is difficult to envision that the simultaneous authority of both texts—despite its eventual reality, with both Deuteronomy and the Covenant Code preserved in the final Torah—was intended from the outset: given both Deuteronomy's extensive use of the Covenant Code and its significant and persistent alteration of it, the creation of such a text with the expectation that it would exist alongside and in parity with its predecessor, rather than superseding it, is unlikely.

ruler."[47] His case is built on the basis of thematic similarities, especially the hubristic pursuit of divine prerogative and ironic reversal of expectations.[48] Though not implausible, as such, the argument's weakness lies in the vagueness of the similarities; not only are they not especially precise, they are neither particularly distinctive nor particularly numerous. That the audience of Isa 14 would recognize these similarities as deliberate allusions is doubtful.[49]

By contrast, Hamori has made a much more successful argument regarding the narrative about Jacob's wrestling match at the river Jabbok, arguing that the Genesis account uses several highly distinctive features of the story of Gilgamesh's hand-to-hand combat with Enkidu to make a theological point.[50] Although the similarities Hamori adduces are not lexical, they comprise a large number of extremely unusual elements: unarmed, non-lethal combat with an unknown assailant who is either divine or a divine agent, occurring at night and culminating in blessing.[51] Taken individually, these features are highly distinctive, satisfying the criterion for identifying allusions that warns against the coincidental duplication of common terms or ideas. Reiterating and strengthening the case is that these are elements that are not otherwise found together, in either biblical or extra-biblical literature. This further reduces the likelihood of their appearance in both texts as being due merely to coincidence. Hamori's argument is especially pertinent to what follows in that it reiterates how, in the absence of specific lexical similarities, a compelling case for intentional allusion must rely heavily on the distinctiveness and volume of the proposed parallels.[52]

---

[47] R. H. O'Connell, "Isaiah XIV 4b–23: Ironic Reversal through Concentric Structure and Mythic Allusion," *VT* 38 (1988): 407–18, here 416.

[48] Ibid., 414–15.

[49] A more influential explanation of Isa 14 is that it refers to the ignominious death of Sargon II in battle (thus H. L. Ginsberg, "Reflexes of Sargon in Isaiah after 715 B.C.E.," *JAOS* 88 [1968]: 49–53; more recently M. A. Sweeney, *Isaiah 1–39: With An Introduction to Prophetic Literature* [FOTL 16; Grand Rapids, Mich.: Eerdmans, 1996], 232–33). There has been no suggestion that this was an allusion to a literary work, however; merely a reference to and interpretation of an historical event.

[50] E. Hamori, "Echoes of Gilgamesh in the Jacob Story," *JBL* 130 (2011): 625–42.

[51] Ibid., 625–32.

[52] Hutton's argument that Isa 51:9–11 is simultaneously subverting a Canaanite Hymn of Anat, anticipated by KTU 1.3 iii 38–46, as well as a Yahwistic hymnic tradition, attested by Ps 74:13–15 and Ps 89:19–11 (itself already subverting the Canaanite tradition), is also worth note here (Hutton, "Isaiah 51:9–11"). Though the triangulation of an Iron Age Hymn of Anat from the extant texts adds an additional level of difficulty, it is again the lexical, syntactic, and thematic similarities among these texts on which Hutton relies in formulating his proposal.

SIGNALING THROUGH TRANSLATION

Before turning to focus on the importance of the audience to the subversive effort, one final issue to do with signaling a source requires attention: the existence of Deuteronomy in Hebrew, while VTE and other Assyrian treaties and loyalty oaths are in Akkadian, renders language a potential obstacle with regard to the recognition of a relationship between Deuteronomy and an Assyrian source. The intention to signal a relationship with a specific source text requires a high level of specificity in the choice of signal. As such precision is most likely to be achieved through the use of specific, distinguishing words and phrases from the source, the means by which such words and phrases are translated from the source text's language into the new text's language is of particular relevance to the ability of the new work to allude to its foreign-language source. Rough or approximate translation of the signal material from the source text, insofar as it obscures the specific and distinctive language of the original, will inhibit its recognition: if the relationship of the "signal" (the repeated words and phrases) to the source is itself unrecognizable, the relationship of the adaptation to its source will be equally unrecognizable. The social implications of these texts' linguistic differences will be addressed in chapter five; here our attention will be limited to how a Hebrew text intending to subvert a foreign-language source might address the translational difficulties posed by this situation and how this intention might be revealed by the resulting text.

In attempting to anticipate and interpret the translational challenges posed by the proposed subversive scenario, it is useful to consider briefly the nature of translation itself. Biblical scholars are accustomed most usually to think of translation as the very tightly coordinated representation of an original source text in a second (target) language, insofar as the representation of Hebrew, Aramaic, and Greek source texts in English, German, or other modern scholarly language forms the foundation for subsequent analysis. Beyond the narrow scholarly context, however, translational activities constitute a much broader set of language phenomena.

Especially useful in appreciating the scope of such phenomena is the approach to translation advocated by Toury, grounded in empirical analysis and going under the name Descriptive Translation Studies.[53] Toury's approach focuses on the target text in the translational relationship, with particular emphasis on the importance of this target

---

[53] See especially G. Toury, *Descriptive Translation Studies—and Beyond* (rev. ed.; Benjamins Translation Library 100; Amsterdam: John Benjamins, 2012).

text's wider cultural context and the social and cultural parameters of the target language:

> translations do not come into being in a vacuum. Not only is the act performed in a particular cultural environment, but it is designed to meet certain needs there, and/or occupy a certain 'slot' within it ... It is the prospective function of the translation ... which yields and governs the strategies which are resorted to during the production of the TL (target language) text in question.[54]

Toury's priority in translational investigation is thus to consider the intended function of a(n assumed) translation, insofar as this function is the driving force behind the translation strategies adopted by the translator.

For the present purposes, a critical aspect of this target-oriented approach is its ability to address the peculiar translational decisions arising from an intended subversive function: how might a subversive function affect the way in which the translator approaches the task of translation? Particularly useful here is Toury's discussion of the two defining, yet competing, features of a translation: its final location in the target text's linguistic and cultural milieu, which necessitates its conformity to the existing norms of that language and culture, and its origins in the source text's language and culture, which the translation is expected somehow to represent. Toury speaks of the former pressure in terms of the "acceptability" of the translated text as a text in the target language and of the latter in terms of its "adequacy" as a representation of the source text.[55] In the biblical studies context this will be familiar as the struggle between the desire to render a passage in "natural" English (or German, *et cetera*), the syntax and vocabulary of which will not offend the linguistic sensibilities of a native speaker or reader of the language, and the desire to render it in such a way as to adequately represent the original Hebrew, Aramaic, or Greek text. Where on the spectrum between acceptability and adequacy a translator will position his or her translation will depend on the intended function of the translation: a scholarly article intending to dissect the Hebrew syntax of a verse will tend to favor adequacy, while a popular translation aiming for accessibility to the general public will more strongly favor acceptability.

---

[54] Ibid., 6.

[55] Ibid., 69–70. These are similar, though not identical, to the notions of "dynamic" and "formal" equivalences advocated by Nida (E. Nida, *Toward a Science of Translating: With Special Reference to Principles and Procedures Involved in Bible Translating* [Leiden: Brill, 1964]).

Returning to the particular problem at hand: a subversive function for a target text suggests that the translational strategies of the translator will need to reflect the requirements of subversive intent. The demands of subversion, as already noted, favor recognizability and therefore precision; the more specific (and more extensive) the similarities between two texts, the more likely it is that an audience will recognize their relationship. When translation is involved, therefore, the translator will need to favor adequacy, in order to facilitate the signaling necessary to subversion, over the acceptability of the translation according to the norms of the target language. Indeed, though a base level of acceptability is necessary for the target text's actual comprehensibility in the target language, a subversive function for the target text provides a strong counter-thrust to this impetus: if the target text is *too* acceptable, even to the point of obscuring the (existence of a) source text, it will undermine its own need to signal to that source text.

It is of course true that the intended function of a translation is not necessarily the actual function that that translation obtains in the target culture.[56] It is possible, in other words, for subversive intent on the part of a translation to fail on account of the translation's over-estimation of the target audience's ability to recognize the signs of a source text that occur in the translation. Even in the absence of subversive intent, however, a persistent feature of translated texts is their tendency to mark their status as translation through a degree of deliberate deviation from the normal language patterns of the target language. Translation is, in fact, a form of adaptation; whether the translator wishes it to be recognized as such affects the extent to which he or she strives to normalize the translation into the target language. In the context of subversive intent, obscuring the existence of a source text would be counterproductive.

Given these considerations, we should expect to see a notable preference in Deuteronomy away from the norms of the target language in favor of the norms of the language of the source text. The preservation of such source language norms in a translated text are described as linguistic interferences: the norms of the source language are understood to interfere with the norms of the target language, such that, although a text "is on the face of it in a single language ... there is reason to think that another language played a part in its formation."[57] In linguistic

---

[56] Toury, *Descriptive Translation Studies*, 8.

[57] J. N. Adams and S. Swain, "Introduction," in *Bilingualism in Ancient Society* (ed. J. N. Adams, M. Janse, and S. Swain; Oxford: Oxford University Press, 2002), 2 n. 8.

terms, then, features attributable to interference from Akkadian, reflecting the material's origins, should be expected in the Deuteronomy text.[58]

There are a number of ways in which such interference might manifest itself. One of the most obvious is "aesthetic symmetry in translation," or "a conscious effort to aim at symmetry between the two texts."[59] In other words, the most obvious signal of a target text's reliance on a source text is for the target text to conform to the content, style, and form of the source text, such that each of its source text's syntactical components and each of its units of meaning are represented in the new text. However—anticipating chapter five—such symmetry is notably absent in instances in which the relationship between the two texts is not important to the target text's meaning. In Toury's language: non-symmetry represents a case in which acceptability has dominated the translational strategy, with the translation's ability (or inclination) to adequately represent the source text reduced in priority.[60] At its extreme, this scenario reaches towards the limits of what may be conventionally understood as "translation"; though the physical juxtaposition of two texts may incline interpreters to attempt to incorporate such bilingual phenomena at the fringes of translation—Toury discusses multilanguage train signage and Taylor bilingual funerary inscriptions—the object of such texts is not the establishment of a relationship between a particular source text and its translation in the target text. This type of "translator," as Taylor contends, "did not start with a text in one language and then translate it into another, but had some essential information that he

---

[58] If Deuteronomy is working from an Aramaic translation, it should be similarly possible to identify signs of interference from the Aramaic text, although the hypothetical form of any Aramaic text, not to mention the greater syntactic and lexical similarity of Aramaic to Hebrew, makes this practically more difficult (and on the question of Aramaic translations of Akkadian treaty and oath texts, see chapter five).

[59] I. Rutherford, "Interference or Translation? Some Patterns in Lycian-Greek Bilingualism," in *Bilingualism in Ancient Society* (ed. J. N. Adams, M. Janse, and S. Swain; Oxford: Oxford University Press, 2002), 203–16. Such symmetry is often visible in translations of religious texts in particular, reflecting the authoritative weight granted to such material (M. Janse, "Aspects of Bilingualism in the History of the Greek Language," in *Bilingualism in Ancient Society* [ed. J. N. Adams, M. Janse, and S. Swain; Oxford: Oxford University Press, 2002], 338–46; D. G. K. Taylor, "Bilingualism and Diglossia in Late Antique Syria and Mesopotamia," in *Bilingualism in Ancient Society* [ed. J. N. Adams, M. Janse, and S. Swain; Oxford: Oxford University Press, 2002], 324–30).

[60] Toury, *Descriptive Translation Studies*, 79: "target norms will be triggered and set into motion, thus relegating the source text and its unique web of relations based on SL [source language] features to a secondary position as a source of constraints."

wished to communicate in two different languages."[61] The relationship between the two texts—absolutely essential to subversion—is not the point. Symmetry, therefore, is functionally superfluous.

Bearing nevertheless in mind that the bounds of acceptability in the target language—as well as other considerations regarding the target text's intended function—may proffer certain limitations on absolute symmetry, other signs of linguistic interference—"evidence that one language has come into contact with another or is being spoken by people whose first language is different"—in a particular text are worth note.[62] These might include "foreign arrangements of semantic and syntactic structures"; "a feature of syntax or an item of morphology or, at the level of writing, a form of spelling"; the use of foreign vocabulary; calques; duplication of nomenclature; preposition and article use; word order; or syntax.[63] If Deuteronomy is translating from an Akkadian source—especially if it is grappling with a need to retain recognizable source language/text features in the target text—this might be revealed by syntactical, vocabulary, or grammatical peculiarities in Deuteronomy's Hebrew. The text might exhibit a preference for the subject-object-verb syntax typical of Akkadian, for example, rather than the verb-subject-object order most common in Hebrew; it might make significant use of Akkadian loan words (more, in this context, than might be expected of general linguistic diffusion); or it might contain peculiarities in its use of vocabulary, prepositions, or phrasing as it attempts to produce a target text that adequately reflects its source.

Each of these are means by which a translation may be recognizable as translation. Anticipating the generally loose relationship between Deuteronomy and VTE in particular, however, it is also worth considering potential reasons that a translated text might diverge in

---

[61] Taylor, "Bilingualism and Diglossia," 320–24; cf. Toury, *Descriptive Translation Studies*, 115–29.

[62] P. Fewster, "Bilingualism in Roman Egypt," in *Bilingualism in Ancient Society* (ed. J. N. Adams, M. Janse, and S. Swain; Oxford: Oxford University Press, 2002), 232–33.

[63] With regard to signs of interference in ancient texts see D. R. Langslow, "Approaching Bilingualism in Corpus Languages," in *Bilingualism in Ancient Society* (ed. J. N. Adams, M. Janse, and S. Swain; Oxford: Oxford University Press, 2002), 42; J. N. Adams, "Bilingualism at Delos," in *Bilingualism in Ancient Society* (ed. J. N. Adams, M. Janse, and S. Swain; Oxford: Oxford University Press, 2002), 121; Fewster, "Bilingualism in Roman Egypt." For a discussion of interferences in modern spoken languages, see R. Appel and P. Muysken, *Language Contact and Bilingualism* (London: Edward Arnold, 1987), 153–74.

certain respects from its source. The first and foremost reason, as already noted, is that the adequacy of the target text *vis-à-vis* the source text is simply not a priority for the translator. If adequacy is desired but not fully achieved, divergences from the source text tend to cluster in the translation of "culture-specific items," such as proper names, references to economic, political, or judicial systems, and cultural phenomena.[64] The underlying issue in such cases is usually (un)familiarity: if a translator believes that a direct or literal translation of the source material might not make sense to the translation's audience, or if the translator is unable to find an appropriately equivalent word or phrase in the second language, then the translator may choose to alter the source material in an attempt to render it comprehensible to the new audience. Again, this reflects the conflict of interest between adequacy and acceptability, with the former deaccentuated for the sake of the latter.

Faced with a culture-specific item, a translator might render it in the translation in one of several ways: she might use the original, foreign word, without attempting to translate it into the target language, thus indicating that the entity or phenomenon it represents is alien to the target language's culture; she might gloss it, to a greater or lesser extent, in an attempt to explain the alien idea to its new audience; she might translate it into more familiar terms, by using native cultural phenomena or universalizing it; she might choose to avoid the incomprehensibility by deleting the problematic passage; or she might abandon the original, untranslatable material and create a largely new phrase or passage to compensate.[65]

Discussions of Deuteronomy that have envisioned its work in terms of a direct literary relationship to either VTE or to a text very similar to it usually rely heavily (albeit implicitly) on the last three of these strategies to explain its divergences from its assumed source. In certain respects this makes good sense: for Deuteronomy to omit Assyrian deity names, for example, makes contextual theological sense. However, there are three reasons to be cautious about the degree of license granted in such a scenario, at least insofar as the scenario is supposed to form the background of Deuteronomy's subversive intent.

First, there is the question of the recognition of the translation as a subversive adaptation if significant portions of the material are substantially altered. In other words, if the author of Deuteronomy was

---

[64] J. F. Aixelá, "Culture-specific Items in Translation," in *Translation, Power, Subversion* (ed. R. Álvarez and M. C.-Á. Vidal; Topics in Translation 8; Philadelphia, Pa.: Multilingual Matters, 1996), 52–78.

[65] Ibid., 61–64.

obliged to delete, compensate, or recast its source material in native or universalized terms in order to render it comprehensible to its audience, the relationship of the new work to its source would have been substantially obscured in the process: the need for acceptability will have trumped the need for adequacy. Temporarily ignoring the question of whether the audience would even be sufficiently aware of the contents of the source text as to be able to recognize Deuteronomy's use of that material in translation—a question to which we will return in chapter five—a source that is heavily altered in the process of translation declines in its ability to be adequately specific or distinctive as to function as a signal of the new work's relationship to the old one.

Second, the extent of the translational license demanded by difficult culture-specific items is related to the familiarity of the source language culture to the target language culture and to their relative similarity: "'translatability is high when the textual traditions involved are parallel' and when 'there has been contact between the two traditions.'"[66] A translation from British English into American English or a translation from Portuguese into Spanish, for example, is facilitated by overall similarities between source and target cultures; although not identical, the cultural and linguistic traditions of these pairs are closely related and are thus generally mutually comprehensible. The translation of a source text into a target language, if the translation intends the relationship between the texts to be recognizable, may in these circumstances be achieved with a relatively high degree of precision; only occasionally will the target text be obliged to deviate from the source material to compensate for an unintelligibly culture-specific item. Although some of the cultural nuances of an Akkadian source text may have been obscure for a Hebrew-reading audience, necessitating occasional deviations in the process of translation, the extent and duration of the cultural contact between Mesopotamia and the southern Levant, as well as the extent of shared cultural features in the ancient Near East (not, by any means, wholly identical, but nevertheless with substantial cultural property in common), means that the process of translating VTE or other Assyrian-Judahite treaty or loyalty oath into Hebrew should have been, for the most part, reasonably straightforward. In other words, if the object was a translation whose relationship to its source remained recognizable, there

---

[66] Ibid., 54, referring to G. Toury, "The Nature and Role of Norms in Literary Translation," in *In Search of A Theory of Literary Translation* (Tel Aviv: Porter Institute for Poetics and Semiotics, 1980), 25.

is no reason to expect a need to accommodate substantial alteration for the sake of an acceptable target language translation.

Finally, it is pertinent that mechanisms for translating culture-specific items are used sparingly—for a few words or the occasional difficult phrase—and do not characterize entire translated works.[67] Insofar as a translation is a kind of adaptation, this makes sense: in order for the new work's relationship with the original to be recognizable, it must retain the specific material of that source. It is only at the boundaries of translation phenomena that this relationship breaks down: when the objective has little, if anything, to do with the relationship between the two texts.

The implications of these translational considerations will need to be borne in mind in the analyses that follow. The very fact of translation, compounded by an intent to function subversively, suggests that Deuteronomy ought—if it is in fact both translation and subversive—to reflect its translator's efforts to produce an adequate representation of its source material, even if this meant making certain concessions with regard to the norms of the target language. Such a degree of precision in the relationship between the two texts is what will enable it to act as an effective signal of that relationship to the audience.

Subversion and the Audience

Thus far we have established that an adaptation must be recognized as having a relationship with some other work in order to function as an adaptation and have explored the ways in which such a relationship might be made known by the adaptation's use of source material. Emphasizing the importance of the audience in this process, Hutcheon suggests that

> If we do not know that what we are experiencing actually *is* an adaptation or if we are not familiar with the particular work that it adapts, we simply experience the adaptation as we would any other

---

[67] It is also possible, of course, to appeal to the weaknesses of the translator to explain a low level of correspondence between a text and its source (Aixelá, "Culture-specific Items in Translation," 66–67). If we have a poor translator in the case of Deuteronomy, however, the immediate question that arises is why such an incompetent translator was entrusted with the job. The obvious answer would be that there was no better-equipped translator available; the implication, in turn, is that the text's eventual audience would have been even less able to discern the relationship between Deuteronomy and its source than the author was able to convey it.

work. To experience it *as an adaptation* ... we need to recognize it as
such...[68]

The discussion thus far has addressed the issue of recognition from the
perspective of the adapting text: what is required of such a text in order
to signal its relationship with its source? A text's ability to successfully
signal its use of a source, however, is only half of the subversive
equation: implicit in all the preceding is a presumption that the intended
audience is actually capable of recognizing these signals and the source
to which they point. It is worth making this aspect of adaptation and
subversion explicit. Because an adaptation's effect requires that the
difference between source and adaptation be recognized—the
recognition that the new work involves "repetition, but repetition
without replication"—adaptation ultimately relies on the audience's
knowledge of the source, whether that source is a single text or a wider
tradition. In Hutcheon's words, in order to recognize and experience an
adaptation as an adaptation the audience must also "know its adapted
text, thus allowing the latter to oscillate in our memories with what we
are experiencing."[69] Even the most skillfully signaled adaptation will fail
in the face of an ignorant audience: no number of crosses will signal
Jesus' crucifixion if the audience is unaware of the Christian gospel
tradition; no number of missing slippers will evoke Cinderella if the
audience has no knowledge of fairy tales (or Disney). The requirements
of adaptation thus also favor the use of well known, even "canonical,"
sources:

> If readers are to be alert to the comparative and contrastive
> relationships ... the texts cited or reworked need to be well known.
> They need to serve as part of a shared community of knowledge, both
> for the interrelationships and interplay to be identifiable and for these in
> turn to have the required impact on their readership.[70]

If the audience does not know the source to which the adaptation refers,
it will be unable to interpret the new work in light of its intentional
differentiation from the source and the new work will be read as a stand-
alone creation. Most fundamentally, therefore, the success of an

---

[68] Hutcheon, *Theory of Adaptation*, 120–21; cf. Sanders, *Adaptation and Appropriation*, 6–9.

[69] Hutcheon, *Theory of Adaptation*, 120–21.

[70] Sanders, *Adaptation and Appropriation*, 97.

adaptation relies on the audience's knowledge of the source being adapted.

Further complicating matters is the possibility of an audience which is "differently knowing"—that is, an audience that knows related sources in addition to or other than the specific adapted text. This kind of audience may read or see an adaptation "through the lenses of other ones" rather than as an adaptation of the "original" work: Hutcheon offers as an example the possibility that a film buff might experience Branagh's 1989 film version of *Henry V* in light of Olivier's 1944 version, rather than in light of Shakespeare's play.[71] Similarly, an audience unaware of Grimm's version of Cinderella might know the Disney adaptation; if the Disney manifestation of the tradition is the only form of the tradition with which the audience is familiar, signaling "Cinderella" using lost slippers will signal a relationship with the Disney version, even if the author intended it to signal a relationship to the wider tradition or—potentially more problematically—a relationship only with the Grimm version. In the former case the adaptation is read more specifically than intended; in the latter it is read as specifically as intended, but with reference to the "wrong" version of the tradition. In attempting a subversive endeavor, an author must factor audience knowledge into decisions regarding the appropriate signal as well as the determination of whether, in the face of an ignorant or differently (or "wrongly") knowing audience, an adaptation has no hope of success.

While no author can fully anticipate the extent of audience knowledge—and complete ignorance is nearly impossible to circumvent—it may be observed that the risk of an audience interpreting an adaptation with reference to the "wrong" specific source becomes progressively more acute the less specific and less extensive the author makes the signal. In order to signal that a new work is to be read in relationship to the Grimm version specifically, and not some other Cinderella story, a new adaptation needs to provide a signal—or combination of signals—otherwise found exclusively in the Grimm version of the tradition; ideally (albeit difficult to achieve in practice), this would be sufficiently specific as to disallow the possibility that the adaptation might be read as an adaptation of the Disney film. Luhrmann's *Romeo + Juliet* is a similar case: although there are numerous film, stage, and musical adaptations of Shakespeare's play, some of which were no doubt more familiar to the 1996 audience, Luhrmann

---

[71] Hutcheon, *Theory of Adaptation*, 125, with reference to *Henry V* (dir. K. Branagh; Renaissance Films, 1989) and *Henry V* (dir. L. Olivier; Two Cities Films, 1944); similarly Sanders, *Adaptation and Appropriation*, 106–108.

ensured that the film was fixed in relation to the original play by means of the extensive use of Shakespeare's original dialogue (not to mention that title). If a signal is not thus secured, but remains multivalent, the author risks the audience understanding the adaptation not as an adaptation of the source actually used by the author but as an adaptation of another adaptation, or as a signal to the general tradition rather than a specific manifestation of the tradition.

SUBVERSION AND DEUTERONOMY

The foregoing suggests that, in order to function as a subversive adaptation, Deuteronomy's audience would have needed to recognize Deuteronomy's relationship with the source it intended to subvert: either VTE in particular or the Assyrian tradition more generally. Deuteronomy's success in this regard implies, in the one direction, its ability to clearly signal the source to which it relates and, in the other, its audience's knowledge of that source. If Deuteronomy does not signal a relationship with its source with the level of precision required by that source's relative location within a wider tradition (or does not signal its source at all) or if its audience does not know the source to which it refers, Deuteronomy's audience experiences Deuteronomy as any other work: no more, no less.

As Deuteronomy clearly lacks a titular or similarly explicit declaration of its source, its success as a subversive adaptation requires that it signal its source through its content; it also requires that its audience is capable of recognizing these signals. The following chapters are therefore designed to investigate Deuteronomy's clarity and precision in signaling relationships with either a specific Assyrian text or a specifically Assyrian tradition and to determine, insofar as possible, the audience knowledge in the context of which any such signals would have been received. Whether Deuteronomy signals a relationship with a specific Assyrian text, VTE, is considered in chapter two. Whether Deuteronomy signals a relationship with a specifically Assyrian form of a wider treaty and loyalty oath tradition is addressed in chapter three. The wider treaty, loyalty oath, and curse tradition of which Deuteronomy's audience is likely to have been aware, along with the implications of this knowledge for the audience's interpretation of Deuteronomy, is considered in chapter four. Finally, whether Deuteronomy's audience would have been familiar with the Assyrian source material—or to what extent—such that it could recognize a signal to it, is considered in chapter five.

2
DEUTERONOMY AND VTE

In the discussion of subversion as adaptation in chapter one it was argued that the interpretation of an adaptation as adaptation—that is, as a work that has a relationship with some other, pre-existing work— depends on the new work's ability to signal that relationship such that the audience is able to recognize the author's intention for the new work to be interpreted in light of the old. Applied to the case of Deuteronomy and VTE, Deuteronomy's subversive potential *vis-à-vis* VTE depends on Deuteronomy's ability to signal its relationship with that text such that its audience is able to recognize Deuteronomy's use of VTE as a source and to acknowledge that Deuteronomy should be interpreted in light of this relationship. Whether Deuteronomy's audience had the requisite knowledge to make such recognition possible will be addressed by chapter five; here the focus is on whether Deuteronomy intended to indicate an interpretive relationship with VTE by using material from it as a signal. In chapter three the net will be cast more broadly, testing the plausibility of an allusive relationship between Deuteronomy and a more general Assyrian treaty, loyalty oath, and curse tradition. The question in this chapter is whether Deuteronomy is signaling a relationship with VTE by using material that is specific to VTE. In the classical biblical language: is Deuteronomy alluding to VTE through the use of words and phrases from that text? In this chapter we will thus be concerned with the narrowest version of the subversion hypothesis: that it is VTE specifically to which Deuteronomy is signaling, through use of treaty, loyalty oath, and curse material characteristic of that text.[1]

TREATIES, LOYALTY OATHS, AND CURSES
IN THE ASSYRIAN TRADITION

For the present purposes this focus entails the consideration of whether Deuteronomy is related to VTE in particular or if it reflects elements that are common to a wider Assyrian tradition. The main source for information on the latter is naturally the treaties and loyalty oaths that have been preserved from the Assyrian period. There are about a dozen of these, primarily from the seventh century height of Assyria's power—under Esarhaddon and Assurbanipal, whose records are especially well-represented—in addition to one each from the ninth and eighth centuries.[2] None are preserved from either Tiglath-pileser III or Sargon II, though other records indicate that they did use such materials to structure relations between Assyria and other states.[3] There is no real doubt that the preserved exemplars are merely a small proportion of those extant in antiquity.[4] The particular concentration of material from the reigns of Esarhaddon and Assurbanipal may be attributable either to the upheaval surrounding the succession of the former especially and/or to the location of these kings and their respective libraries toward the end of the Assyrian empire's existence. None of the kings after Assurbanipal ruled for more than a few years; their reigns are poorly

---

[1] VTE specifically, or a text that is identical to it in the relevant passages.

[2] The standard edition is S. Parpola and K. Watanabe, *Neo-Assyrian Treaties and Loyalty Oaths* (SAA 2; Helsinki: The Neo-Assyrian Text Corpus Project, 1988). The version of VTE found recently at Tell Tayinat should also be noted; its *editio princeps* is in J. Lauinger, "Esarhaddon's Succession Treaty at Tell Tayinat: Text and Commentary," *JCS* 64 (2012): 87–123.

[3] A. K. Grayson, "Akkadian Treaties of the Seventh Century B.C.," *JCS* 39 (1987): 131; the texts include Tiglath-pileser III 12 3'; 20 18'; 21 12'; 22 8'b; 35 i 21'; 47 19b (as enumerated by H. Tadmor and S. Yamada, *The Royal Inscriptions of Tiglath-pileser III (744–727 BC) and Shalmaneser V (726–722 BC)* [RINAP 1; Winona Lake, Ind.: Eisenbrauns, 2011]); note also the declaration in Sennacherib's inscriptions that Padi was bound by oath to him (Sennacherib 4 42 and parallels, in A. K. Grayson and J. Novotny, *The Royal Inscriptions of Sennacherib, King of Assyria (704–681 BC), Part 1* [RINAP 3/1; Winona Lake, Ind.: Eisenbrauns, 2012]).

[4] Especially K. Radner, "Assyrische *ṭuppi adê* als Vorbild für Deuteronomium 28,20–44?," in *Die deuteronomistischen Geschichtswerke: redaktions- und religionsgeschichtliche Perspektiven zur "Deuteronomismus"-Diskussion in Tora und Vorderen Propheten* (ed. M. Witte, et al.; BZAW 365; Berlin: de Gruyter, 2006), 51–378.

attested in the texts overall and, given the indications that the empire was collapsing from within, international affairs are unlikely to have been a priority.[5] Occasional references will also be made to curses in other types of texts.

DEUTERONOMY'S RELATIONSHIP WITH VTE

The analysis will focus first on Deut 28, as its relationship with VTE represents the original form of the subversion hypothesis and has been more extensively discussed, before turning to more recent observations regarding the relationship between VTE and Deut 13.

DEUTERONOMY 28

Beginning with the publication of Wiseman's *editio princeps* of VTE in 1958, scholars have observed certain similarities between the curse section of that document and the curse material in Deut 28.[6] These observations quickly gave rise to proposals of a more direct relationship

---

[5] For the former point and on the seventh century material as a group see Grayson, "Akkadian Treaties"; on the Nineveh texts see S. Parpola, "Neo-Assyrian Treaties from the Royal Archives of Nineveh," *JCS* 39 (1987): 161–89. The Neo-Assyrian material is in its own turn related to earlier Mesopotamian sources; for a summary of this material, its development, and its relationship to non-Mesopotamian traditions see N. Weeks, *Admonition and Curse: The Ancient Near Eastern Treaty/Covenant Form as a Problem in Inter-Cultural Relationships* (JSOTSup 407; London: T&T Clark, 2004), 13–54.

[6] D. J. Wiseman, "The Vassal Treaties of Esarhaddon," *Iraq* 20 (1958): 26. The observant reader will note that the following discussion focuses on Deut 28:20–44, rather than the entire chapter. This shorter section comprises the verses in which the claims of dependence on Assyrian material have been concentrated; these are therefore the verses to which a critique of such claims should most closely attend. It is also opportune to note here that the decision to approach Deut 13 and 28 from the perspective of subversion-as-adaptation means that the conclusions drawn from this analysis are not contingent upon a particular redactional theory. Where individual words or phrases have the potential to act as a signal, these are examined on their own merits; no attempt to extricate them from the situation with an editorial scalpel has been undertaken. An extensive discussion of these chapters' redactional development has therefore been deemed largely superfluous; regardless of whether the chapters are taken in their entirety or whittled down to a more limited set of verses, the sum of the material with any potential to act as a signal remains the same. Even at the extreme end of the latter situation, the poverty of this material is fatal to any claim of subversive intent.

between the two texts, beginning with the studies by Weinfeld and Frankena, both published in 1965. Though subject to a range of further nuance, the conclusions drawn by these early scholars have profoundly shaped scholarly understanding of Deuteronomy over the subsequent half century. Following in the footsteps of Frankena's conclusion that "the phrasing of some curses of Deut. xxviii may be supposed to be an elaboration of an Assyrian 'Vorlage,'" scholars such as Steymans and Otto have made extended arguments in favor of the direct literary transposition of VTE curses into Deuteronomy.[7] As the precision of such direct transposition would suggest, the conclusion of a literary dependence of Deut 28 on VTE has been widely understood to reflect Deuteronomy's intention to be understood in relation to the VTE text. Its adaptation of this material constitutes an attempt to subvert a familiar, hated instrument of Assyrian political power through its use and presentation of the VTE material in a recognizable but altered form: taking the source material of VTE and adapting it to supplant the subject of VTE's power, the Assyrian king, with YHWH, the Israelite god. In light of the foregoing discussion of the requirements for successful adaptation, the focus here is on the precision of this purported transposition: how precise actually are Deuteronomy's similarities with VTE? More to the point: are they precise enough, distinctive enough, and frequent enough to justify the belief that Deuteronomy is deliberately alluding to VTE?

Even allowing for the translational frustrations that would have been faced by an author-translator attempting to allude to a source text in another language, it is difficult to view the language used by the curses of Deut 28 as intentional signals to curse passages in VTE; there is no sign of an attempt to produce an adequate translation of the Akkadian text, no sign of any attempt at symmetry between the new and the old, and no signs of linguistic interference in the extant Hebrew. The relationships between the two texts are indistinct, erratic, and directed toward no apparent purpose. An analysis of this material in terms of its

---

[7] R. Frankena, "The Vassal-Treaties of Esarhaddon and the Dating of Deuteronomy," *OTS* 14 (1965): 145; H. U. Steymans, *Deuteronomium 28 und die Adê zur Thronfolgeregelung Asarhaddons: Segen und Fluch im Alten Orient und in Israel* (OBO 145; Göttingen: Vandenhoeck & Ruprecht, 1995); idem, "Eine assyrische Vorlage für Deuteronomium 28:20–44," in *Bundesdokument und Gesetz: Studien zum Deuteronomium* (ed. G. Braulik; HBS 4; Freiburg: Herder, 1995), 119–41; followed by E. Otto, "Treueid und Gesetz: Die Ursprünge des Deuteronomiums im Horizont neuassyrischen Vertragsrechts," *ZABR* 2 (1996): 45–47; idem, *Das Deuteronomium: Politische Theologie und Rechtsreform in Juda und Assyrien* (BZAW 284; Berlin: de Gruyter, 1999), although he sees its incorporation into Deut 12–26 as a later development (idem, "Treueid," 47–52).

supposed function casts into serious doubt Deuteronomy's ability to signal a relationship with VTE which might, once recognized, be understood as subversive. Rather, it recalls the warnings about reading too much into superficial similarities that, upon closer inspection, turn out to be illusory—reminding us that it would be hardly surprising to find that two substantial blocks of text, employing a common literary type and addressing similar subjects, share language and imagery commonly used to articulate such issues.[8]

The first sign of Deuteronomy's lack of interest in producing a text capable of signaling to VTE is the extent to which the texts' similarities constitute topics which each text mentions repeatedly. Both VTE and Deuteronomy are highly repetitive in the subjects they choose to address; this repetition draws attention to the terminological and phraseological imprecision of the purported parallels by highlighting the multiplicity of possibilities regarding the "allusions" involved. Deportation, for example, is mentioned no less than five times in Deuteronomy (Deut 28:21, 25, 32, 36, 41), while lists of mental and physical illnesses also appear repeatedly (Deut 28:22, 27, 34–35). Similarly, illnesses appear several times in VTE (VTE §§38a–40, 60, 72–73), as do famine (VTE §§47, 62, 74, 85) and descriptions of the other physical fates awaiting those who break their oath (VTE §§41, 48–56, 58–60, 77–84, 88–90, 95–99). The repetitiveness of both texts emphasizes the extent to which they are each imagining variations on common threats: threaten death and suffering enough times and similarities eventually arise.[9]

Examined more closely, however, the essential superficiality of these similarities is apparent. Deuteronomy 28:22 threatens illness and agricultural plagues ("YHWH will afflict you with consumption, fever, inflammation, with fiery heat and drought, and with blight and mildew; they shall pursue you until you perish"[10]): should we therefore see in it an allusion to VTE §62 ("May Girra, who gives food to small and great,

---

[8] B. D. Sommer, "Exegesis, Allusion and Intertextuality in the Hebrew Bible: A Response to Lyle Eslinger," *VT* 46 (1996): 484 n. 10; cf. G. Toury, *Descriptive Translation Studies—and Beyond* (rev. ed.; Benjamins Translation Library 100; Amsterdam: John Benjamins, 2012), 119 and below.

[9] On the common logic and resultant overlap of ancient Near Eastern curses see A. M. Kitz, "Curses and Cursing in the Ancient Near East," *Religion Compass* 1 (2007): 615–27.

[10] יככה יהוה בשחפת ובקדחת ובדלקת ובחרחר ובחרב ובשדפון ובירקון ורדפוך עד אבדך

burn up your name and your seed"[11])? Should the warning about deportation in Deut 28:41 ("You shall have sons and daughters, but they shall not remain yours, for they shall go into captivity"[12]) be interpreted in light of VTE §67 ("may your [see]d and the seed of y[our] s[ons] and your daughters disappear [from] the face of your ground"[13]), VTE §82 ("may you, your [women], your brothers, your sons and your daughters be seized by the hand of your enemy"[14]), or VTE §45 ("May Zarpanitu, who grants name and seed, destroy your name and your seed from the land"[15])? Deuteronomy's failure to use specific and recognizable material from any of these suggests, rather, none of the above. The multiplication of topical similarities between these texts establishes in practice what was already suspected in theory: in order to signal a relationship with VTE, Deuteronomy will need to use specific and preferably distinctive language—recognizable words and phrases—drawn from specific passages of VTE. The myriad permutations of a common vocabulary of disaster, already within these two texts, indicates that an allusion to a general topic is unlikely to have succeeded as a signal to VTE.

The use of shared language—and, barring that, the use of shared concepts—is, indeed, the locus of most arguments in favor of Deuteronomy's use and manipulation of VTE as its source text. The correlations observed by Weinfeld and Frankena retain the greatest degree of consensus regarding the existence of a specific relationship between the Deuteronomy curses and VTE and are, accordingly, where we begin. Weinfeld's initial analysis proposed, in addition to the parallel to Deut 28:23-24 noted by Wiseman, a specific curse in VTE as the source of each of the verses in Deut 28:26–33, excepting Deut 28:31 and noting that the parallel for Deut 28:26 occurs out of sequence.[16] We should of

---

[11] ᵈGIŠ.BAR *na-din ma-ka-le-e a-na* TUR.MEŠ GAL.MEŠ MU-*ku-nu* NUMUN-*ku-nu liq-mu* (transliterations and translations of VTE are according to SAA 2 6).

[12] בנים ובנות תוליד ולא יהיו לך כי ילכו בשבי (translations of biblical texts are according to the NRSV).

[13] [NUMU]N-*ku-nu* NUMUN.MEŠ *šá* ŠEŠ.MEŠ-[*ku-nu* DUMU.MEŠ]-*ku-nu* DUMU.MÍ.[MEŠ-*ku-nu*] [TAʾ] UGU *pa-ni ša kaq-qa-ri li-iḫ-liq*; cf. VTE §66, "may your name, your seed, and the seed of your sons and your daughters disappear from the land" (NUMUN-*ku-nu* NUMUN *šá* DUMU.MEŠ-*ku-nu* DUMU.MÍ.MEŠ-*ku-nu* TAʾ KUR *li-iḫ-liq*).

[14] *a*[*t-t*]*u-nu* [MÍ.MEŠ]-*ku-nu* ŠEŠ.MEŠ-*ku-nu* DUMU.MEŠ-*ku-nu* DUMU.MÍ.MEŠ-*ku-nu ina* ŠU.2 LÚ.KÚR-*ku-nu na-aṣ-bi-ta*

[15] ᵈNUMUN-DÙ-*tú na-di-na-at* MU *u* NUMUN MU-*ku-nu* NUMUN-*ku-nu ina* KUR *lu-ḫal-liq*

[16] M. Weinfeld, "Traces of Assyrian Treaty Formulae in Deuteronomy," *Bib* 46 (1965): 418–19.

course recall that Weinfeld himself considered VTE to be merely the most fully known exemplar of an Assyrian treaty—although he implicitly presupposes that such treaties were highly formulaic—rather than assuming that it was VTE from which Deuteronomy was transcribing; the idea that it was VTE itself from which Deuteronomy drew its material derives from Frankena.[17] Published in the same year, Frankena's analysis varies in these verses only in a few details and, overall, is largely similar to Weinfeld's conclusions; the main difference is Frankena's identification of further parallels for most of the verses in Deut 28:20–57.[18] Some of this material will be examined in further detail below and in chapter three; first, however, each of the parallels common to both Weinfeld and Frankena will be examined in turn.

Bearing especially in mind the possibility that Deuteronomy's alteration of its source might indicate points of subversive intent with regard to that source—recalling Sommer's contention that purposeful allusion ought to display a degree of consistency in style and intent—this comparison of the texts draws attention not only to their similarities but also to their differences.[19] As both Sommer and Leonard observe, the existence of material in either or both source and alluding text does not, of itself, demand the rejection of a relationship between the texts in question; divergence, in the form of omission, elaboration, or alteration, is allowable as a legitimate translational technique.[20] The references to Mesopotamian deities, for example, would have been obviously problematic for Deuteronomy—though their incorporation, even in non-divinized form, would have been an excellent signal of Deuteronomy's intended relationship with an Assyrian source. However, the allowance of divergence must be balanced with the intent to function subversively: in translational terms, the functional preference for adequacy over acceptability, and in allusive terms the importance of frequency and density. As Berger points out: "if we observe just a handful of similarities distributed over large expanses of text, an argument in favor of allusion

---

[17] Frankena, "Vassal-Treaties."

[18] Ibid., 145–46; the parallels from Deut 28:35 onwards are, however, noted as very general or as deriving from the treaty with Baal of Tyre.

[19] B. D. Sommer, *A Prophet Reads Scripture: Allusion in Isaiah 40–66* (Contraversions; Stanford, Ca.: Stanford University Press, 1998), 35.

[20] J. Leonard, "Identifying Inner-Biblical Allusions: Psalm 78 as a Test Case," *JBL* 127 (2008): 254; Sommer, "Exegesis," 483–85; Sommer, *A Prophet Reads Scripture*, 32–35; J. F. Aixelá, "Culture-specific Items in Translation," in *Translation, Power, Subversion* (ed. R. Álvarez and M. C.-Á. Vidal; Topics in Translation 8; Philadelphia, Pa.: Multilingual Matters, 1996), 61–64.

will most often fall short."[21] A concentration of distinctive terms and phrases, in the same way as a (nearly) symmetrical text, will make a much more convincing case for allusive intent than a few scattered words. With a nod to Sommer, we ought also to bear in mind that a text employing allusion for deliberately polemical (subversive) intent should exhibit a tendency to use its creative license as an opportunity to further its polemical purpose by conveying its own particular interpretation of the earlier material.[22] Where Deuteronomy does diverge from VTE, in other words, it should be either for polemical purposes or translational acceptability.

VTE §39
May Sin, the brightness of heaven and earth, clothe you with leprosy and forbid your entering into the presence of the gods or king. Roam the desert like the wild-ass and the gazelle![23]

DEUT 28:27
YHWH will afflict you with the boils of Egypt, with ulcers, scurvy, and itch, of which you cannot be healed.[24]

Deuteronomy 28:27, threatening several illnesses upon its addressee, is usually considered to be adapting VTE §39, in which Sin will bring leprosy upon anyone disloyal to Assurbanipal. First we should note that there is none of the specific lexical overlap that would act as the most decisive signal of a relationship between these texts. The skin disease in VTE is *saḫaršubbû*, while Deuteronomy includes שחין מצרים, עפלים (perpetual *qere* טחרים), גרב, and חרס (whether all of these are meant to refer to skin diseases is unclear; none appear elsewhere in contexts that might clarify their remit). Though obscure, none of these are loan words from, or even cognate with, the Akkadian such as might suggest their origins in the VTE text. Indeed, there are no clear terminological points of contact anywhere in the verse to suggest that Deuteronomy is adapting VTE, even making a generous allowance for translational difficulties. In terms of form the Deuteronomy text bears no more than a passing resemblance to the VTE passage, eliminating symmetry between target and source texts as an indicator of the texts' relationship:

---

[21] Y. Berger, "Ruth and Inner-Biblical Allusion: The Case of 1 Samuel 25," *JBL* 128 (2009): 254.

[22] Sommer, *A Prophet Reads Scripture*, 22–31.

[23] ᵈ30 *na-an-nar* AN.MEŠ *u* KI.TIM *ina* SAḪAR.ŠUB-*bu li-ḫal-lip-ku-nu ina* IGI DINGIR.MEŠ *u* LUGAL *e-rab-ku-nu a-a iq-bi ki-i sir-ri-me* MAŠ.DÀ <*ina*> EDIN *ru-up-da*

[24] יככה יהוה בשחין מצרים ובעפלים ובגרב ובחרס אשר לא תוכל להרפא

May Sin	YHWH will
the brightness of heaven and earth	—
clothe you with leprosy	afflict you with the boils of Egypt
—	with ulcers, scurvy, and itch
—	of which you cannot be healed
and forbid your entering into the presence of the gods or king	—
Roam the desert like the wild-ass and the gazelle	—

Such formal comparison makes obvious Deuteronomy's lack of interest in adequately representing its source text in its translation (if it is indeed translating VTE). The description of Sin has no analogy, though some acceptable approximation—נגה שמים וארץ ("brightness of heaven and earth"), בורא שמים וארץ ("creator of heaven and earth"), or even מלך שמים וארץ ("king of heaven and earth")—could have been concocted readily enough. Although explication through multiplication of terms is an allowable translational strategy in cases of unfamiliar culture-specific items, the expansion of the number of illnesses (and probably also their type) undercuts the subversive necessity of linking the target text to its source text as closely as possible.

Conceptually VTE is quite specific in its remit and intent: it names a single skin disease and specifies its consequence as its interference with cultic practice and social intercourse. By contrast, no mention is made by Deuteronomy of the social or cultic implications of its (four) afflictions, only that they will be incurable. Rather, the focus of the curse in the Deuteronomy text is on the perpetuity of these illnesses once inflicted, which is missing from VTE §39. That diseases could have social and cultic implications is attested elsewhere in the Hebrew Bible; it therefore seems unlikely that this change should be attributed to Yahwistic theological concerns or practical reasons.[25] It is equally difficult to understand it as an alteration relating to Deuteronomy's subversive intention *vis-à-vis* VTE. Without such purpose, however, the divergence does nothing other than render the relationship between the texts less precise and less recognizable.

Contributing to the tenuousness of Deuteronomy's connection to VTE are the witnesses to a range of similar curses in the wider Assyrian repertoire. In Sin-sharru-ishkun's treaty with his Babylonian allies (which post-dates VTE), the king asks that "Sin, light of heaven and

---

[25] For discussion see S. Olyan, *Disability in the Hebrew Bible: Interpreting Mental and Physical Differences* (Cambridge: Cambridge University Press, 2008).

earth, clothe them in leprosy as in a cloak (and) destroy their stands from temple and palace,"[26] while the treaty of Assur-nerari V with Mati'ilu of Arpad (which ante-dates VTE) demands that

> Sin, the great lord who dwells in Harran, clothe Mati'-ilu, [his so]ns, his magnates, and the people of his land in leprosy as in a cloak; may they have to roam the open country, and may there be no mercy for them. May there be no more dung of oxen, asses, sheep, and horses in his land.[27]

Like the VTE curse, both of these emphasize the curse's implications for the addressee's social and cultic activities. This point turns up also in Esarhaddon's accession treaty in a curse associated with Assur, "king of the totality of heaven and earth."[28]

Similarly, though the idea of perpetual illness is absent from VTE §39, it is hardly alien to the Assyrian curse repertoire. The Assur-nerari treaty hints at such an idea in its phrase "may there be no mercy," while it is perfectly clear in the laws of Hammurabi:

> May the goddess Ninkarrak, daughter of the god Anu, who promotes my cause in the Ekur temple, cause a grievous malady to break out upon his limbs, an evil demonic disease, a serious carbuncle which cannot be soothed, which a physician cannot diagnose, which he cannot ease with bandages, which, like the bite of death, cannot be expunged; may he bewail his lost virility until his life comes to an end.[29]

The treaty of Shamshi-adad V with Marduk-zakir-shumi of Babylon also invokes perpetual bodily illness—"[May Sin, the lord of heaven, whose] punishment is renowned among the gods, [inflict upon him] a severe puni[shment] which is not to be removed from his body; may he [make

---

[26] ᵈ30 ᵈŠEŠ.KI A[N-e u KI.TIM] [SAḪAR].ŠUB-pu ki-ma na-aḫ-lap-tilu-u-ḫal-lip-šú-[nu] maⁱ-za-sa-šuⁱ¹-nu TAˀ ŠÀ É.KURÉ.GAL lu-ḫal-liq [0] (SAA 2 11 10'–12').

[27] ᵈ30 EN GAL-u a-šib URU.KASKAL a-na ᵐma-ti-iˀ—DINGIR DUM[U—MEŠ-šú] GAL.MEŠ-šú UN.MEŠ KUR-šú SAḪAR.ŠUB.BA-a GIM na-ḫa-lap-ti l[i-ḫal-lip] EDIN li-ir-pu-du a-a TUK-šú-nu re-e-mu kaⁱ-buⁱ-utⁱ GUD ANŠE UDU.MEŠ ANŠE.KUR.RA.MEŠ ina KUR-šú a-aib-ši (SAA 2 2 iv 4–7).

[28] [AN.ŠÁR AD DINGIR.MEŠ LUGAL k]iš-šat AN-e u KI.TIM še-ret-s[u kab-tú li-mid-su] [x x x x x x x]x-ma ina ma-ḫar DINGIR u LUGAL e-[reb-šú a-a iq-bi] (SAA 2 4 16'–17').

[29] Ninkarrak mārat Anim qābiat dumqija ina Ekur murṣam kabtam asakkam lemnam simmam marṣam ša la ipaššeḫu asûm qerebšu la ilammadu ina ṣimdi la unaḫḫušu kīma nišik mūtim la innassaḫu ina biniātišu lišāṣiaššumma adi napištašu ibellû ana eṭlūtišu liddammam; (M. T. Roth, Law Collections from Mesopotamia and Asia Minor [2d ed.; SBLWAW 6; Atlanta, Ga.: Scholars Press, 1997], 8 li 50–69).

the days, months and years] of his reign [end] in sighing and [moaning]"[30]—while the treaty with Baal of Tyre appeals to Gula to put "an unhealing sore in your body."[31] VTE itself may hint in the same direction, many curses later, with its hope that "When your enemy pierces you, may there be no honey, oil, ginger or cedar-resin available to place on your wound" (VTE §99).[32]

These other texts raise for us two points. First, the idea of threatening one's enemy or disloyal ally with physical ill health, even in perpetuity, is at home in the wider Assyrian conceptual world. Second, the implication of this wider context is that the VTE rendering is likely to have required a certain degree of precision.[33] Deuteronomy 28:27, however, does not use terms or phrases—or even an overall symmetry of structure—from the purported VTE source text that might, by such specificity, successfully signal its use of VTE. Distinctiveness and frequency do not enter the picture, since there are no specific terms to qualify according to such criteria. Conceptually the orientation of the Deuteronomy material is also different from VTE; while this may, if persistent through what follows, highlight a focus of the Deuteronomy text, perpetuity of punishment is difficult to construe as subversive *vis-à-vis* Assyrian imperial power. The only real similarity between these texts is the use of skin disease as curse material, and that is far from distinctive.

VTE §40
May Shamash, the light of heaven and earth, not judge you justly. May he remove your eyesight. Walk about in darkness![34]

---

[30] [ᵈ30 EN AN-*e šá*] *še-reṭ'-su ina* DINGIR.MEŠ *šu-pa-a*[*t 0*] [*x x x x šir-t*]*a ra-bi-ta šá ina* SU-*šú la* KÚR-*ru* [*li-mid-su-ma*] [UD.MEŠ ITI.MEŠ MU.MEŠ *pa*]-*le-e-šú i-na ta-né-ḫi* ˹*ù*˺ [*dim-ma-ti li-šaq-ti*] (SAA 2 1 10–12).

[31] *si-im-mu la-zu* (SAA 2 5 iv 4′).

[32] *ki-i* LÚ.KÚR-*ku-nu ú-pa-ta-ḫu-ka-nu-ni* LÀL Ì.MEŠ *zi-in-za-ru-*˹*u*˺ MÚD—GIŠ.ERIN *a-na šá-kan pi-it-ḫi-ku-nu li-iḫ-liq*; already D. R. Hillers, *Treaty-Curses and the Old Testament Prophets* (BibOr 16; Rome: Pontifical Biblical Institute, 1964), 64.

[33] Part of the inevitable difficulty here, of course, concerns whether Deuteronomy's audience or author would have known of these other texts, such that Deuteronomy would need to differentiate its use of VTE from these others. This anticipates and is ultimately pre-empted by the conclusions of chapter five, however, and therefore will not be discussed more fully here.

[34] ᵈUTU *nu-úr šá-ma-mi u kaq-qar di-inket-ti* <*me-šá-ri*> *a-a i-di-in-ku-nu ni-ṭil* IGI.2.MEŠ-*ku-nu li-ši-ma ina ek-le-ti i-tal-la-ka*

DEUT 28:28–29
[28]YHWH will afflict you with madness, blindness, and confusion of mind; [29]you shall grope about at noon as blind people grope in darkness, but you shall be unable to find your way; and you shall be continually abused and robbed, without anyone to help.[35]

The similarity between Deut 28:28–29 and VTE §40 is blindness. Here, at least, there is a little terminological overlap: the mention of movement "in darkness" (Hebrew באפלה, Akkadian *ina eklēti*). One might also allow the appearance of "blindness" (עורון) in Deuteronomy as a simplification of "removal of eyesight" (*ni-ṭil* IGI.2.MEŠ-*ku-nu li-ši-ma*) in VTE, but this would seem an unnecessary deviation from the Akkadian syntax, diminishing the symmetry of the texts rather than maintaining it. Indeed, the symmetry of these two passages is so poor as to defy visual representation; at best, Deuteronomy is doing no more than what Toury describes as the translation of an entire textual entity, without attempt to break down the source into smaller units.[36] Even if such a relationship still constitutes translation, the relationship itself is irrelevant for the resulting target text, whose meaning is independent of its source. Such translational practice is antithetical to subversion. From the perspective of allusive practice such vague correlations are likewise all but useless: whether one (two?) term(s) satisfies the criterion of frequency is doubtful; neither, in any case, constitutes distinctive terminology: language regarding vision and lack thereof is common to both Hebrew and Akkadian. Affirming this are curses in the Assur-nerari-Mati'ilu treaty ("may […] blind their eyes"[37]) and, in almost identical terms to VTE, in Assurbanipal's treaty with his Babylonian allies ("May Šamaš, the great judge of heaven and earth, [……] render an unjust judgment [against us ……]. May he remove our eyesight, [may we wander about in darkness]"[38]). What little overlap there is, in other words, is highly unlikely to have functioned successfully as a signal—especially not one on which the entirety of the allusion, in the absence of additional terminological overlap, was obliged to rely.

---

[35] יככה יהוה בשגעון ובעורון ובתמהון לבב: והיית ממשש בצהרים כאשר ימשש העור באפלה ולא תצליח את דרכיך והיית אך עשוק וגזול כל הימים ואין מושיע:

[36] Toury, *Descriptive Translation Studies*, 119; see further below.

[37] [*x x x x*]*x-ma* IGI.2-*šú-nu lu-na-pi-il* (SAA 2 2 vi 2). For the biblical material see chapter four.

[38] ᵈUTU! DI.KUD.GAL AN-*e u* KI.TIM *be*[*x x x x x x x x x x x x x*] *di-i-ni pa-rik-ti li-di-n*[*a-na-ši x xx x x x x x x x x x*] *ni-iṭ-lu* IGI.2-*ni liš-ši i-n*[*a ek-le-tini-tal-la-ka*] (SAA 2 9 8'–10').

Exacerbating these minimal terminological affinities are the texts' conceptual divergences. Deuteronomy again multiplies the afflictions invoked. Its governing motif, mental illness, is entirely absent from VTE. The issue of blindness in Deuteronomy, in fact, is introduced in reference to the "madness" and "confusion of mind" with which the curse is primarily concerned, rather than constituting the primary focus of the curse. Thus, though the mention of blindness is normally interpreted as parallel and alluding to VTE's mention of loss of eyesight, Deuteronomy's usage is more obviously understood as an elaboration of the theme of madness, culminating in a description of the addressee's consequent social vulnerability. Bar the interpretation of VTE's mention of Shamash as shorthand for that deity's responsibility for justice and injustice in all its forms, the Deuteronomy addressee's subjection to abuse and theft may hardly be traced to VTE; even if Deuteronomy were inspired by VTE, it is clearly not concerned to signal this relationship to its audience. Again, therefore, though the texts bear superficial similarities, their relationship is so generalized as to render all but impossible the contention that Deuteronomy intends to allude to VTE.

VTE §41
May Ninurta, the foremost among the gods, fell you with his fierce arrow; may he fill the plain with your blood and feed your flesh to the eagle and the vulture.[39]

DEUT 28:26
Your corpses shall be food for every bird of the air and animal of the earth, and there shall be no one to frighten them away.[40]

The blindness curse is followed in VTE by the threat of violent death at the hand of the war god Ninurta, whose excesses will extend to the entire plain of battle. Death is compounded by the condemnation of the corpse to the indignity of consumption by carrion birds: the eagle and the vulture. Similar cultural concerns lie behind Deut 28:26, in which the addressees are warned of the consumption of their corpses by birds and animals, without respite. The language of these two texts bears some similarities, most especially in the references to carrion birds and the description of the addressee as food for or feeding the animals. Conceptually, both curses draw on a common fear of unrest for the dead

---

[39] ᵈMAŠ *a-šá-rid* DINGIR.MEŠ *ina šil-ta-ḫi-šu šam-ri li-šam-qit-ku-nu* MÚD.MEŠ-*ku-nu li-mal-li* EDIN UZU- [*k*]*u-nu* Á.MUŠEN *zi-i-bu li-šá-kil*

[40] והיתה נבלתך למאכל לכל עוף השמים ולבהמת הארץ ואין מחריד

whose bodies are not honored with proper burial.[41] We will return to this issue in chapter three; here it will suffice to observe that the same concept arises in Sin-sharru-ishkun's treaty with his Babylonian allies— "May [......] of heaven and earth cover (sic) them with an evil, irremovable curse. Above, may [he uproot] them from amongst the living, (and) below, in the underworld, deprive [their] ghosts of water"[42]—as well as in a curse in one of Assurbanipal's inscriptions, invoked in prayer to Assur and Ishtar: "May his corpse be cast before his enemy and may they bring me his bones."[43] Esarhaddon declares that he "let the vultures eat the unburied bodies of their [his enemies'] warriors."[44] Multiple reports of the deliberate desecration of enemy dead as a form of post-mortem punishment or humiliation confirm this as a well-established component of the Assyrian understanding of death and its implications for the afterlife.[45] The Deuteronomy curse reflects a similar cultural logic, but gives little indication of dependence on the VTE formulation. Again, the terminological overlap is limited and the symmetry is weak:

May Ninurta	—
the foremost among the gods	—
fell you with his fierce arrow	—
may he fill the plain with your blood	—
and feed your flesh	Your corpses shall be food
to the eagle and the vulture	for every bird of the air
	and animal of the earth
—	and there shall be no one to
	frighten them away

---

[41] C. B. Hays, *Death in the Iron Age II and in First Isaiah* (FAT 79; Tübingen: Mohr Siebeck, 2011), 11–132; cf. F. Stavrakopoulou, "Gog's Grave and the Use and Abuse of Corpses in Ezekiel 39:11–20," *JBL* 129 (2010): 67–76.

[42] [x x] *šá* AN-*e u* KI.TIM *ar-rat la na*[*p-šu-ri*] [GIG-*t*]*ú li-ri-im-šú-nu e-liš i-na* T[I.LA.MEŠ] [*li-su-uḫ-š*]*ú-nu šap-liš i-na* KI.TIM *ꞌeꞌ-*[*ṭím-ma-šú-nu*] [A.ME]Š *lu-u-za-am-me* (SAA 2 11 7'–10'); cf. SAA 2 9 13'–14'.

[43] *pa-an* ˡᵘ*kúr-šú pa-gar* ‖ *adda-šú li-ø* ‖ *in-na-di-ma liš-šu-u* ‖ *ø-ni* gìr-PAD-DU ‖ *da-meš-šú* (R. Borger, *Beiträge zum Inschriftenwerk Assurbanipals: Die Prismenklassen A, B, C = K, D, E, F, G, H, J und T sowie andere Inschriften, mit einem Beitrag von Andreas Fuchs* [Wiesbaden: Harrassowitz, 1996], A ii 116–117, with fulfilment noted in A ii 117–118).

[44] *pa-gar qu-ra-di-šú-un ina la qe-bé-ri ú-šá-kil zi-i-bu* (Esarhaddon 1 v 6; cf. Esarhaddon 1019 16, as enumerated in E. Leichty, *The Royal Inscriptions of Esarhaddon, King of Assyria (680–669 BC)* [RINAP 4; Winona Lake, Ind.: Eisenbrauns, 2011]).

[45] For details of such reports see C. L. Crouch, *War and Ethics in the Ancient Near East: Military Violence in Light of Cosmology and History* (BZAW 407; Berlin: de Gruyter, 2009).

As with the curses discussed already, these curses differ noticeably, though they are superficially quite similar. The deity, his descriptor, and the military context are absent in Deuteronomy. The military context of the VTE threat is overtly expressed by the curse itself: it is the warrior felled on the plain of battle whose body will be denied burial. Though a military context for Deut 28:26 may be inferred from Deut 28:25 (inclusion of which, for the sake of the parallel to VTE, dilutes the similarities even further), the envisaged scenario remains quite different: neither verse describes the occasion or nature of the death of the person whose corpse is now threatened. If anything, the description of flight "seven ways" in Deut 28:25 implies survival on the battlefield only to suffer an ignominious afterlife when death does arrive. While the curse in VTE constitutes a simple threat of non-burial and corpse humiliation, there is a significant additional emphasis on the unceasing nature of this fate in Deuteronomy, in which the warning that "there shall be none to frighten them away" demolishes any hope of deliverance. Rather than relating to a VTE source, this divergence anticipates the similar iterations of immutability in the following verses ("of which you cannot be healed," אשר לא תוכל להרפא, Deut 28:27; "continually abused and robbed, without anyone to help," והיית אך עשוק וגזול כל הימים ואין מושיע, Deut 28:29; "without anyone to help you," ואין לך מושיע, Deut 28:31). Though clearly a particular interest of Deuteronomy, the relevance of such an emphasis to a subversive agenda is opaque.

The Akkadian refers to two types of carrion birds, while the Hebrew generalizes with "every bird of the air" and diverges further in its expansion of the consumers of the corpses to include land animals in addition to the birds. Perhaps the differences in the phrasing—the passive "your corpses shall be food for every bird of the air" (והיתה נבלתך למאכל לכל עוף השמים) instead of the active "(may he) feed your flesh to the eagle and the vulture" (UZU-[k]u-nu Á.MUŠEN zi-i-bu li-šá-kil) are attributable to the demands of acceptability in Hebrew, but it serves to emphasize that the texts' only specific terminological overlap is in their use of the root 'kl: as a verb in VTE and as a noun by Deuteronomy. The weight placed on this limited evidence by the interpretation of the Deuteronomy curse as an allusion to VTE is considerable. In this verse as in those that follow, the relationship between Deuteronomy and its purported VTE source text is neither specific, nor frequent, nor distinctive. It is generalized at the point of its similarity and, where divergent, without apparent subversive purpose.

VTE §42
May Venus [Ishtar], the brightest of the stars, before your eyes make your wives lie in the lap of your enemy; may your sons not take possession of your house, but a strange enemy divide your goods.[46]

DEUT 28:30–33
[30]You shall become engaged to a woman, but another man shall lie with her. You shall build a house, but not live in it. You shall plant a vineyard, but not enjoy its fruit. [31]Your ox shall be butchered before your eyes, but you shall not eat of it. Your donkey shall be stolen in front of you, and shall not be restored to you. Your sheep shall be given to your enemies, without anyone to help you. [32]Your sons and daughters shall be given to another people, while you look on; you will strain your eyes looking for them all day but be powerless to do anything. [33]A people whom you do not know shall eat up the fruit of your ground and of all your labors; you shall be continually abused and crushed.[47]

VTE §42 articulates the spoils of war as experienced by the defeated, whose wives are raped by the victors and whose property is plundered, denied as an inheritance to the addressees' sons. The points of overlap between Deuteronomy and this text are twofold. First, the named people and things involved are similar: there is the woman of whom the addressee expects exclusive access; the man's sons; and his house. In Akkadian these are *ḫirtu*, *māru* (DUMU), and *bītu* (É), respectively; in Hebrew they are אשה, בנים, and בית. Both also reference the addressee's enemy: *nakru* ([lú]KÚR) and איבים. In terms of frequency of terminological overlap, the Deuteronomy curse(s) might conceivably be successful in signaling to VTE §42, although the overall extent of the Deuteronomy material over which these terms are spread does work against it. Whether these particular terms are specific or distinctive enough to work as signals is also doubtful. Women, sons, and houses are not entities distinctive to any human society but rather entities common to nearly all and certainly to both Mesopotamia and the southern Levant. As common

---

[46] [d]*dil-bat na-bat* MUL.MEŠ *ina ni-ṭil* IGI.2-*ku-nu ḫi-ra-a-te-ku-nu ina* ÚR LÚ.KÚR-*ku-nu li-šá-ni-il* DUMU.MEŠ-*ku-nu a-a i-bé-lu* É-*ku-un* LÚ.KÚR *a-ḫu-u li-za-i-za mim-mu-ku-un*

[47] אשה תארש ואיש אחר ישגלנה בית תבנה ולא תשב בו כרם תטע ולא תחללנו: שורך טבוח לעיניך ולא תאכל ממנו חמרך גזול מלפניך ולא ישוב לך צאנך נתנות לאיביך ואין לך מושיע: בניך ובנתיך נתנים לעם אחר ועיניך ראות וכלות אליהם כל היום ואין לאל ידך: פרי אדמתך וכל יגיעך יאכל עם אשר לא ידעת והיית רק עשוק ורצוץ כל הימים: The redactional status of Deut 28:33 is in some doubt; as it is a summary of the preceding verses and not in any specific way linked to VTE, however, its inclusion or exclusion has little effect on the overall analysis.

phenomena they lack the distinctiveness of good signals: to recall Berger, "if the features in question are unexceptional, or if we observe just a handful of similarities distributed over large expanses of text, an argument in favor of allusion will most often fall short."[48] Nor are the terms themselves distinctive: both VTE and Deuteronomy use the common word for each of these entities in their respective languages.[49] The fact that the only specific points of overlap between these texts are in common terminology does not bode well for Deuteronomy's ability—or intent—to signal its use of VTE.

The content of these curses also levies against the interpretation of Deut 28:30–33 as drawing on VTE §42. In this respect it is worth highlighting, first, that the concepts behind VTE §42 are not, in themselves, distinctive: the collocation of sons, houses, and sexual deprivation appears, for example, in the Assur-nerari-Mati'ilu treaty:

> If our death is not your death, if our life is not your life, if you do not seek (to protect) the life of Aššur-nerari, his sons and his magnates as your own life and the life of your sons and officials, then may Aššur, father of the gods, who grants kingship, turn your land into a battlefield, your people to devastation, your cities into mounds, and your house into ruins.
>
> If Mati'-ilu sins against this treaty with Aššur-nerari, king of Assyria, may Mati'-ilu become a prostitute, his soldiers women, may they receive [a gift] in the square of their cities like any prostitute, may one country push them to the next; may Mati'-ilu's (sex) life be that of a mule, his wives extremely old; may Ištar, the goddess of men, the lady of women, take away their bow, bring them to shame, and make them bitterly weep ...[50]

---

[48] Berger, "Ruth," 254.

[49] Of the four, only the words for house (bītu, בית) are cognate. It is difficult to conclude whether, or to what extent, Deuteronomy might have been clearer in signaling use of VTE with respect to the remaining terms while still remaining acceptable in the target language: it might conceivably have used נכרים in lieu of איבים to nearer resemble nakru, but the options for the woman and the sons are more limited.

[50] šúm-mu mu-a-tin-ni la mu-at-kašúm-mu ba-[la-ṭi]n-ni la ba-laṭ-ka-ni ki-i šá TI.LA šá Z[I.MEŠ]-ka DUMU.MEŠ-ka GAL.MEŠ-ka ku-[nu]-ni TI.LA šá ᵐaš-šur—ERIM.GABA DUMU.MEŠ-šú GAL.MEŠ-šú la tú'-[b]a-'u-u-ni aš-šur AD DINGIR.MEŠ na-din LUGAL-ti KUR-ka ana tú-šá-ri UN.MEŠ-ka ana GÌR.BAL URU.MEŠ-ka ana DUL.ME É-ka ana ḫar-ba-ti lu-tir // šúm-mu ᵐKI.MIN ina a-de-e an-nu-tiša ᵐaš-šur—ERIM.[GABA] MAN KUR—aš-šur iḫ-ti-ṭi ᵐKI.MIN lu MÍ.ḫa-rim-tú LÚ'.ERIM.[MEŠ-šú] lu MÍ.MEŠ GIM MÍ.ḫa-rim-tú ina re-bit URU-šú-n[u nidᵊ-n]u lim-ḫu-ru KUR ana KUR lid-ḫu-šú-nu

In this category Koch also draws attention to a curse associated with the goddess Astarte in Esarhaddon's treaty with Baal of Tyre: "May Astarte break your bow in the thick of battle and have you crouch at the feet of your enemy, may a foreign enemy divide your belongings."[51] The use and abuse of females is so common to the antagonistic relations among men as to hardly—in this context, at least—merit a second thought; the targets of military destruction and the exploitation of conquered property are similarly mundane. Cities are destroyed; property is destroyed or commandeered; people are humiliated, killed, or both. The VTE curse resides conceptually and terminologically in a wider Assyrian context that, in turn, is itself part of a common conceptualization of the effects of military engagement. Although both texts more or less explicitly concern loss resulting from military defeat, the lack of conceptual distinctiveness in their similarities works against identifying these similarities as a convincing case of allusion.

Closer inspection of the curses also reveals that these similarities are essentially superficial. As already noted, the Deuteronomy text is much more extensive, including agriculture and animals; this dilutes the strength of its connection to VTE.[52] Even more importantly, the relations among the overlapping components differ significantly. VTE relates the house to the sons who will not inherit; in Deuteronomy the two elements appear separately, with the house of the addressee built but not inhabited and the sons—mentioned alongside daughters—appearing as destined for deportation. The woman is the wife in VTE and the betrothed in Deuteronomy.

This last also highlights a significant difference in the overall function of the texts. Though both threaten the addressee with loss, the loss in VTE is explicitly articulated in terms of loss to another, with both wife and property transferred to the possession of the enemy. The loss in Deuteronomy, on the other hand, is loss primarily in the sense of non-consummation or non-fulfilment: it is the woman to whom the addressee is engaged but not yet married, not the wife he already has, whom he will lose before his sexual access to her is consummated; it is the vineyard and livestock that he possesses of which he will not enjoy the yield. Both texts operate, more or less explicitly, against a background of

---

TI' *ša* ^mKI.[MIN *lu šá*ʾ] ANŠE.GÌR.NUN *áš-šá-tu-šú li-tu-tu* [^d15 *be-l*]*it* NITA.MEŠ GAŠAN MÍ.MEŠ GIŠ.BAN-*su-nu li-kim* [*x*]*x bal-tu-šú-nu liš-kun* (SAA 2 2 v 1–13).

[51] ^d*aš-tar-tú ina ta-ḫa-zi dan-ni* GIŠ.BAN-ʾ*ku-nu li-<iš>-bir ina šap*ʾ-*l*[*a* LÚ*.KÚR-ku-nu*] *li-še-ši-ib-ku-nu* LÚ*.KÚR *a-ḫu-u li-za-i-za mim-*[*mu-ku-nu*] (SAA 2 5 iv 18′–19′); Koch, *Vertrag*, 222–223.

[52] Steymans concludes that much of this text is secondary (Steymans, "Eine assyrische Vorlage," 125).

war and plunder, but the VTE focus on it being the enemy who will possess the addressees' property is a minor theme in Deuteronomy, which is much more explicitly concerned with the addressee's failure to experience the use of his possessions. In sum, the similarities between these texts are superficial and concern only the most general of their respective features, rather than any of their distinctive or specific ones. Reliance on such indistinct components of the source to signal an intentional, subversive allusion to VTE is unlikely to have succeeded.

VTE §§63–64

[63]Ditto, ditto, may all the gods that are [mentioned by name] in th[is] treaty tablet make the ground as narrow as a brick for you. May they make your ground like iron (so that) nothing can sprout from it. [64]Just as rain does not fall from a brazen heaven so may rain and dew not come upon your fields and your meadows; instead of dew may burning coals rain on your land.[53]

DEUT 28:23–24

[23]The sky over your head shall be bronze, and the earth under you iron. [24]YHWH will change the rain of your land into powder, and only dust shall come down upon you from the sky until you are destroyed.[54]

The final parallel between VTE and Deuteronomy concerns VTE §§63–64 and Deut 28:23–24. These are the texts that are generally considered to be the most closely related of any of those proposed as indicating Deuteronomy's dependence on VTE: appearing in both texts are the sky, described as bronze, the earth, specified as iron, and the descent of various substances from the sky in place of rain. The sky (šamû [AN], שמים), bronze (sipparu [UD.KA.BAR], נחשת), earth (q/kaqqaru, ארץ), and iron (parzillu [AN.BAR], ברזל) overlaps are terminological; the overlap in the idea of the god sending non-rain from the sky as punishment is more broadly conceptual, except for the use of words for rain in both texts (zunnu [n.], zananu [v.], מטר). In Deut 28:23–24, then, the terminological overlap with regard to specific words from VTE is more extensive than in any of the other texts considered, consisting of as many as five individual terms. It is also reasonably frequent, insofar as the overall length of the two VTE curses and the two Deuteronomy verses is not so

---

[53] KI.MIN KI.MIN DINGIR.MEŠ ma-la ina ṭup-pi a-d[e]-e an-[ni-e MU-šú-nuzak-ru] am—mar SIG₄ kaq-qu-ru lu-si-qu-ni-ku-nu kaq-qar-ku-nu ki-i AN.BAR le-pu-šume-me-ni ina ŠÀ-bi lu la i-par-ru-ʾa

[54] והיו שמיך על ראשך נחשת והארץ אשר תחתיך ברזל: יתן יהוה את מטר ארצך אבק ועפר מן השמים ירד עליך עד השמדך:

much as to dilute the terms' appearance into a sea of other verbiage. If Deuteronomy is intending to signal a relationship with and an intent to subvert VTE by using specific words and phrases from VTE, this degree of frequency just might succeed in doing so. There remain, nevertheless, some points of concern which hinder the conclusion that Deuteronomy here intends to allude to VTE.

As with Deut 28:30–33 and VTE §41, one issue is the lack of distinctiveness of the overlapping terminology. The similarities again occur in the form of several common concepts: the natural world, represented by the earth and the sky, and its natural phenomena, represented by the rain or its withholding. Iron and bronze are common metals. Whether these five terms, taken together, might have successfully signaled Deuteronomy's intention to allude to another text that also contained these five terms is difficult to determine; we will be obliged to return to it in chapter four. However, the relative commonality of each of the individual components of this set renders the adequate transference of their original constellation of meaning into the new work all the more important. Yet: the VTE material can hardly be said to have been precisely rendered into Deuteronomy, either with regard to syntax or with regard to meaning; instead Deuteronomy plays havoc on the relative relations and purpose of these lexemes' counterparts in VTE, with no apparent objective in doing so. Thus the least awkward juxtaposition of these two texts might look something like the following (and even this demands the dislocation of Deut 28:23b):

[63]may all the gods that are [mentioned — by name] in th[is] treaty tablet make the ground as narrow as a brick for you	—
May they make your ground like iron	[23b]and the earth under you iron
(so that) nothing can sprout from it	—
[64]Just as rain does not fall from a brazen heaven	[23a]The sky over your head shall be bronze
—	[24]YHWH will change the rain of your land into powder
so may rain and dew not come upon your fields and your meadows	—
instead of dew may burning coals rain on your land	and only dust shall come down upon you from the sky
—	until you are destroyed

As before, the superficial similarity of these texts is betrayed by their substantial divergences, with even the texts here juxtaposed reflecting,

upon direct comparison, only limited similarities. Nearly the entirety of
VTE §63 is without a Deuteronomy counterpart; this includes the
description of the ground as "as narrow as a brick," which, in VTE, is the
first iteration of the idea expressed by the analogization of the earth to
iron. While it is explicit in both VTE §63 and VTE §64 that the curse will
inhibit agricultural production, this is absent from Deuteronomy.
Additional issues arise from the fact that the VTE material comprises, in
this exceptional case, not one but two curses. The first, VTE §63, impels
the deities to render the earth like a brick, like iron, for the purpose of
preventing agricultural production; the second, VTE §64, evokes the
analogy of a bronze sky, from which rain does not fall, to demand that
no hydration of any kind grace the fields. In lieu of rain, the curse
invokes burning coals. The elements of the two VTE curses that do
appear in Deuteronomy are garbled: the bronze sky and iron earth are
joined together in Deut 28:23, while the abnormal precipitation appears
in Deut 28:24. The generalized destruction in Deuteronomy is rendered
in VTE much more specifically as agricultural depredation. The
Deuteronomy text introduces spatial notations absent from VTE—the
bronze sky is over the addressee, while the iron earth is under—and
while the idea is hardly alien to Hebrew both the heavens and earth are
well able to appear without this reminder.[55] The text also declares that
the abnormal precipitation will be powder and dust, rather than the
burning coals of VTE, even though something like גחלי אש would surely
have been acceptable within target norms.[56] The omission of the initial
curse that the earth be like brick, the alteration of the purpose of the
curse(s), the change in what will now fall from the heavens, and the
abandonment of the bronze sky's rhetorical function all distance the
Deuteronomy text from the VTE text. Perhaps some of these divergences
might be attributed to acceptability in the target language, but when
combined with the overall asymmetry of the two texts they do nothing
but weaken the new text's ability to evoke VTE as its source.[57] More than

---

[55] Note also that the texts that do make spatial annotations almost always use
שמים ממעל and ארץ מתחת (Deut 4:39; Exod 20:4 // Deut 5:8; Josh 2:11; 1 Kgs 8:23; cf. Isa
51:6). The phrasing in Deut 28:23–24 is thus unusual within the Hebrew repertoire—
but there is no indication that its phrasing reflects an underlying Akkadian phrase.

[56] Cf. Pss 18:9, 13–14; 140:10; 2 Sam 22:9, 13; Ezek 1:13; 10:2; Job 41:13.

[57] The curses also occur against a background in which the deprivation of normal
precipitation, with attendant consequences, was part of a common curse repertoire;
compare the Shamshi-adad-Marduk-zakir-shumi and Assur-nerari-Mati'ilu treaties.
The latter invokes "Adad, the canal inspector of heaven and earth" to put an end
Mati'ilu's land, "deprived of Adad's thunder so that rain becomes forbidden to

a top-level "translation" of the VTE material will have been necessary to signal VTE as the source text.

At this point it is useful to reintroduce Toury and, in particular, his discussion of the margins of translational activity. As observed in chapter one, most usually biblical scholars think of translation in terms of word by word, or at least phrase by phrase, transposition of a source text into a target language. If the relationship between the source text and the target text is intended to be retained for the interpretation of the target text, as in a case of subversion, this is the kind of translation we may expect. At the fringes of "translation," however, there is the possibility of the "translation" of an entire textual entity *en bloc*: that is, the replacement of an entire text, or section thereof, with another block of text that, though designed to convey broadly the same information, possesses no finer connection to the source text. Discussing the relationship between various warnings on English and German trains, Toury discusses how, in such a case, "the source text itself had not been broken down during the act, so that replacement was indeed performed on the level of the textual repertoire: a habitual entity for another habitual entity of the same rank."[58]

In Toury's example, the texts are warnings in German and English on German trains. The English text functions entirely on its own; its relationship to the German text is inconsequential to its interpretation. It is only the fact of the texts' physical juxtaposition that raises the possibility that the English text should be construed as a translation of the German text. We will return to this idea in chapter five; the salient point for the current discussion is this:

> It is not that no lower-rank coupled pairs could have been established in this case too (e.g., "pull + *ziehen*", "handle + *Griff*", "penalty + *wird bestraft*" and "improper use + *Mißbrauch*"); it is only that those pairs would be irrelevant for the mode of transition from one text to the other (i.e., the reconstructed translation process): they would have reflected the mere fact that similar (but not identical!) verbal formulations have

---

them": "May dust be their food ..." (*ik-kil* ᵈIM *li-za-me-ú-ma* A.AN.MEŠ *a-na ik-ki-bi-šú-nu liš-šá-kín*; SAA 2 2 iv 8–16). The former demands that "[May Adad, the canal inspector of heaven and earth, deprive him of rain] from the heaven, and of seasonal flooding from the underground water; may he destroy [his land through famine, roar fiercely at his city], and turn his [land into ruins by means of a flood]" ([ᵈIM GÚ.GAL AN-*e u* KI.TIM A.A]N *ina* AN-*e* A.KAL *ina nag-bi* [*li-ṭir-šu*] [KUR-*su ina ḫu-šaḫ-ḫi*] *li-ḫal-*[*liq* 0] [UGU URU-*šú ez-zi-iš li-is-si-ma* KUR]-*su¹ a¹-n*[*a* DU₆ *a-bu-bi*]; SAA 2 1 13–15).

[58] Toury, *Descriptive Translation Studies*, 119.

been selected by members of different societies to indicate similar norms of behaviour under similar circumstances.[59]

In attempting to understanding the relationship between Deuteronomy and VTE, a narrow focus on "coupled pairs" obscures the importance of the wider dissimilarities between the two texts for understanding their relationship. That such pairs exist is not evidence for the translation of an Akkadian text into a Hebrew text, but rather evidence for the use of similar words to refer to similar circumstances in different societies. In the case of Deuteronomy and VTE, the fact that the two texts—both using curse formulae to threaten natural upheaval and disaster—share similar terminology is hardly surprising. This fact must remain subordinate to the overall relationship of the textual entities in which these terms appear.[60]

Two final points are in order. Further problematizing the ability of Deut 28:23–24 to signal a relationship to VTE is that the VTE material to which Deut 28:23–24 is supposed to allude is entirely isolated from the other passages claimed as Deuteronomy's source material: VTE §63 and VTE §64 are twenty sections further into VTE than the passages previously discussed. Though Deut 28:23–24 initially appears to be a concentrated use of VTE source material, therefore, the allusive potential of this material—if such it is—is immediately countermanded by the text's failure to reinforce these signals with further ones. Rather than continuing in Deut 28:25 with material from VTE §65, Deut 28:25 uses nothing recognizable from VTE at all, while Deut 28:26 is supposed to backtrack two dozen curses to VTE §41. The concentration of references to which we might appeal in support of allusive intent in Deut 28:23–24, despite the overall evidence to the contrary, is thus undermined. If Deuteronomy is deliberately alluding to VTE, we should expect to see this intention reiterated in the accumulation of further evidence, with developing patterns in the texts to which Deuteronomy alludes.[61] Such patterns are not evident. Indeed, the material ostensibly chosen from

---

[59] Ibid., 119.

[60] We may especially wish to note that the German and English texts in Toury's example are a mere nine and ten words each; it is possible, in other words, to produce a quite significant number of coupled pairs (Toury offers four) in a quite short passage without this necessitating the conclusion that the one is translating the other—not, at least, at the level of adequacy that would suggest the relevance of the relationship between the two texts for the interpretation of the "target" text (see further chapters one and five).

[61] Sommer, *A Prophet Reads Scripture*, 32–72.

VTE by the author of Deut 28:23–24 is a bizarre passage to have chosen for any purpose, let alone a subversive one. It occurs in the middle of VTE's extensive curse section and its content bears no relation to Deuteronomy's purportedly subversive intent. Only with significant difficulty, therefore, may Deut 28:23–24 be understood as alluding to VTE §63 and VTE §64 for the purpose of signaling Deuteronomy's subversive relationship with VTE.

Considered in terms of the criteria for successful subversion—especially the specificity, distinctiveness, and frequency of the text's signals to its source, such that the relationship between the texts might be recognizable and understood as aimed at subversion—these verses must be acknowledged as a failure. The relationship between the individual verses of Deut 28:23–24, 26–33 and VTE §§39–42, 63–64 constitutes little more than a series of loosely related ideas. Only rarely do they involve the sharing of specific terms and phrases. The terms common to the two texts are quite ordinary, rather than terms that might be deemed distinctive to VTE and thus trigger the recognition of Deuteronomy's allusive intent. Conceptually, the texts rarely share more than a general idea or image; the concepts that they do share are not unique to these texts. Ultimately the extent of the similarities between Deut 28 and VTE is limited to the superficial resemblances of curses involving illness; blindness; loss of possessions; denial of burial and the consumption of the corpse by carrion; and the imagery of an iron earth and a bronze sky. While this list seems at first remarkable, establishing a specific and recognizable relationship between individual Deuteronomy and VTE curses on its basis is well-nigh impossible. None of the similarities are sufficiently precise as to warrant the claim that Deuteronomy has deliberately used specific, distinctive, and recognizable words and phrases from VTE to signal a relationship with that specific source text; the frequency of the overlap that does exist is underwhelming. Without successfully signaling its relationship with and intention to be understood in contrast to VTE through the use of specific and distinctive words and phrases at a frequency that facilitates the recognition of this relationship, Deuteronomy's ability to subvert VTE is undermined before it even begins.

In light of the foregoing, it is perhaps no surprise that sequential similarities between Deuteronomy's and VTE's contents have received particular attention in the analysis of the two texts' relationship. Weinfeld, for example, already contended that the sequence of curses in Deut 28:27–33 were explicable only in reference to the deity hierarchy (Sin–Shamash–Ninurta–Ishtar) reflected in VTE §§39–42, and variations on this remain common; Koch has recently argued that Deut 28:25–36 is based on a palindromic rendering of the deities Ninurta, Sin, Shamash, and Ishtar (i.e., Ninurta–Sin–Shamash–Ishtar–Shamash–Sin–Ninurta).[62] Another recent variant is Steymans' contention that the structure of (an original, shorter version of) Deut 28:20–44 is based on VTE §56, arguing that not only the correlations between the individual curses of Deut 28:23–24, 26–33 and VTE §§39–40, (41,) 42, 63–64 are sufficiently specific to signal a relationship between these texts but that their overall structure is also sufficiently similar to VTE §56 to signal a specific literary relationship between Deuteronomy and VTE.[63] To Steymans' argument we will turn momentarily; first, however, there are already immediate problems with the more traditional claims for Deuteronomy's reliance on the sequential structure of VTE §§39–42.

First, the Deuteronomy text does not actually follow the VTE sequence: the Deuteronomy curse associated with Ninurta appears before the others, in Deut 28:26, and is followed by curses associated with the VTE curses attributed to Sin, Shamash, and Ishtar. This disordering has no discernable purpose with respect to subversive

---

[62] Weinfeld, "Traces of Assyrian Treaty Formulae," 420–23 (similarly B. M. Levinson and J. Stackert, "Between the Covenant Code and Esarhaddon's Succession Treaty: Deuteronomy 13 and the Composition of Deuteronomy," *JAJ* 3 [2012]: 123–40); C. Koch, *Vertrag, Treueid und Bund: Studien zur Rezeption des altorientalischen Vertragsrechts im Deuteronomium und zur Ausbildung der Bundestheologie im alten Testament* (BZAW 383; Berlin: de Gruyter, 2008), 241–44. Koch's suggestion is, in part, connected to his efforts to dissociate Deuteronomy from VTE specifically; if Deuteronomy is assumed to be borrowing a sequential logic based on the respective remits of the deities of the Assyrian pantheon, it need not be doing so on the basis of VTE in particular, as there are other texts through which Deuteronomy might have picked up such a sequence (ibid., 218–22). (One might also observe that the relative hierarchy of Assyrian deities is not the sort of information that must necessarily have been derived from a textual source—and that this is complicated by the variability in the pantheon even over the relatively brief period in question.) In making this argument, however, Koch appears to unwittingly strengthen the text's connection to the Assyrian tradition more generally. As, if correct, such an association poses a potential counter-thrust to the present argument, it is worth further attention, although it anticipates somewhat the discussions of chapters three and four. Its downfall, however, is quite readily identified: Koch himself admits that the association between Deut 28:36 with Ninurta is tenuous, while the justification for associating Deut 28:25, 36 with Ninurta and Deut 28:34, 35 with Shamash and Sin are no stronger—no more specific, frequent, or distinctive—than the usual association of Deut 28:26–33 with these deities plus Ishtar.

[63] Steymans, "Eine assyrische Vorlage," 119–41; idem, *Deuteronomium 28*, 284–312.

intent; it is difficult to imagine, for example, how the prioritization of the war god Ninurta over his colleagues might be construed as subverting a program of Assyrian imperial domination. The remarkable clumsiness with which Deuteronomy must be supposed to have borrowed this sequence from VTE—mis-ordering it and thus disordering the theological significance of such a sequence—makes it difficult to view the order of Deuteronomy's curse material in Deut 28:26–33 as a deliberate allusion to a VTE source text.

In addition to spoiling the hierarchy of deities reflected by VTE, this group of curses is buried in the middle of the Deuteronomy curse section (Deut 28:20–44). While it is, of course, possible to eliminate some of the surrounding material—on account of strong deuteronomistic affinities, for example—the dissolution of the entirety of the material that cannot be closely linked to VTE §§39–42 finds no support beyond the purported reliance of an original author on the VTE text. The strongest case for a connection between the texts—VTE §§63–64 and Deut 28:23–24—is not part of this sequence at all. From the perspective of VTE, it is difficult to fathom the unifying logic of the curses that Deuteronomy is supposed to have extracted for its purposes: they are neither the first nor the last, nor do they form an obvious unit within the VTE curse section (which is extensive, constituting nearly half of VTE and containing several dozen curses). Perhaps most notably, the first three curses in VTE—attributed to Assur, Mullissu, and Anu—are overlooked entirely, despite these deities' status: surely, if Deuteronomy intended to undermine VTE and the Assyrian ideology it represented, the route to doing so ought to have incorporated the Assyrians' eponymous deity at the very least.[64] It may also be pertinent to observe that the deities of VTE appear to have no qualms about appearing in mixed company; of the deities in VTE §§39–42, both Ishtar (who is not, in fact, named in VTE §42 as such, but as Venus) and Shamash appear twice later in the text, while Assur and Mullissu appear once more each. Making the significance of Deut 28:26–33 contingent on its relationship to a hierarchy that the Assyrians themselves do not appear to have held sacrosanct is precarious.

Recognizing that VTE §§39–40, (41,) 42, 63–64 appear to be randomly selected VTE passages, Steymans attempts to explain their choice as

---

[64] Note too that Assur is invariably present in Assyrian treaty curse sequences; while problematic in the immediate context for Deuteronomy's relationship to VTE, therefore, it also casts doubt on the variant hypothesis to be considered in more detail in chapter three—namely that it is some other Assyrian treaty, or an abstraction thereof, that Deuteronomy intends to subvert: any such entity would have involved reference to Assur, and the absence of any material in Deut 28 associable with that deity invites explanation.

reflecting Deuteronomy's intention to use material that in VTE is associated with solar deities, linking this to YHWH's solar manifestations.[65] They are integrated into a coherent whole through their relationship to an overall structure based on VTE §56. The difficulty in viewing the relationship between Deut 28:23–24, 26–33 and VTE §§39–42, 63–64 as deliberately signaling the former's intention to be interpreted in light of the latter has already been assessed and deemed wanting. Perhaps, however, Deut 28:20–44 is successful in signaling a relationship with VTE §56; if so, the otherwise general similarities between Deut 28:23–24, 26–33 and VTE §§39–42, 63–64 may stand in a supporting role. As with the individual curses, the argument requires that Deuteronomy be able to distinguish its use of VTE specifically, as opposed to some other source, and suggests that the degree of correlation between these parallels ought to be quite precise and reasonably extensive, probably involving the use of specific and distinctive words and phrases with a frequency that attracts attention to the relationship and its intentionality. A brief foray into the proposition readily establishes that it does not fulfil these requirements.

Steymans' outline of Deut 28 according to VTE §56 begins by aligning the first ten lines of VTE §56 with Deut 28:20–22.[66]

VTE §56

[472–475]May all the great[t go]ds of heaven and earth who inhabit the universe and are mentioned by name in this tablet, strike you, look at you in anger, uproot you from among the living and curse you grimly with a painful curse. [476]Above, may they take possession of your life; [476–479]below, in the netherworld, may they make your ghost thirst for water. May shade and daylight always chase you away, and may you not find refuge in a hidden cor[ner]. [479]May food and water abandon you; [480–481]may want and famine, hunger and plague never be removed from you.[67]

---

[65] Steymans, "Eine assyrische Vorlage," 121–22, 137–40; idem, *Deuteronomium 28*, 284–312.

[66] The logic involved in these correlations is detailed most clearly in Steymans, "Eine assyrische Vorlage," 122–23, 128. As VTE §56 is extensive, the line numbers are used for additional clarity.

[67] DIN[GIR.MEŠ G]AL.MEŠ *šá* AN-*e* KI.TIM *a-ši-bu-tu kib-ra-ʾa-tiˋ ma-la ina ṭup-pi an-ni-e* MU-*šú-nuzak-r*[*u*] *lim-ḫa-ṣu-ku-nu li-kil-mu-ku-nu ár-ra-tu ma-ru-uš-tu ag-giš li-ru-ru-ku-nu e-liš* TI.LA.MEŠ *li-sa-ḫu-ku-nu šap-liš ina* KI.TIM *e-ṭím-ma-ku-nu* A.MEŠ *li-ṣa-mu-u* GIŠ.MI *u* UD.DA *li-ik-ta-ši-du-ku-nu ina pu-uz-ri šá-ḫ*[*a-ti*] *la ta-nim-me-da* ˋNINDAˋ.MEŠ *u* A.MEŠ *li-z*[*i-b*]*u-ku-nu su-un-qu ḫu-šaḫ-ḫu bu-bu-tu* NAM.[Ú]Š.MEŠ TA IGI-*ku-nu a-*[*a*] *ip-pi-ṭirˊ*

DEUT 28:20–22

²⁰YHWH will send upon you disaster, panic, and frustration in everything you attempt to do until you are destroyed and perish quickly, [on account of the evil of your deeds, because you have forsaken me]. ²¹YHWH will make the pestilence cling to you until it has consumed you from the land [that you are entering to possess]. ²²YHWH will afflict you with consumption, fever, inflammation, with fiery heat and drought, and with blight and mildew; they shall pursue you until you perish.[68]

After an introduction mentioning the deity in VTE §56 ll. 472–475, linked to Deut 28:20a, and a reference to death in VTE §56 l. 476, linked to Deut 28:20bα, Steymans equates an elaboration of the death curse with regard to thirst and persecution by the deities (VTE §56 ll. 476–479) with a curse of pestilence (Deut 28:21a). He claims that the curse of famine and disease in VTE §56 ll. 480–481 has been rendered as the illnesses and crop failure of Deut 28:22, whereupon the author diverted his attention momentarily from VTE §56 in order to introduce material based on VTE §§63–64, also implying agricultural failure, in Deut 28:23–24.[69]

⁴⁷²⁻⁴⁷⁵May all the great[t go]ds of heaven and earth who inhabit the universe and are mentioned by name in this tablet,	²⁰YHWH will send upon you
strike you, look at you in anger, uproot you from among the living and curse you grimly with a painful curse.	disaster, panic, and frustration in everything you attempt to do until you are destroyed
⁴⁷⁶Above, may they take possession of your life;	and perish quickly [on account of the evil of your

---

[68] ישלח יהוה בך את המארה את המהומה ואת המגערת בכל משלח ידך אשר תעשה עד השמדך ועד אבדך מהר מפני רע מעלליך אשר עזבתני: ידבק יהוה בך את הדבר עד כלתו אתך מעל האדמה אשר אתה בא שמה לרשתה: יככה יהוה בשחפת ובקדחת ובדלקת ובחרחר ובחרב ובשדפון ובירקון ורדפוך עד אבדך: Brackets indicate Steymans' own redactional conclusions.

[69] Steymans, "Eine assyrische Vorlage," 122-23, 129, 137–38. An English rendering of Steymans' own visualization of this relationship is provided for the sake of the reader, who should nevertheless note that the small units into which Steymans has broken the text, the variant syntaxes of English and German, and the severe limitations of the proposed similarities have rendered this rather awkward.

476–479below, in the netherworld, may they make your ghost thirst for water.

May shade and daylight always chase you away,
and may you not find refuge in a hidden cor[ner].

479May food and water abandon you;

480–481may want and famine, hunger and plague

never be removed from you.

deeds, because you have forsaken me].
21YHWH will make the pestilence cling to you

until it has consumed you from the land
[that you are entering to possess.]

22YHWH will afflict you with

consumption, fever, inflammation, with fiery heat

and drought, and with blight and mildew; they shall pursue you until you perish.

Over the course of two significant sections of text the only points of contact are the threats of death and plague/pestilence. The opening of both texts is generic, with no specific correlation between them beyond a summarizing promise of suffering. Both openings culminate with threats of death, but this is the obvious climax for series of generalizing maledictions and not distinctive enough to indicate a more specific use of VTE by Deuteronomy. VTE's subsequent interest is in the oath-taker's fate after death; Deuteronomy's is not. Deuteronomy's opening focuses on a range of illnesses before addressing the threat of drought, while VTE focuses on famine.

There is nothing specific in the content of these curses to suggest that Deuteronomy is drawing on the VTE text. We might continue through the rest of the analysis, but the results are the same; the material in Deuteronomy is neither specific, nor distinctive, nor frequent enough to make this a convincing case of allusion. Even supposing that the author of Deuteronomy was possessed of VTE and used it for inspiration, the resultant text of Deuteronomy cannot be understood as intending to signal a specific relationship with that text or its desire to be interpreted in its light. The imprecision of the similarities that do exist, exacerbated by the frequent interjections of material from elsewhere in VTE, would have severely hindered the text's ability to signal its use of VTE §56.

In fact, Steymans is obliged to rely heavily on the idea that translations may involve divergences from their sources in terminology and phraseology, as well as concluding that the author of Deut 28 was engaged in significant creative activity in the process of transforming this VTE source material.[70] Though creativity is inherent to the adaptive process, it is limited by the need to signal to the new work's audience that the adaptation should be understood *as* adaptation. The extent of the differentiation between Deut 28 and VTE §56 goes beyond what can be attributed to either translational limitations or creative license while still retaining the degree of specificity necessary to successfully signal an adaptation.

Last but not least, the points of divergence between the texts—the overwhelming majority of their content—produce no meaning. Recalling that it is an adaptive text's divergence from its source that reveals its intent, especially if subversive—lost boots in lieu of lost slippers—it is antithetical to the subversive argument that there is no point on which the differences between the material in VTE and the material in Deuteronomy converge. Though Steymans claims that the use of VTE §56 as a framework and the interjection of VTE §§63, 64, 41, 39, 40, 42 into this framework reflect Deuteronomy's intention to use curses pertaining to the sun god, this can hardly be sustained. VTE §56 is a generic invocation of "all the great gods," as is VTE §§63–64 ("all the gods"), while the others include Sin, Shamash, Ninurta, and Ishtar. A categorical stretch to allow that the adapted texts included all those relating to celestial deities of any kind (sun, moon, stars) might include all four of these deities, but becomes largely meaningless given the tendency for all prominent deities to be thus characterized.[71] It also

---

[70] Steymans, *Deuteronomium 28*, 380: "Moreover, he expanded his *Vorlage* according to his own concerns. In the transfer of his (probably Aramaic) version of VTE, he followed literary compositional techniques (amplification, permutation, *ellu-ebbu-namru*-Strukturen) like those used by Assyrian scribes in the revision of battle reports, and cast his text into the prescribed mold (e.g., *futility curses*) and idiomatic phrases of the target language, as attested by multilingual ancient Near Eastern curse and blessing texts as well as the translation of this text genre." ("Außerdem ergänzte er seine Vorlage nach eigenen Aussageanliegen. Bei der Übertragung der ihm wohl aramäisch vorliegenden VTE-Version folgte er literarische[n] Gestaltungstechniken (amplification, permutation, *ellu-ebbu-namru*-Strukturen), wie sie assyrische Schreiber zur Überarbeitung von Feldzugsberichten anwendeten, und goß seinen Text in vorgegebene Muster (z.B. *futility curses*) und idiomatische Wendungen der Zielsprache, wie es mehrsprachige altorientalische Fluch- und Segenstexte auch sonst für Übersetzungen dieser Textgattungen bezeugen.").

[71] The association between YHWH and the sun, which Steymans' entire argument about VTE §56 presupposes, is also problematic, despite the success with which the idea has permeated the literature. See J. Day, *Yahweh and the Gods and Goddesses of Canaan* (JSOTSup 265; Sheffield: Sheffield Academic, 2002), 151–63; S. A. Wiggins, "Yahweh: The God of Sun?," *JSOT* 71 (1996): 89–106; idem, "A Rejoinder to J. Glen

returns to the question of why these particular deities are singled out; they are not the first on the VTE curse list nor the most important if the objective is to challenge pretenders to YHWH's dominance.

In sum: an allusion to VTE by Deut 28 is far from recognizable, even by a highly literate modern audience with the advantage of being able to view and compare these texts in tandem. Were the similarities between the texts intended purposefully, they should be more extensive, more distinctive, and more specific, with the entirety of the Deuteronomy sequence paralleling a lengthy, recognizable sequence of VTE through the use of terms and phrases characteristic of and distinctive to VTE. Though discussing the (supposed) allusive relationship between Gen 38 and the Succession Narrative, Noble's lamentation sums the situation up nicely:

> The basic methodological flaw in these arguments, I think, is that the standards for identifying resemblances have been set far too low. Finding resemblances then becomes very easy; yet, although at first glance this seems to show that there is abundant evidence for a connection between these passages, a more careful assessment in fact suggests just the opposite. Taken as a whole, the resemblances are a disorderly hotch-poch of generally quite imprecise parallels, sometimes bubbling up in clusters ... sometimes all but disappearing from quite long stretches of the narrative ... often jumbling across each other, and all with very little sign of any intelligible plan or design informing the whole. In other words, they are far more suggestive of the sort of

---

Taylor," *JSOT* 73 (1997): 109–12; contra M. S. Smith, "When the Heavens Darkened: Yahweh, El, and the Divine Astral Family in Iron Age II Judah," in *Symbiosis, Symbolism, and the Power of the Past: Canaan, Ancient Israel, and Their Neighbors—From the Late Bronze Age through Roman Palaestina* (ed. W. G. Dever and S. Gitin; Winona Lake, Ind.: Eisenbrauns, 2003), 265–77; idem, "The Near Eastern Background of Solar Language for Yahweh," *JBL* 109 (1990): 29–39; H. P. Stähli, *Solare Elemente im Jahweglauben des Alten Testaments* (OBO 66; Göttingen: Vandenhoeck & Ruprecht, 1985); J. G. Taylor, *Yahweh and the Sun: Biblical and Archaeological Evidence for Sun Worship in Ancient Israel* (JSOTSup 111; Sheffield: JSOT, 1993); idem, "A Response to Steve A. Wiggins, 'Yahweh: The God of Sun?'," *JSOT* 71 (1996) 107–19. Note especially the recent attempt to trace the solarisation of YHWH to Assyrian influence, based on the interpretation of Psalm 72 as a subversive, Josianic reappropriation of Assurbanipals' coronation hymn (SAA 3 11), by Arneth (M. Arneth, *„Sonne der Gerechtigkeit"*: *Studien zur Solarisierung der Jahwe-Religion im Lichte von Psalm 72* [BZABR 1; Wiesbaden: Harrassowitz, 2000]). Following the example set by Steymans, Arneth attempts to demonstrate Psalm 72's subversive intention on the basis of a very limited set of terminological and structural correspondences; subjected to closer scrutiny, this holds up no better than Steymans' analysis of Deuteronomy and VTE.

random half-similarities which may arise between two texts simply by chance, than of a subtle author who is trying to intimate to his readers that he is covertly commenting upon another story that they know.[72]

The extent of the relationship between Deuteronomy and VTE is limited, and the connections that do exist are neither specific nor distinctive enough to VTE to signal a relationship with that text. The links are more often in terms of general subject rather than in specific terminology, and where there is terminology in common the overall phrasing and purpose of the Deuteronomy material diverges—often substantially—from the supposed VTE source, without an apparent reason for doing so. Given the vagueness and imprecision of the relationship between Deuteronomy and VTE, Deut 28 fails to produce a signal capable of identifying VTE as its source.

Deuteronomy 13

Though the roots of the subversion hypothesis lie in the correlations observed in Deut 28, the argument is no longer limited to that chapter. Much more pertinent to the alleged intention of Deuteronomy to challenge Assyrian power, in fact, are the proposed similarities between Deut 13 and VTE's section on treason, VTE §10. Here, given the source text's focus on the issue of loyalty and its addressees' potential failures in that quarter, combined with the subversion hypothesis's contention that it is loyalty with which Deuteronomy's interests in VTE are concerned— or, more precisely, to whom loyalty is due, Assurbanipal or YHWH—it is more readily conceivable that Deuteronomy's adaptation of such material might signal its subversive intent with regard to the Assyrian king. Whether Deuteronomy does so, however, depends on the same criteria used to assess the relationship between VTE and Deut 28: as it is a specific source involved, the precision of the allusions used to indicate the relationship may be expected to be relatively high.

VTE §10 forms part of the second section of VTE, after the introductory material: one of a long list of instructions to the oath-takers regarding their responsibilities. Among the other tasks with which the oath-takers are charged are the facilitation of Assurbanipal's ascent to the throne after Esarhaddon's death, delivery of good advice and support for Assurbanipal once he becomes king, and the provision of protection for him against threats: those against his person as well as those against his throne. Though less prominent, the treaty also

---

[72] P. R. Noble, "Esau, Tamar, and Joseph: Criteria for Identifying Inner-Biblical Allusions," *VT* 52 (2002): 227–28.

admonishes its addressees to ensure that Assurbanipal's brother, Shamash-shumu-ukin, ascends the Babylonian throne and to deal honestly with his other brothers, born of the same mother. The potential source of threats to Assurbanipal and his brothers is envisioned broadly and includes members of Assurbanipal's family, his counsellors and advisors, members of the Assyrian administration at a variety of levels, family members of the addressees, the empire's vassal and Assyrian populations, and divinatory experts, as well as the addressees themselves, who are enjoined to protect Assurbanipal against all enemies, both foreign and domestic. The text goes on to instruct the oath-takers in the proper actions to be taken upon the discovery of such threats, including reporting the danger to Assurbanipal and taking steps to apprehend the offender.

Comprising approximately half the text of VTE, these instructions are, like the curses that follow, highly repetitive, with the text imagining threats in innumerable permutations. Even to distinguish a specific one of these sections from others that resemble it, therefore, requires a relatively high degree of precision. VTE §6, for example, reads nearly identically to VTE §10:

VTE §6
If you hear any improper, unsuitable or unseemly word concerning the exercise of kingship which is unseemly and evil against Assurbanipal, the great crown prince designate, either from the mouth of his brothers, his uncles, his cousins, his family (var. his people), members of his father's line; or from the mouth of magnates and governors, or from the mouth of the bearded and the eunuchs, or from the mouth of the scholars or from the mouth of any human being at all, you shall not conceal it but come and report it to Assurbanipal, the great crown prince designate.[73]

VTE §10
If you hear any evil, improper, ugly word which is not seemly nor good to Assurbanipal, the great crown prince designate, son of Esarhaddon, king of Assyria, your lord, either from the mouth of his enemy or from

---

[73] *šum-ma at-tu-nu a-bu-tú la* DÙG.GA-*tú la ba-ni-tú la ta-ri-su ša e-peš* LUGAL-*te šá ina* UGU ᵐ*aš-šur*−DÙ−A DUMU−MAN GAL-*u šá* É−UŠ-*te la tar-ṣa-tú-u-ni la ṭa-bat-u-ni lu-u ina pi-I* ŠEŠ.MEŠ-*šú* ŠEŠ.MEŠ−AD.MEŠ-*šú* DUMU−ŠEŠ.MEŠ−AD.MEŠ-*šú qin-ni-šú* NUMUN É−AD-*šú lu ina pi-i* LÚ.GAL.MEŠ LÚ.NAM.MEŠ *lu ina pi-i* LÚ.*šá*−*ziq-ni* LÚ.SAG.MEŠ *lu-u ina pi-i* LÚ.*um-ma-ni lu-u ina pi-i nap-ḫar ṣal-mat*− SAG.DU *ma-la ba-šu-u ta-šam-ma-a-ni tu-pa-za-ra-a-ni la ta-lak-a-ni-ni a-na* ᵐ*aš-šur*− DÙ−A DUMU−MAN GAL-*u šá* É−UŠ-*ti la ta-qab-ba-a-ni*

the mouth of his ally, or from the mouth of his brothers or from the mouth of his uncles, his cousins, his family, members of his father's line, or from the mouth of your brothers, your sons, your daughters, or from the mouth of a prophet, an ecstatic, an inquirer of oracles, or from the mouth of any human being at all, you shall not conceal it but come and report it to Assurbanipal, the great crown prince designate, son of Esarhaddon, king of Assyria.[74]

Again, VTE's own internal repetitiveness reminds us that an adaptive text dealing with VTE is presented with a particularly acute challenge, by virtue of the commonality of the ideas and language involved. This is further emphasized by the continuity between the loyalty material of VTE and the wider universe of Assyrian treaties and loyalty oaths. As will be discussed further in chapter three, loyalty and disloyalty are concepts central to the nature of these texts; this is equally true of all of the Assyrian material extant. In phrasing closely aligned to VTE §6 and VTE §10, Esarhaddon's accession text warns that

Should I he[ar an ug]ly word about him [from the mou]th of his progeny, [should I hear it] from the mouth of one of the magnates or [governors], [from the mouth of one o]f the bearded or from the mouth of [the eunuchs], I will go and tell it to Esarhaddon, my lord; I [will] be [his servant] and speak good of him, I [will be] loyal to him ...[75]

Similar sentiments appear in Sennacherib's succession text[76] and in an unidentified, fragmentary treaty text.[77] Against this common background, therefore, efforts to link Deuteronomy's ideas about loyalty to YHWH to VTE in particular will have required a significant degree of

---

[74] š[u]m-ma a-bu-tú la DÙG.GA-tú la de-iq-tú la ba-ni-tú ina UGU ᵐaš-šur−DÙ−A DUMU−MAN GAL ša É−UŠ-ti DUMU ᵐaš-šur−PAB−AŠ MAN KUR−aš-šur EN-ku-nu la tar-ṣa-at-u-ni la ṭa-bat-u-ni lu-u ina pi-i LÚ.KÚR-šú lu-u ina pi-i sal-me-šú lu ina pi-i ŠEŠ.MEŠ-šú ŠEŠ.MEŠ−AD.MEŠ-šú DUMU−ŠEŠ.MEŠ−AD.MEŠ-šú qin-ni-šu NUMUN É−AD-šu lu-u ina pi-i ŠEŠ.MEŠ-ku-nu DUMU.MEŠ-ku-nu DUMU.MÍ.MEŠ-ku-nu lu ina pi-i LÚ.ra-gi-me LÚ.maḫ-ḫe-e DUMU šá-ʾi-li a-mat DINGIR lu-u ina pi-i nap-ḫar ṣal-mat−SAG.DU mal ba-šú-u ta-šam-ma-a-ni tu-pa-za-ra-a-ni la ta-lak-a-ni-ni a-na ᵐaš-šur−DÙ−A DUMU−MAN GAL-u šá É−UŠ-te DUMU ᵐaš-šur−PAB−AŠ MAN KUR−aš-šur la ta-qab-ba-a-ni

[75] [ù šúm-ma a-na-k]u a-bat-su la ʿdeʾ-i[q-t]ú [TAˀ pi]-i NUMUN-šú a-šam-mu-[u-ni] [ú-la-a šúm-ma] TAˀ pi-i ša 1-en T[Aˀ ŠÀ L]Ú.GAL.MEŠ [LÚ.NAM.MEŠ] [TAˀ pi-i 1-en T]Aˀ ŠÀ LÚ.šá−ziq-ni ú-la-a TAˀ pi-ˀiˀ [1-en LÚ.SAG.MEŠ] [a-šam-mu-u-ni] ù a-na ᵐaš-šur−PABⁱⁱ−[SUM]-na EN-ía la a-qab-b[u-u-ni] (SAA 2 4 4′−7′).

[76] SAA 2 3 2−4.

[77] SAA 2 13.

precision, combined with an unmistakable frequency of specific and distinctive elements of that text.

Even in its current form, including a number of later additions, Deut 13 is much shorter than the material concerned with loyalty to the king in VTE. The chapter is split into three cases, each dealing with the importance of the addressee's exclusive loyalty to YHWH and detailing potential sources of danger to that loyalty: the diviner (Deut 13:2–6), the family member (Deut 13:7–12), and the city (Deut 13:13–19).[78] In each case an individual or group pursues the worship of deities other than YHWH and encourages others to do the same; in the first two cases it is the addressee thus inveigled, while the last is a second hand report of the corruption of an entire city. Using political language inspired by VTE, this is understood to be articulating Israel's loyalty to YHWH in terms more commonly used of the loyalty due to a royal sovereign, with the betrayal of that loyalty expressed as sedition.[79]

As already noted, the primary focus of discussion regarding the relationship of Deut 13 to VTE has been on the similarity between their lists of people who might threaten the addressees' loyalty and the actions prescribed in response to such threats. According to Levinson, there is a direct relationship between the list in VTE §10, the persons in Deut 13, and the responses the texts instruct with regard to these persons; he argues that the VTE prohibitions, discussing the possibility of incitement to conspiracy and comprising warnings about disloyalty, "are reworked by Deuteronomy's authors into laws that prohibit apostasy."[80] The

---

[78] A variety of approaches to the compositional history of this chapter have been proposed; those interested may peruse the commentaries as well as the numerous specific studies (many of which, unsurprisingly, undertake such analysis as a direct result of their interest in its relationship to the Assyrian material). As, however, the question under current consideration is whether any part of the text might have constituted a signal to some other source, the necessity is here to err on the side of redactional generosity. We cannot, in other words, eliminate potential signals and then conclude that there are no signals.

[79] Implicit in the idea that such a presentation is subverting Assyrian imperial ideology is also the assumption that the depiction of YHWH as king (which Deuteronomy does explicitly only at Deut 33:5) is somehow inherently incompatible with the recognition of the sovereignty of the Assyrian king. It also assumes that the depiction of YHWH as king would have been interpreted in relation to the Assyrian king rather than in relation to native traditions. On this see further below; also M. Zehnder, "Building on Stone? Deuteronomy and Esarhaddon's Loyalty Oaths (Part 1): Some Preliminary Observations," *BBR* 19 (2009): 370–71.

[80] B. M. Levinson, "Textual Criticism, Assyriology, and the History of Interpretation: Deuteronomy 13:7a as a Test Case in Method," *JBL* 120 (2001): 236.

similarities between the texts, he suggests, "can be accounted for only in terms of the Deuteronomic authors having access to the treaty material, either directly or in Aramaic translation."[81] If this is the case, and if Deuteronomy intended to adapt this VTE material subversively, we should expect to observe specific correspondences between the Deuteronomy and VTE texts, satisfying the criteria of distinctiveness and frequency as well as producing consistency of style and content.

In VTE the possible perpetrators of disloyalty are extensive, with permutations enumerated over dozens of lines. As with the discussions of Deut 28 and VTE, however, there are a few sections that have gained particular attention, with VTE §10 foremost among them. VTE §10—noted already for its near indistinguishability from VTE §6—includes among its possible sources of disloyalty to Assurbanipal persuasions that come

> from the mouth of his enemy or from the mouth of his ally, or from the mouth of his brothers or from the mouth of his uncles, his cousins, his family, members of his father's line, or from the mouth of your brothers, your sons, your daughters, or from the mouth of a prophet, an ecstatic, an inquirer of oracles, or from the mouth of any human being at all.

This is followed by a general warning in VTE §11 against "[anything] that is evil or improper" and concerning the maintenance of exclusive loyalty to Assurbanipal and, in VTE §12, instructions of what to do if the addressees should discover anyone plotting against Assurbanipal.

Deut 13, in its turn, imagines threats from "prophets or those who divine by dreams" (נביא או חלם חלום; Deut 13:2), "your brother, your mother's son, or your son or daughter, or the wife you embrace, or your most intimate friend" (אחיך בן אמך או בנך או בתך או אשת חיקך או רעך אשר כנפשך; Deut 13:7). Later in the chapter there is a threat from "scoundrels from among you [who] have gone out and led the inhabitants of the town astray" (אנשים בני בליעל מקרבך וידיחו את ישבי עירם; Deut 13:14). Each of these possibilities prompts instructions regarding the addressee's

---

[81] Ibid., 236–37; cf. idem, "'But You Shall Surely Kill Him!': The Text-Critical and Neo-Assyrian Evidence for MT Deuteronomy 13:10," in *Bundesdokument und Gesetz: Studien zum Deuteronomium* (ed. G. Braulik; HBS 4; Freiburg: Herder, 1995), 37–63; idem, "The Neo-Assyrian Origins of the Canon Formula in Deuteronomy 13:1," in *Scriptural Exegesis: The Shapes of Culture and the Religious Imagination: Essays in Honour of Michael Fishbane* (ed. D. A. Green and L. S. Lieber; Oxford: Oxford University Press, 2009), 25–45; idem, "Esarhaddon's Succession Treaty as the Source for the Canon Formula in Deuteronomy 13:1," *JAOS* 130 (2010): 337–48; Otto, "Treueid und Gesetz"; idem, *Deuteronomium*, 57–88. Similarly, R. D. Nelson, *Deuteronomy* (OTL; London: Westminster John Knox, 2004), 168 calls it a "deliberate imitation of Assyrian forms."

appropriate response. The diviners "shall be put to death for having spoken treason against YHWH your God" (יומת כי דבר סרה על יהוה אלהיכם; Deut 13:6).[82] The addressee is to show no pity or compassion to his brother, children, or wife: "you shall surely kill him," stoning him (or her) to death (הרג תהרגנו; Deut 13:10–11). The town and its inhabitants are to be completely destroyed (Deut 13:16).

Attending to Deut 13, Levinson places particular emphasis on the mention of "your brother, the son of your mother" in Deut 13:7 (אחיך בן אמך); he contends that it is linked directly to the Akkadian phrase aḫḫēšu mar'ē ummišu (in the third person language of VTE, "his brothers, the sons of his mother") and argues that the fact that the phrase occurs only in VTE, and not in any of the other known Assyrian treaties, indicates that it must have been adapted from VTE specifically.[83] As Levinson observes, however, this phrase is the means by which VTE refers to Assurbanipals' brothers who might be the target of a conspiracy, rather any of Assurbanipals' brothers who might be instigating a conspiracy against him.[84] Levinson is therefore obliged to suggest that Deut 13 has taken over the phrase with a meaning opposite to its VTE usage. We will return to the question of the distinctiveness of this phrase and its attendant ability to signal a relationship with another text in chapter three. Here two observations will suffice.

First, the transformation of such a phrase—from a reference to those in danger to a reference to those posing the danger—is difficult to contextualize as part of a subversive message. While the plurality of entities threatened by disloyal machinations in VTE is obviously incompatible with the monolatrous Yahwistic agenda of Deuteronomy, the simple omission of other entities from the adaptation and the use of material from VTE more obviously related to the central question of loyalty to the sovereign would seem a much more effective allusive mechanism than the use of a phrase whose significance must be substantially altered in order to fit the subverting text's paradigm.

Equally problematic to the identification of this phrase as allusive is its essentially mundane character: family members, as already observed with regard to Deut 28, do not involve the kind of distinctive terminology necessary for making compelling allusions. It seems most

---

[82] On the translation of דבר סרה, here "to speak treason" with the NRSV, see chapter four.

[83] Levinson, "Textual Criticism," 212, 233. The versions create symmetry through the addition of "the son of your father"; see Levinson's discussion in ibid., 211–23. Note also that the phrase does not actually appear in VTE §10.

[84] Ibid., 240.

likely that (MT) Deuteronomy's mention of the brother who is the son of the same mother is used as a normal means of articulating the idea that even the nearest and dearest of the addressee's family and friends—the brother who shares not one but both parents with the addressee—could pose a threat to the addressee's loyalty to YHWH, rather than being a specific adaptation of language from VTE.

The methodological analysis in chapter one, however, noted that even relatively mundane language may function as a signal to a source text if it appears in conjunction with an abundance of other such material that, collectively, becomes distinctive. What then of the other individuals and groups named by these texts? Are there adequate and sufficiently specific similarities elsewhere that might have acted as a signal of Deuteronomy's use of VTE such that the transformation of *aḫḫēšu marʾē ummišu* into אחיך בן אמך would have been understood as part of a cumulative allusion?

While there are certain general similarities between the persons who might pose a danger to Assurbanipal's authority in VTE §10 and the persons who might tempt the addressee away from YHWH in Deut 13, and both address concerns about loyalty, these similarities are not specific or distinctive enough to support the claim that Deuteronomy is using VTE material with the intention of signaling a relationship with VTE. In VTE, the list begins with a merism, "from the mouth of his enemy or from the mouth of his ally." It then lists a number of family members, including (any of) Assurbanipal's brothers, uncles, cousins, other royal (paternal) family members, and the sons and daughters of the addressees, then mentions three different types of diviners before concluding with another phrase meant to cover all eventualities: "any human being at all." The Deuteronomy chapter addresses its concerns in three parts, beginning with two types of diviners in Deut 13:2–6; then family members in Deut 13:7–12, naming the maternal brother, the children and the wife as well as the close friend; and, finally, considering an entire city in Deut 13:13–19. There is no equivalent to this last in VTE, and the first two groups overlap with VTE only erratically. As with Deut 28, direct comparison makes these differences readily apparent.

VTE §10
If you hear any evil, improper, ugly word which is not seemly nor good to Assurbanipal, the great crown prince designate, son of Esarhaddon, king of Assyria, your lord, either from the mouth of his enemy or from the mouth of his ally, or from the mouth of his brothers or from the mouth of his uncles, his cousins, his family, members of his father's line, or from the mouth of your brothers, your sons, your daughters, or from the mouth of a prophet, an ecstatic, an inquirer of oracles, or from the

mouth of any human being at all, you shall not conceal it but come and report it to Assurbanipal, the great crown prince designate, son of Esarhaddon, king of Assyria.[85]

DEUT 13:2–12

[2]If prophets or those who divine by dreams appear among you and promise you omens or portents, [3]and the omens or the portents declared by them take place, and they say, "Let us follow other gods" (whom you have not known) "and let us serve them," [4]you must not heed the words of those prophets or those who divine by dreams; for YHWH your God is testing you, to know whether you indeed love the Lord your God with all your heart and soul. [5]YHWH your God you shall follow, him alone you shall fear, his commandments you shall keep, his voice you shall obey, him you shall serve, and to him you shall hold fast. [6]But those prophets or those who divine by dreams shall be put to death for having spoken treason against YHWH your God—who brought you out of the land of Egypt and redeemed you from the house of slavery—to turn you from the way in which YHWH your God commanded you to walk. So you shall purge the evil from your midst. [7]If anyone secretly entices you—even if it is your brother, your mother's son, or your son or daughter, or the wife you embrace, or your most intimate friend—saying, "Let us go and worship other gods," whom neither you nor your ancestors have known, [8]any of the gods of the peoples that are around you, whether near you or far away from you, from one end of the earth to the other, [9]you must not yield to or heed any such persons. Show them no pity or compassion and do not shield them. [10]But you shall surely kill them; your own hand shall be first against them to execute them, and afterwards the hand of all the people. [11]Stone them to death for trying to turn you away from YHWH your God, who brought you out of the land of Egypt, out of the house of slavery. [12]Then all Israel shall hear and be afraid, and never again do any such wickedness.[86]

---

[85] š[u]m-ma a-bu-tú la DÙG.GA-tú la de-iq-tú la ba-ni-tú ina UGU ᵐaš-šur—DÙ—A DUMU—MAN GAL ša É—UŠ-ti DUMU ᵐaš-šur—PAB—AŠ MAN KUR—aš-šur EN-ku-nu la tar-ṣa-at-u-ni la ṭa-bat-u-ni lu-u ina pi-i LÚ.KÚR-šú lu-u ina pi-i sal-me-šú lu ina pi-i ŠEŠ.MEŠ-šú ŠEŠ.MEŠ—AD.MEŠ-šú DUMU—ŠEŠ.MEŠ—AD.MEŠ-šú qin-ni-šu NUMUN É—AD-šu lu-u ina pi-i ŠEŠ.MEŠ-ku-nu DUMU.MEŠ-ku-nu DUMU.MÍ.MEŠ-ku-nu lu ina pi-i LÚ.ra-gi-me LÚ.maḫ-ḫe-e DUMU šá-'i-li a-mat DINGIR lu-u ina pi-i nap-ḫar ṣal-mat—SAG.DU mal ba-šú-u ta-šam-ma-a-ni tu-pa-za-ra-a-ni la ta-lak-a-ni-ni a-na ᵐaš-šur—DÙ—A DUMU—MAN GAL-u šá É—UŠ-te DUMU ᵐaš-šur—PAB—AŠ MAN KUR—aš-šur la ta-qab-ba-a-ni

[86] כי יקום בקרבך נביא או חלם חלום ונתן אליך אות או מופת: ובא האות והמופת אשר דבר אליך לאמר נלכה אחרי אלהים אחרים אשר לא ידעתם ונעבדם: לא תשמע אל דברי הנביא ההוא או אל חולם החלום ההוא כי מנסה יהוה אלהיכם אתכם לדעת הישכם אהבים את יהוה אלהיכם בכל לבבכם ובכל נפשכם:

As with Deut 28, the overlap between the texts is very generalized, consisting of terms that might be expected of any list of persons to whom an addressee might be supposed to listen: the immediate family members of brother, son, and daughter, as well as common ancient Near Eastern religious functionaries. None of these are specified with a precision that might suggest that Deuteronomy's use of them derives from VTE or is intended to signal an interpretive relationship with VTE.

Both lists include family members—VTE in numerous other passages besides VTE §10, revealing Esarhaddon's particular fears *vis-à-vis* his decision to establish one of his younger sons as crown prince—but the overlap is minimal, with Deuteronomy's list much more limited than VTE's and with numerous differences, including attention to the maternal brother, mention of the wife, and mention of the friend. VTE, by contrast, is more attuned to the risks of Assurbanipal's paternal relatives—logical enough in the context of a royal succession—and includes uncles, cousins, and Assurbanipal's brothers; regarding the addressees' relatives it notes brothers, sons, and daughters but makes no mention of wives or friends. Inclusion of all of these, by virtue of the extensive quotation of what is otherwise a fundamentally generic list, might have served to indicate VTE as Deuteronomy's specific source, but the apparently random selection of only some persons works instead to dilute the connection.

Both lists also mention diviners: Deuteronomy includes the prophet and the dreamer (נביא, חלם חלום), while VTE names the prophet, ecstatic, and enquirer (*raggimu, maḫḫu, ša 'ili amat ilī*). Yet there is no more meaningful correlation: Deuteronomy goes from three divinatory functionaries to two, and one of these (the dreamer) is certainly not present in VTE.[87] Indeed the diviners, as more distinctive personnel than

---

אחרי יהוה אלהיכם תלכו ואתו תיראו ואת מצותיו תשמרו ובקלו תשמעו ואתו תעבדו ובו תדבקון: והנביא ההוא או חלם החלום ההוא יומת כי דבר סרה על יהוה אלהיכם המוציא אתכם מארץ מצרים והפדך מבית עבדים להדיחך מן הדרך אשר צוך יהוה אלהיך ללכת בה ובערת הרע מקרבך: עי יסיתך אחיך בן אמך או בנך או בתך אט אשת חיקך או רעך אשר כנפשך בסתר לאמר נלכה ונעבדה אלהים אחרים אשר לא ידעת אתה ואבתיך: מאלהי העמים אשר סביבתיכם הקרבים אליך או הרחקים ממך מקצה הארץ ועד קצה הארץ: לא תאבה לו ולא תשמע אליו ולא תחוס עינך עליו ולא תחמל ולא תכסה עליו: כי הרג תהרגנו ידך תהיה בו בראשונה להמיתו ויד כל העם באחרנה: וסקלתו באבנים ומת כי בקש להדיחך מעל יהוה אלהיך המוציאך מארץ מצרים מבית עבדים: וכל ישראל ישמעו ויראון ולא יוספו לעשות כדבר הרע הזה בקרבך:

[87] Considering the relationship between these lists, Pakkala suggests that the "dreamer of a dream" may have been adopted from some other source but that VTE's enquirer—for which קסם or similar would have been expected—is unlikely to have been the inspiration for this particular term (J. Pakkala, "Der literar- und religionsgeschichtliche Ort von Deuteronomium 13," in *Die deuteronomistischen Geschichtswerke: redaktions- und religionsgeschichtliche Perspektiven zur*

the family members, might have served as especially effective signals and, since the intention in Deuteronomy would be—like in VTE—to reject the message of such persons, their inclusion would have been acceptable—even advantageous—to Deuteronomy's overall message concerning divinatory figures. This potential is not pursued.

The biblical text thus exacerbates the differences between the texts by including its own categories of threatening persons who do not appear in VTE: the dreamer, the brother who is specifically identified as the son of the same mother, the wife, the friend, and, of course, the entire city of apostate men.[88] With such erratic connections between the lists, it is difficult to imagine that the author of Deuteronomy was deliberately alluding to VTE in order to signal to Deuteronomy's audience a desire that the new text be read in relation to VTE.

In addition to the list of persons who might be involved in disloyalty, there are three other points on which Deuteronomy's use of VTE has been proposed: the phrase דבר סרה, the so-called "canon formula" in Deut 13:1, and the instruction regarding the fate of the disloyal friend or family member in Deut 13:10. The second of these requires the least attention: the "canon formula" of Deut 13:1 is perhaps conceptually similar to instructions in VTE against alteration, but not even Levinson is inclined to see a translation here. It is probably better to understand the interest in non-alteration in connection with the development of an authoritative written culture.[89] Non-alteration

---

"Deuteronomismus"-Diskussion in Tora und Vorderen Propheten [ed. M. Witte, et al.; BZAW 365; Berlin: de Gruyter, 2006] 132–33); contrast Dion, who sees the dreamer as indicative of foreign influence and concludes that it must have come from VTE (P. E. Dion, "Deuteronomy 13: The Suppression of Alien Religious Propaganda in Israel during the Late Monarchical Era," in Law and Ideology in Monarchic Israel [ed. B. Halpern and D. W. Hobson; JSOTSup 124; Sheffield: JSOT, 1991], 200). Divination by dreams is well attested elsewhere in the Hebrew Bible, however, and is unlikely to have served as an effective signal to an Assyrian source. Pakkala also rejects the correlation between the lists of persons in VTE §10 and Deut 13 on the basis that VTE speaks in the plural while Deuteronomy speaks in the singular.

[88] On the large number of individuals present in only one of the texts and the fact that that Deuteronomy separates the prophet from the family, addressing them in two separate legislative units rather than the continuous list of VTE §10, see Pakkala, "Deuteronomium 13," 130–31 (cf. also Koch, Vertrag, 160; U. Rütersworden, "Dtn 13 in neueren Deuteronomiumforschung," in Congress Volume: Basel 2001 [ed. A. Lemaire; VTSup 92; Leiden: Brill, 2002], 185-203). Koch notes that the friend, absent from VTE, does appear in the treaty between the Assyrian queen mother Zakutu and the Arabs (SAA 2 8) (Koch, Vertrag, 154–55).

[89] Levinson, "Neo-Assyrian Origins"; idem, "Esarhaddon's Succession Treaty."

instructions also appear elsewhere in Akkadian texts, including the Tel Fekheriye "A" text, which includes a warning against anyone who "removes my name and writes his name."[90]

With regard to the last, the MT of Deut 13:10 is notorious as legislating immediate execution in cases of proposed worship of non-Yahwistic deities. Levinson suggests that this is "perfectly reflecting normative neo-Assyrian practice" regarding sedition and concludes that Deuteronomy is using VTE §12 in formulating its instructions here.[91]

> VTE §12
> If anyone should speak to you of rebellion and insurrection (with the purpose) of ki[lling], assassinating, and eliminating Assurbanipal, the [great crown] prince designate, son of Esarhaddon, king of Assyria, your lord, concerning whom he has concluded (this) treaty with you, or if you should hear it from the mouth of anyone, you shall seize the perpetrators of insurrection, and bring them before Assurbanipal, the great crown prince designate. If you are able to seize them and put them to death, then you shall destroy their name and their seed from the land. If, however, you are unable to seize them and put them to death, you shall inform Assurbanipal, the great crown prince designate, and assist him in seizing and putting to death the perpetrators of rebellion.[92]

The ability of Deut 13:10 to signal a relationship between Deuteronomy and VTE §12 is as problematic as the suggestion that Deuteronomy's list of dangerous persons originated as VTE §10. First, it is questionable whether VTE §12 is actually instructing its oath-takers to take matters into their own hands: although it refers to the addressees being "able to seize them and put them to death," this follows immediately on from instructions to "seize the perpetrators of insurrection, and bring them before Assurbanipal." In order for the analogy to work, Levinson is

---

[90] J. C. Greenfield and A. Shaffer, "Notes on the Akkadian-Aramaic Bilingual Statue from Tell Fekherye," *Iraq* 45 (1983): 113.

[91] Levinson, "'But You Shall Surely Kill Him!'," 37–63.

[92] *šum-ma me-me-ni a-na* ᵐ*aš-šur*—DÙ—A DUMU—[MAN GAL *š*]*á* É—UŠ-*te* DUMU ᵐ*aš-šur*—PAB—AŠ MAN KUR—*aš-šur* EN-*ku-nu šá ina* [U]GU-*ḫi-šú a-de-e is-si-ku-nuiš-ku-nu-u-ni si-ḫu bar-tú šá* d[*u-a-ki*]-*šu ša-mut-ti-šu ḫul-lu-qi-šú a-na ka-šu-nu* [*i*]*q-ba-ka-nu-u-ni ù at-tu-nu ina pi-i me-me-ni ta-šam-ma-a-ni e-piš-a-nu-te šá bar-te la ta-ṣab-bat-a-ni-ni ina* UGU ᵐ*aš-šur*—DÙ—A DUMU—MAN GAL *ša* É—UŠ-*ti la tu-bal-a-ni-ni šum-ma am*—*mar ṣa-ba-ti-šú-nu du-a-ki-šú-nu ma-ṣa-ku-nu la ta-ṣab-bat-a-šá-nu-ni la ta-du-ka-a-šá-nu-ni* MU-*šú-nu* NUMUN-*šú-nu ina* KUR *la tu-ḫal-laq-qa-a-ni šum-ma am*—*mar ṣa-ba-te-šú-nu du-a-ki-šú-nu la ma-ṣa-ku-nu* PI.2 *šá* ᵐ*aš-šur*—DÙ—A DUMU—MAN GAL-*u ša* É—UŠ-*ti la tú-pat-ta-a-ni is-si-šú la* [*t*]*a-za-za-a-ni e-piš-a-nu-ti šá bar-te la ta-*[*ṣ*]*ab-bat-a-ni la ta-du-ka-a-*[*ni*]

obliged to argue that the language of seizure, followed as it usually is by references to putting the seized person to death, is tantamount to an expectation that to seize means to kill.[93] The location of the initial instruction to seize in the context of delivery to Assurbanipal, however, casts doubt on this premise. The reference to the informant putting the perpetrator of insurrection to death should be interpreted as an elliptical expression for the longer process of report and prosecution.[94]

Even more notably, Deuteronomy does not itself use the language of seizure. It emphasizes the addressee's involvement—as would be expected in the family context—but is more interested in warning against compassion than in the means by which the individual is apprehended and punished. The repetition of "seize and put to death" (ṣabātu u duāku) in VTE—in VTE §12 and elsewhere—would make the phrase a potentially potent signal, as its repetition in the source would have rendered its use more likely to evoke that source. Deuteronomy, however, gives no indication of its awareness of the Akkadian idiom. Further situating the Deuteronomy instructions within their own context is the apparent relationship of the instructions in each of the three cases to the nature of the addressee's evidence; in the cases of the diviner and the family member the disloyalty is discovered first hand and responded to directly, while in the case of the city it is reported second hand and requires verification prior to punitive action.[95]

Last but not least in the arsenal of arguments in favor of a relationship between Deut 13 and VTE is the resemblance of the phrase דבר סרה in Deut 13:6 to Akkadian dabābu surrātu in VTE §57 l. 502. Weinfeld, having noted the Akkadian phrase's appearance also in several of the inscriptions of Sargon II and Assurbanipal, suggested that it appears to be "an expression taken from the political vocabulary of the period."[96] Given its wider use beyond VTE, the phrase is difficult to construe as a recognizably distinctive signal to VTE; with our criteria in

---

[93] Levinson, "'But You Shall Surely Kill Him!'," 58–59.

[94] Rütersworden, "Dtn 13," 199-203 and Koch, *Vertrag*, 162–164 also discuss this passage and conclude that the idea of capital punishment in cases of disloyalty is at home in both Mesopotamian and southern Levantine concerns about royal dynastic successions; the origin of the influence on the Deuteronomy formulation is therefore indeterminable.

[95] For further discussion see C. L. Crouch, *The Making of Israel: Cultural Diversity in the Southern Levant and the Formation of Ethnic Identity in Deuteronomy* (VTSup 162; Leiden: Brill, 2014), 120–28.

[96] M. Weinfeld, *Deuteronomy and the Deuteronomic School* (Winona Lake, Ind.: Eisenbrauns, 1992), 99; more recently, Koch, *Vertrag*, 160–62.

mind we might also note that its sole appearance in VTE, in VTE §57, is isolated from other passages appearing in discussions of this relationship and is not conducive to the frequency of good allusive signaling.[97] Nevertheless, it is construed as "central evidence for the influence of the Neo-Assyrian treaty tradition on Deuteronomy 13*."[98] Otto goes so far as to render the phrase as "to speak a word[s] of high treason," as part of his wider contention of Deuteronomy's subversive intention.[99]

For purposes of subversion, however, the question is not merely whether this Hebrew phrase may be traced to an Akkadian one, but whether the phrase would have signaled an intention for the audience to interpret Deuteronomy's meaning in relation to Assyrian ideas about loyalty to the Assyrian sovereign. The ability of דבר סרה to succeed in such a task is doubtful. From the Akkadian perspective it should be noted, first, that the phrase does not appear elsewhere in the known treaty corpus (in other words, though worries about loyalty are rife in these texts, these worries are not expressed in fixed terms using this phrase) and, second, that it does appear elsewhere in the inscriptions but neither very frequently nor as part of a fixed formula. In VTE *dabāb surrātu* is not a stand-alone phrase but part of a longer description: *mušamḫiṣūtu mušadbibūtu liḫšu dabāb surrāti la kīnāti* ("someone who makes trouble, someone who speaks whispers: lying, disloyal talk"). In a few of Assurbanipal's other inscriptions *surrātu* appears in the phrase "to speak lying speech" (*dabābu dabāb[ti] surrāti*, i.e., duplicating *dbb* as both noun and verb) but appears also with the verb *epēšu*.[100] Two occurrences in Esarhaddon's inscriptions prefer *dabābu surrātu la šalmāti*, "to speak insincere/unwholesome lies."[101] The variations in the Akkadian usage suggest that this is not a technical or idiomatic phrase but the everyday use of ordinary vocabulary. In other words: to see in the Hebrew דבר סרה an adaptation of an Akkadian *dabābu surrātu*, intended to carry the weight of Deuteronomy's allusion to an Assyrian treaty and loyalty oath tradition or text, is to ask a great deal of two isolated words. To recall Noble: "they are far more suggestive of the sort of random half-similarities which may arise between two texts simply by chance, than of

---

[97] Except, of course, VTE §56, but that has already been deemed the weakest of any proposals regarding Deuteronomy's ability to signal a relationship with VTE.

[98] Koch, *Vertrag*, 162 ("zentraler Beleg für den Einfluss der neuassyrischen Vertragsrechtstradition auf Dtn 13*").

[99] Otto, *Deuteronomium*, 51 ("Hochverrat das Wort reden").

[100] CAD 15: 409–10.

[101] Leichty, *The Royal Inscriptions of Esarhaddon*, Esarhaddon 1 i 27–28; Esarhaddon 33 i 20. Interestingly, the one instance of simple *dabābu surrātu* is in Esarhaddon's Letter to Aššur (Esarhaddon 104 i 24), in reference to the neglect of certain deities.

a subtle author who is trying to intimate to his readers that he is covertly commenting upon another story that they know."[102]

Loyalty and disloyalty are concepts central to the nature of treaties and loyalty oaths, including all of Assyrian material. The common language and conceptualization of these texts—and their application, as witnessed not least by the regular descriptions in the Assyrian royal inscriptions of military campaigns waged in response to disloyalty— means that Deuteronomy's ability to signal a relationship with VTE (or with Assyrian ideology, as will be tested in chapter three) is dictated by its ability to distinguish a specific manifestation of these ideas from the general morass.[103] Rather than the relatively easy task of alluding to a text whose distinctiveness renders it readily recognizable with a minimum of signaling—the distinctiveness compensating for any weaknesses in frequency or specificity—an attempt to allude to the loyalty and disloyalty issues of VTE has, as a result of the indistinctness of these concepts, very little leeway for imprecision in its choice of words or phrases. The generality of the concept means that Deuteronomy is only likely to be successful in signaling a relationship with VTE if it uses material from it extensively and frequently. In order to successfully signal an allusive and subversive relationship with VTE, Deuteronomy requires "an announced and extensive transposition" of its source material, in order to make its "overt relationship to another work or works" apparent to its audience.[104]

Such systematic use of VTE material by Deut 13 is not apparent. At most Deut 13 may use two phrases employed by VTE: דבר סרה, from *dabābu surrātu*, and אחיך בן אמך, from *aḫḫēšu marʾē ummišu*. Whether either of these two phrases are likely to have triggered audience recognition of Deuteronomy's use of an outside source will be revisited in chapter four. Even if they attracted a degree of interest, however, they are surrounded by material possessed of general similarities to the ideas and language of VTE—but not specific ones. Rather like the iron earth and bronze sky of Deut 28:23–24, the limited nature of the specific links to VTE material weighs heavily against their interpretation as deliberate attempts to signal a relationship to another text. Clearly Deut 13 is concerned with

---

[102] Noble, "Esau, Tamar, and Joseph," 227–28; recall also Toury, *Descriptive Translation Studies*, 119: "… similar (but not identical!) verbal formulations have been selected by members of different societies to indicate similar norms of behaviour under similar circumstances."

[103] See B. Oded, *War, Peace and Empire: Justifications for War in the Assyrian Royal Inscriptions* (Wiesbaden: Ludwig Reichert, 1992), 61–100.

[104] L. Hutcheon, *A Theory of Adaptation* (New York, N.Y.: Routledge, 2006), 7, 6.

the Israelites' relationship with YHWH—as is most of the book—and especially with the exclusivity of this relationship and the Israelites' loyalty to YHWH alone. Its articulation of such concerns doubtless draws on a wider vocabulary of ideas about loyalty, in much the same way that Deut 28 uses the genre of curses. In neither case, however, does the nature of the relationship between Deuteronomy and VTE support the identification of a program of distinctive, frequent, and meaningful allusions to the latter by the former.

CONCLUSIONS

The requirements of subversion demand that a subversive work signal to its audience its relationship with its source text such that the audience is able to recognize the source and interpret the new work in light of the old. The relationship between the adaptation and its source must be specific enough that both the relationship itself and the points at which the adaptation diverges from the source—the points at which its subversive effect is achieved—are recognizable by the audience. If Deuteronomy's intention was to subvert VTE, its use of specific source material from VTE ought to result in a relatively high correlation between the two texts. The similarities between occasional elements of VTE and the text of Deut 13 and 28 hardly achieve this effect. The relationship between the texts is of a general, imprecise character; though some elements of Deuteronomy exhibit superficial similarities to parts of VTE, this material is neither distinctive nor frequent enough to signal an intentional relationship between the texts. Their divergences, from overall orientation and conceptualization to syntax and vocabulary, are apparent as soon as they are subject to close scrutiny. The lack of specificity, distinctiveness, and frequency in the supposed similarities between Deuteronomy and VTE means that Deuteronomy is not recognizable as an adaptation of VTE. It cannot, therefore, take advantage of the subversive potential that such recognition might enable. The likelihood that Deuteronomy intends to signal its position as an adaptation of VTE, meant to be read in relation to that text, is minimal.

3
DEUTERONOMY AND ASSYRIA

The preceding has argued that the relationship between Deut 13 and 28 and VTE is not specific, frequent, or distinctive enough to warrant the conclusion that the similarities between the two texts were intended by the author of Deuteronomy to function as allusions to VTE. Abandoning the suggestion that Deuteronomy is signaling a relationship to VTE means that the ability of Deuteronomy to subvert VTE must be likewise forsaken. An exception to this relates to the question of a wider tradition: if VTE were the only exemplar of loyalty oath and curse traditions known to Deuteronomy's audience, even the sloppy allusions contained in Deuteronomy might successfully function as signals of its intention to be read as a polemical, subversive interpretation of a VTE source text. We will return to the question of audience knowledge in chapters four and five. First, however, we must address another possibility: that Deuteronomy alludes not to VTE but to the Assyrian treaty and loyalty oath tradition more generally or, alternatively, to another Assyrian treaty or loyalty oath text.

As already established in chapter two, VTE is certainly not the only treaty, loyalty oath, or curse text produced by the Assyrian empire. In fact, much of the caution in scholarly analyses of the relationship between VTE and Deuteronomy derives from a recognition of this fact, combined with an acknowledgement that VTE does not, in any extant version, address Judah. The exceptions in chapter two notwithstanding, the more common variant of the subversion hypothesis therefore takes

VTE as a representative of the Assyrian treaty and loyalty oath tradition, arguing that the similarities between Deuteronomy and VTE reflect VTE's inclusion within this Assyrian tradition.[1] Deuteronomy's failure to signal a relationship with the specific text of VTE, in other words, does not on its own equate to a failure to signal a subversive relationship with the Assyrian tradition of which VTE forms a part. If this Assyrian treaty and loyalty oath tradition were the only such tradition in the ancient Near East—and thus, by default, the only such tradition with which Deuteronomy's audience might be expected to be familiar— Deuteronomy's allusions to this tradition might be relatively inexact yet still recognizable to its audience, for whom "treaty" effectively means "Assyrian treaty."

That Assyria was a major user of ancient Near Eastern treaties and that Deuteronomy's audience would have known this, however, is not the same as saying that Deuteronomy's audience would have taken all references to treaties as references to Assyrian treaties. Not only was the Assyrian tradition part of an extensive ancient Near Eastern treaty, loyalty oath, and curse tradition, but there is significant evidence to suggest that Deuteronomy's audience would have been aware of this tradition. To the details of the latter issue we will return in chapter four. Here the focus remains on the relationship between the new work (Deuteronomy) and its proposed source (the Assyrian treaty and loyalty oath tradition), investigating whether Deuteronomy may be understood to be signaling a relationship with this tradition. Rather than requiring Deuteronomy to signal VTE through the use of material specific to VTE, this version of Deuteronomy's subversive intent requires that Deuteronomy signal the Assyrian treaty and loyalty oath tradition through the use of material that is specific to that tradition and that is

---

[1] On the implications of the very large number of treaties and loyalty oaths for the relationship between Deuteronomy and VTE both Pakkala (who suggests "hundreds or even thousands" of these in existence in antiquity) and Radner have been particularly emphatic; both conclude that, while VTE is the text most familiar to modern scholarship, the odds in favor of VTE actually representing the one single text on which Deuteronomy was based are slim (J. Pakkala, "Der literar- und religionsgeschichtliche Ort von Deuteronomium 13," in *Die deuteronomistischen Geschichtswerke: redaktions- und religionsgeschichtliche Perspektiven zur "Deuteronomismus"-Diskussion in Tora und Vorderen Propheten* [ed. M. Witte, et al.; BZAW 365; Berlin: de Gruyter, 2006], 133; K. Radner, "Assyrische *ṭuppi adê* als Vorbild für Deuteronomium 28,20–44?," in *Die deuteronomistischen Geschichtswerke: redaktions- und religionsgeschichtliche Perspektiven zur "Deuteronomismus"-Diskussion in Tora und Vorderen Propheten* [ed. M. Witte, et al.; BZAW 365; Berlin: de Gruyter, 2006], 351–78).

distinguishable from other ancient Near Eastern treaty and loyalty oath traditions.[2]

Recalling the discussion in chapter one of the factors influencing an adaptation's choice of signaling techniques, it will be remembered that the specificity of an adaptation's signals relates to the source with which the adaptation wishes to indicate a relationship and, in particular, to the location of that source in a wider tradition: an adaptation of Disney's *Cinderella* requires a more specific signal than an adaptation of the general Cinderella tradition. Just as Deuteronomy's relationship to VTE was affected by VTE's location in a constellation of Assyrian treaties and loyalty oaths, the question of Deuteronomy's subversive intent *vis-à-vis* the latter is contingent on the relationship of the Assyrian tradition to other treaties and loyalty oaths. In order to be understood as adapting and subverting Assyrian ideology, Deuteronomy's allusions need to signal to the Assyrian manifestation of the treaty and loyalty oath tradition. That is, Deuteronomy must mark this interpretive relationship by using ideas and concepts characteristic of the Assyrian form of the tradition; by their associations with the Assyrian material, these may successfully distinguish Assyria as the object of Deuteronomy's interests. If Deuteronomy's audience is not able to recognize the Assyrian tradition as Deuteronomy's source, the audience will not experience Deuteronomy as an adaptation. In the absence of a juxtaposition of the new against the old, the meaning intended to arise from this juxtaposition will be lost on the audience.[3] Subversion, dependent on awareness of differentiation, will be impossible.

---

[2] As a relationship with a tradition rather than an individual text, this is less likely to be signaled by the precise verbal and syntactical parallels sought in chapter two than by the use of ideas and concepts specific to the tradition. On the problems associated with attempts to identify cases of allusion on the basis of ideas rather than specific terms and phrases, see J. Leonard, "Identifying Inner-Biblical Allusions: Psalm 78 as a Test Case," *JBL* 127 (2008): 246–47; recall also the degree of distinctiveness, the level of specificity, and the overall frequency of conceptual similarities that rendered Hamori's discussion of the story of Jacob at Jabbok convincing, by contrast to O'Connell's analysis of Isa 14 (E. Hamori, "Echoes of Gilgamesh in the Jacob Story," *JBL* 130 [2011]: 625–42 and R. H. O'Connell, "Isaiah XIV 4b–23: Ironic Reversal through Concentric Structure and Mythic Allusion," *VT* 38 [1988]: 407–18).

[3] The fact that, even in this case, this is still only a potential for subversion (rather than a guarantee of it) may be witnessed by the extensive adoption and adaptation of Assyrian imagery and language in positive terms by the rulers of Sam'al (see M. W. Hamilton, "The Past as Destiny: Historical Visions in Sam'al and Judah under Assyrian Hegemony," *HTR* 91 [1998]: 215–30).

Finally: in addition to asking whether Deuteronomy is signaling to the Assyrian treaty and loyalty oath tradition in general, a further object of this exercise concerns the possibility that Deuteronomy's target may have been a specific loyalty oath or treaty text, but one that is no longer extant. The kind of analysis undertaken in chapter two regarding the relationship between VTE and Deuteronomy cannot, naturally, be undertaken on a specific text that is unavailable for comparison. However, as the text in question is invariably understood to be one regulating the relationship between Judah and Assyria (and its rendering by Deuteronomy thus understood to be subverting Assyrian authority), the possibility addressed by the present chapter will address this alternative by implication: if Deuteronomy is related to a specific Assyrian text, albeit one that is no longer preserved, the location of that text within the Assyrian tradition of treaty and loyalty oath texts means that there should be recognizable affinities between Deuteronomy and the specifically Assyrian form of the tradition of which the absent text was a part. This variant on the hypothesis of Deuteronomy's subversive intentions has the potential to account for the shortcomings in Deuteronomy's relationship with VTE while still maintaining its subversive intentions with regard to Assyria.

With this in mind, this chapter explores the possibility that Deuteronomy's subversive intentions *vis-à-vis* Assyria are reflected in its relationship with an Assyrian form of the treaty and loyalty oath tradition. The focus will therefore be on whether the material in Deuteronomy that has treaty and oath affinities has affinities to a tradition that is recognizable as Assyrian.

TREATIES, LOYALTY OATHS, AND CURSES IN ANCIENT NEAR EASTERN TRADITION

There is a major ongoing argument regarding the extent of a West Semitic, non-Mesopotamian treaty tradition. The relevance of this argument for the current purposes has to do with the nature of the treaty and loyalty oath tradition in which Deuteronomy is situated: is this tradition wholly Assyrian, such that any allusion to it functions as a signal to a specifically Assyrian interpretive context for Deuteronomy by default, or is this a wider ancient Near Eastern tradition, such that a desire to signal to the Assyrian treaties and loyalty oaths would require a signal with specifically Assyrian elements?

In the immediate context, the Sefire treaties are at the center of this debate. These texts comprise three fragmentary treaties, two (Sefire I and Sefire II) apparently copies of a single treaty between "Bar-ga'yah, king of KTK" and "Mati'el ben 'Attarsamak, king of Arpad" and a third (Sefire III) recounting the treaty stipulations between a king of Arpad and an unknown treaty partner, perhaps the same Bar-ga'yah if the restoration of his name in Sef III 25 is correct. All three of these treaties are written in Aramaic. Some scholars contend that they represent a West Semitic treaty tradition; others argue that they are Assyrian treaties translated into Aramaic. The issue at stake in these arguments is whether these treaties, as West Semitic treaties differentiable from Assyrian treaties, are witnesses to a wider ancient Near Eastern treaty (and loyalty oath) tradition or if, as variants of but nevertheless still fundamentally Assyrian treaties, they are merely additional exemplars of the Assyrian tradition elsewhere witnessed, even now, by more than a dozen treaties and loyalty oaths.

The major case in favor of the Sefire treaties as Assyrian was made in a monograph by Lemaire and Durand, culminating in a new edition of the texts. Developing an earlier suggestion by Malamat, Lemaire and Durand argued that Bar-ga'yah should be understood as one and the same man as an Assyrian *turtanu* of the eighth century, Shamshi-ilu, and that KTK, of which Bar-ga'yah is said to be king, should be identified as Til Barsip, the seat of Shamshi-ilu's governance in the region of Bit-Adini.[4] Neither of these associations has been universally accepted: the toponym has been the subject of ongoing debate since the discovery of the texts, with its identification as Til Barsip challenged by, among others, Von Soden, advocating for its identification as Kiski; Ikeda, suggesting that KTK represents an acronym for a federation of cities in the area of Bit-Adini, comprised of Carchemish, Til Barsip, and Kummah; and Hawkins, who has shown that the Hittite name for Til Barsip was Masuwari.[5] While most have been inclined to see the

---

[4] A. Lemaire and J.-M. Durand. *Les inscriptions araméennes de Sefiré et l'Assyrie de Shamshi-ilu* (Hautes études orientales 20; Paris: Librairie Droz, 1984).

[5] W. Von Soden, "Das Nordsyrische Ktk/Kiski und der Turtan Šamši-ilu: Erwängungen zu einem neuen Buch," *Studi epigraphici e linguistici sul Vincino Oriente antico* 2 (1985): 133–41; cf. S. C. Layton and D. Pardee, "Literary Sources for the History of Palestine and Syria: Old Aramaic Inscriptions," *BA* 51 (1988): 179–80; Y. Ikeda, "Looking from Til Barsip on the Euphrates: Assyria and West in Ninth and Eighth Centuries BCE," in *Priests and Officials in the Ancient Near East: Papers of the Second Colloquium on the Ancient Near East—The City and Its Life, Held at the Middle Eastern Culture Center in Japan (Mitaka, Tokyo) March 22–24, 1996* (ed. K. Watanabe; Heidelberg: Universitätsverlag C. Winter, 1999), 287–78; J. D. Hawkins, "The Hittite Name of Til-Barsip: Evidence from a New Hieroglyphic Fragment from Tell Ahmar," *Anatolian Studies* 33 (1983): 131–36. For a history of interpretation of the mysterious

identification of Bar-ga'yah as Shamshi-ilu as probable nevertheless, Dion—similarly appealing to the hieroglyphic evidence against the identification of KTK with Til Barsip—has contested Lemaire and Durand's interpretation more fundamentally, contending that the challenge to KTK as Til Barsip "casts considerable doubt" on the identification of Bar-ga'yah with Shamshi-ilu.[6]

Also entering into the debate is the appearance of one of the parties to Sefire I and Sefire II, Mati'el of Arpad, as a signatory to a treaty with Assur-nerari V, king of Assyria in the middle of the eighth century (754–745). Arguing that "the treaty gods, the structure and formulation of the texts, and the actual treaty terms" imply that the Sefire treaties are with an Assyrian king, the editors of the SAA volume of treaties and loyalty oaths conclude that Bar-ga'yah is a pseudonym for Assur-nerari rather than Shamshi-ilu and that the enigmatic KTK stands for Assyria. The Sefire treaties are, according to Parpola and Watanabe, "the Aramaic counterpart—though not an exact translation" of the fragmentary Akkadian text of the treaty between Mati'el (Mati'ilu in Akkadian) and Assur-nerari.[7]

The close comparison of the Sefire material with Assyrian treaty texts and the treaty of Assur-nerari and Mati'ilu in particular is beyond the scope of the current discussion and has, in any case, been undertaken quite recently by Koch.[8] For the current purposes it is instructive to consider the textual relationship posited by the possibility that the Sefire material is an Aramaic rendering of a treaty agreement with an Assyrian official—either the king himself or his representative. Recalling the preceding discussions of translation and allusion, it comes as no surprise that that assessment of the Sefire texts' relationship to the Assyrian tradition is based primarily on the extent to which these texts may be construed as in keeping with other, unquestionably Assyrian treaty and loyalty oath exemplars and, in particular, the treaty between Mati'ilu and Assur-nerari.

The deities named as witnesses on Face A of Sefire I include several recognizable from the Assyrian pantheon: to note only those whose

---

KTK see J. A. Fitzmyer, *The Aramaic Inscriptions of Sefire* (rev. ed.; BibOr 19A; Rome: Pontifical Biblical Institute, 1995), 167–74.

[6] P. E. Dion, review of A. Lemaire and J.-M. Durand, *Les inscriptions araméennes de Sfiré et l'Assyrie de Shamshi-ilu*, JBL 105 (1986): 512.

[7] S. Parpola and K. Watanabe, *Neo-Assyrian Treaties and Loyalty Oaths* (SAA 2; Helsinki: The Neo-Assyrian Text Corpus Project, 1988), xxvii.

[8] C. Koch, *Vertrag, Treueid und Bund: Studien zur Rezeption des altorientalischen Vertragsrechts im Deuteronomium und zur Ausbildung der Bundestheologie im alten Testament* (BZAW 383; Berlin: de Gruyter, 2008), 52–77.

names are complete, these include *mlš* (Mullissu in Akkadian), Marduk, Nabu, Nergal, and Shamash, among others.[9] Though both texts are missing parts, a number of the gods invoked by Sefire I appear also in Assur-nerari's treaty with Mati'ilu. Apparent from the most cursory comparison of the texts, however, is that even such superficially straightforward material is not simply correspondent. Not only do the number, arrangement, and identities of the deities differ in the two texts, but their invocation occurs at opposite ends of the treaties, with the list prominent at the beginning of Sefire I and at the end of the Akkadian text.[10] The latter is quite fragmentary, but appears to include several passages likening the fate of the recalcitrant treaty partner to the dismemberment of the animal whose slaughter cements the treaty; a section discussing the treaty's stipulations; a section connecting specific curses to various failings on the part of Mati'ilu; and the final list of deities by whom the treaty is sworn. Sefire I, by contrast, begins with an introduction of the parties to the treaty and an accounting of the witnessing deities before proceeding to a list of curses to befall Mati'el should he prove unfaithful (details of which betrayal are not supplied); a section of threats corresponding to ritual actions; reiteration of the deities' involvement; a section concerning what acts will constitute betrayal of the treaty; and, finally, a short section of concluding remarks.

These texts, though possessed of a significant degree of conceptual overlap—involvement of the deities, the importance of the subordinate signatory's loyalty, ritual invocations, curses—are not simply the same text. Rather, they represent related but distinct conventions regarding the literary representation of political and ritual power negotiations, with their respective authors able to record these events and their implications with a remarkably limited degree of correspondence in their structure and content.[11] If these qualify as translations at all, they are

---

[9] On the identity of the missing deity partnered with *mlš* see M. L. Barré, "The First Pair of Deities in the Sefire I God-List," *JNES* 44 (1985): 205–10.

[10] Sef I A 7–14a; SAA 2 2 vi 6–26, followed by a break.

[11] Altman identifies the double presentation of the partners of the treaty (Sef I A 1–6; B 1–6), the presentation of the gods as parties to the treaty, and the public presentation of the treaty by copying it onto a stele as features unique to the Sefire treaties, unknown from either Assyrian or Hittite exemplars (A. Altman, "What Kind of Treaty Tradition Do the Sefire Inscriptions Represent?," in *Treasures on Camels' Humps: Historical and Literary Studies from the Ancient Near East Presented to Israel Eph'al* [ed. M. Cogan and D. Kahn; Jerusalem: Magnes, 2008], 26–40); cf. the distinctive form and syntax—"genuine non-Assyrian features"—noted by W. S. Morrow, "The Sefire Treaty Stipulations and the Mesopotamian Treaty Tradition," in *The World of the*

translations at the margins, of the type that involves the replacement of a source text with a target text situated wholly in the target language and culture.[12] If, in other words, we should understand the Sefire treaties as Aramaic accounts of an agreement between Mati'el of Arpad and Assur-nerari (or his representative, Shamshi-ilu) of Assyria, which was recorded from the Assyrian perspective in Akkadian, this material constitutes evidence not for a monolithic Assyrian treaty tradition but rather for a multivalent and polyphonous tradition of treaty writing, in which the tradition represented by the Sefire material exhibits notable differences in its linguistic and cultural norms when compared to the Assyrian exemplars, combined with a quite remarkable degree of flexibility with regard to the local representation of such agreements. In addition to diverging substantially in the structuring of the account, the author(s) of the Sefire material demonstrate significant creativity in rendering the agreement according to the language and imagery of local norms—with perhaps the preference for curses formulated using the number seven worth particular note. The Sefire texts, in sum, are not simply direct Aramaic translations of obviously Akkadian source material.[13] If this is translation, it is a translation with an acute preference for acceptability in the target language.

Aramaeans III: Studies in Language and Literature in Honour of Paul-Eugène Dion (ed. P. M. M. Daviau, J. W. Wevers, and M. Weigl; JSOTSup 326; Sheffield: Sheffield Academic, 2001), 83–99.

[12] G. Toury, *Descriptive Translation Studies—and Beyond* (rev. ed.; Benjamins Translation Library 100; Amsterdam: John Benjamins, 2012), 119. On whether something like this constitutes "translation" see Toury and chapter one.

[13] Compounding this point is that the three Sefire texts are themselves far from identical. Sefire II is similar to but distinct from Sefire I, while Sefire III is a much more extensive catalogue of treaty stipulations, concerned especially with the subordinate signatory's loyalty to the dominant party, which is of uncertain relationship to Sefire I and Sefire II. Considering Sefire I and Sefire II in particular, it is noteworthy that, though Sefire II is also a treaty between Bar-ga'yah and Mati'el and is thus likely a counterpart to Sefire I, it is apparently not concerned with replicating Sefire I precisely. This internal diversity of witnesses to this treaty relationship between Bar-ga'yah and Mati'el suggests, among other things, that the exact content of treaty formulations was not as important as the general concept of loyalty that the stipulations and curses support. In other words, if at least two and possibly three (or perhaps even more) Aramaic versions of a treaty between Bar-ga'yah and Mati'el could co-exist, it is difficult to contend that the exact wording of such treaties was fundamental to their authors' or their audiences' understanding of their meaning. This is in turn reiterated by the different manifestations of "the" treaty with Mati'el of Arpad in Akkadian and Aramaic, respectively (if, in fact these are to be understood as Akkadian and Aramaic variants of an Assyrian-Aramean agreement at all). For

A major implication of this for the present purposes concerns the extent to which this Aramaic material, from the perspective of its audience, would have evoked an Assyrian framework for interpretation. Though—again, if the identification of Bar-ga'yah as either Shamshi-ilu or Assur-nerari is correct—Mati'el's counterpart in the treaty is of Assyrian extraction, there is very little in the content or form of the Sefire material itself that recommends its interpretation in Assyrian terms. The deities listed as witnesses near the beginning of Sefire I include a number of Mesopotamian deities—albeit probably deities perfectly familiar to and perhaps even worshipped by an audience situated at the northern edge of that region—but, otherwise, the preference in these texts is for language and imagery that is most plausibly identified as native to their Aramaic *milieu*. It is certainly not co-opted from the Assyrian account of the treaty agreement and, without positing another, unidentified influence on the text, the obvious origin for the language and imagery of the Sefire texts is the cultural inheritance native to Mati'el's Arpad. The interpretation of this material by its audience, in other words, would have occurred most naturally against the background of the native treaty and curse tradition on which its author(s) drew in the course of rendering the agreement in Aramaic.

That the Sefire treaties are unlikely to have been and probably were not intended to be understood in Assyrian terms is also supported by the use of an Aramaic name by the gubernatorial signatory, Bar-ga'yah. The use of Aramaic suggests an Aramaic lineage for the person thus named; hence the fact that Shamshi-ilu is generally considered to have been Aramean is construed as part of the case for his identification as Bar-ga'yah.[14] However, none of the other references to Shamshi-ilu—and

---

another case in which multiple versions of what appears to be the same treaty exhibit substantial differences see G. Beckman, *Hittite Diplomatic Texts* (2d ed.; SBLWAW 7; Atlanta, Ga.: Scholars Press, 1999), 17–18. For further discussion of the implications of these relationships see chapter five.

[14] Parpola and Watanabe sidestep this issue when they contend that Bar-ga'yah was a pseudonym or euphemism for Assur-nerari, used because this was "the only feasible way by which Mati'-il could accept the treaty without being ousted from his throne by the anti-Assyrian elements of his population" (Parpola and Watanabe, *Neo-Assyrian Treaties and Loyalty Oaths*, xxviii). If, however, opposition to the treaty were that strong, it is difficult to imagine how such a move could have pacified the treaty's detractors, as—by virtue of being a treaty, not to mention one in which even a cursory reading indicates that Mati'el was the subordinate partner—it would have been quite immediately obvious that Mati'el was swearing loyalty to someone; only a quite remarkable level of assumed ignorance might have enabled Mati'el to enter into such

these are both extensive and inclusive of several of his own inscriptions—use anything other than his Akkadian name.[15] Shamshi-ilu's self-aggrandizing tendencies are known not least from his defacement of Shalmaneser IV's monumental lions at the gates of Til Barsip in favor of inscriptions glorifying himself, yet none of Shamshi-ilu's own inscriptions call him anything other than Shamshi-ilu ([md]*šam-ši-*[f]DINGIR or [md]UTU-DINGIR) (and not even on the Til Barsip lions does he claim the title of king, as he would be doing in the Sefire texts if he is Bar-ga'yah).[16]

If Bar-ga'yah—the senior party of the treaty—is a representative of the Assyrian government, the option of presenting him(self) as an Assyrian, wielding the implements of Assyrian power, was presumably open and available. Nevertheless, this document is recorded in Aramaic, not Akkadian, with Bar-ga'yah presented in Aramaic terms, rather than Akkadian ones: he is not called Shamshi-ilu or Assur-nerari, identifying him in Assyrian terms with an Akkadian name, but rather Bar-ga'yah, an Aramaic name. The prosopographic decision to use an Aramaic name in

---

a treaty thinking that his subjects could be misled regarding the identity of his treaty partner. On the question of whether the Sefire treaties represent a vassal or parity relationship see Altman, "What Kind of Treaty Tradition."

[15] See R. Mattila, "Šamši-ilū," in *The Prosopography of the Neo-Assyrian Empire, Volume 3, Part II: Š–Z* (ed. H. D. Baker; Helsinki: Neo-Assyrian Text Corpus Project, 2011), 1226.

[16] Fuchs draws attention to this weakness in the Shamshi-ilu = Bar-ga'yah equation when he asks "why Šamšī-ilu, if he had been the partner of the Sfire treaties at this time, does not appear in them with his usual name, as is used in his own inscriptions" ("warum Šamšī-ilu, wenn er in dieser Zeit der Partner der Sfire-Verträge gewesen wäre, dort nicht mit seinem üblichen, auch in seinen eigenen Inschriften verwendeten Namen erscheint"; A. Fuchs, "Der Turtān Šamšī-ilu und die große Zeit der assyrischen Großen (830–746)," *WO* 38 [2008]: 93). The purported use of an alternate name for Shamshi-ilu contrasts also with the only direct evidence available for the use of personal names in Aramaic and Akkadian texts: in the Tel Fekheriye inscription the governor/king dedicating the statue is identified using the same Aramaic name in both the Akkadian and Aramaic versions of the text, while his father's Akkadian name is also the same in both texts (for discussion see A. R. Millard and P. Bordreuil, "A Statue from Syria with Assyrian and Aramaic Inscriptions," *BA* 45 [1982]: 138–39; J. C. Greenfield and A. Shaffer, "Notes on the Akkadian-Aramaic Bilingual Statue from Tell Fekherye," *Iraq* 45 [1983]: 114; note that the line numbers for the inscriptions differ in different editions). Elsewhere, Esarhaddon's mother is known to have gone by two names, Naqi'a and Zakutu, but the one translates the other; by contrast, Bar-ga'yah ("son of majesty") is not a translation of either Shamshi-ilu ("my sun is god") or Assur-nerari ("Assur is my help") (A. R. Millard, "Assyrians and Arameans," *Iraq* 45 [1983]: 107).

the Sefire texts suggests that, even if Bar-ga'yah is Shamshi-ilu (or Assur-nerari), in this context this otherwise Assyrianized official of the Assyrian empire is being presented in Aramaic terms rather than in Akkadian ones, with his Assyrian affiliations obscured in favor of his Aramaean ones. Even if Bar-ga'yah's *alter ego* is as an Assyrian *turtanu*, then, the use of an Aramaic name rather than an Assyrian one supports the conclusion that the Sefire texts should be understood in primarily Aramaic, rather than Akkadian, terms. Though the Sefire material shares certain features with the Assyrian treaty and loyalty oath tradition, it also contains features unknown from that tradition and that most probably reflect treaty and loyalty oath elements from native treaty, loyalty oath, and curse traditions.

Before drawing to a close, a brief digression concerning another, more overt case of Akkadian-Aramaic translational activities, the Tel Fekheriye inscriptions, is worthwhile. The statue's text is made up of four parts: two in Akkadian and two in Aramaic. The "A" texts in both languages correspond very closely, with a high degree of symmetry and clear signs of linguistic interferences from the Akkadian in the Aramaic text; the Aramaic is thus generally acknowledged to have been intended as a fairly straightforward translation of the Akkadian text.[17] In his discussion of the development of vernacular writing in the creation of political consciousness, a phenomenon he sees as prompted by the exposure of southern Levantine polities to Assyrian imperial forms, Sanders points to the Tel Fekheriye inscription as "an Assyrian imperial form literally translated into local Aramaic vernacular terms."[18] He suggests that, beginning in the ninth century, local kings in the southern Levant began to "pirate a cosmopolitan genre of empire, the first-person royal conquest inscription, for the new purpose of asserting a local language and territory" and argues that the eighth century Aramaic Sefire treaties are evidence of the "local translation and publication" of Assyrian imperial genres.[19]

---

[17] These include word order that is atypical for Aramaic but normal in Akkadian and the use of "Akkadian words written in Aramaic letters" (see Millard and Bordreuil, "A Statue from Syria," 139). Even if we did not have the original Akkadian text, in other words, the use of an Akkadian source would be evident from the peculiarities of the Aramaic.

[18] S. L. Sanders, *The Invention of Hebrew* (Traditions; Chicago, Ill.: University of Illinois, 2011), 121.

[19] Ibid., 120, 122. On language and identity see R. Appel and P. Muysken, *Language Contact and Bilingualism* (London: Edward Arnold, 1987), 11–20; P. Bourdieu,

The Tel Fekheriye "A" inscriptions are certainly evidence that Akkadian inscriptions could be translated directly into Aramaic or another local language (given the location of the find in Syria, Aramaic could be used in Tel Fekheriye either as the local tongue or as a western *lingua franca*). Yet overall the extant texts also suggest that this was not merely a mono-directional process: the Tel Fekheriye "B" texts exhibit a more complex, symbiotic relationship. They are mostly comprised of a style of curse material that is otherwise almost unknown in Akkadian texts; this has led to suggestions that this material is derived from or has been strongly influenced by the "B" inscription(s)'s Aramaic heritage.[20]

Outline of A Theory of Practice (transl. R. Nice; Cambridge Studies in Social and Cultural Anthropology 16; Cambridge: Cambridge University Press, 2011), 150–51.

[20] The nearest Akkadian analogy to the curse material in these inscriptions is the treaty between Assur-nerari and Mati'ilu of Arpad ("may [a city of] one thousand houses decrease to one house, may one thousand tents decrease to one tent, may (just) one man be spared in the city to (proclaim my) glory"; [URU *šá*] 1-*lim* É.MEŠ *a-na* 1 É *li-tur* [0] 1-*lim* TÚG.*maš-ku-nu a-na* 1 TÚG.*maš-ki-ni li-tur ina* ŠÀ URU 1 LÚ *a-na di-li-li li-ni-zib*; SAA 2 2 vi 3–5) and in an inscription of Assurbanipal describing his campaign against Arabians ("Young camels, young asses, calves and spring lambs sucked their nursing mothers seven times and still could not satisfy their stomachs with milk"; *ba-ak-ru su-ḫi-ru* gu4{amar} udu-nim *ina* ugu 7(imin)-ta-{A}-AN (d.h. –ta-àm) *mu-še-ni-qa-a-te* ‖ *ti* ‖ *e* ‖ *i-ni-qu-u* ‖ *ú* ‖ ø-*ma ši-iz-bu la ú-šab-bu-u ka-ra* ‖ *ras-sún*(A1 *s*[*ún*]ⁱ); R. Borger, *Beiträge zum Inschriftenwerk Assurbanipals: Die Prismenklassen A, B, C* = K, D, E, F, G, H, J *und* T *sowie andere Inschriften, mit einem Beitrag von Andreas Fuchs* [Wiesbaden: Harrassowitz, 1996], A ix 65–67). The Assur-nerari-Mati'ilu treaty has been discussed already; given the geographical origins of Mati'ilu, it is not surprising to see a hint of this more commonly "West Semitic" formulation here. The known treaty between Assurbanipal and the Arabian Qedarites is unfortunately fragmentary (SAA 2 10). The Assurbanipal narrative in which the futility curse appears seems to suggest that the Arabs in question had connections to the west; it refers to an earlier leader as "Uaite', son of Hazael, king of Arabia." While chronology means this can hardly refer to the more famous Hazael of Damascus, both the name and the geographical indications regarding the territory of the Arabians suggest strong connections to the west. There is no systematic discussion of this material but brief discussions of Uaite', including geographical considerations and whether he should be identified with Yauta', may be found in T. C. Mitchell, "Judah until the Fall of Jerusalem (*c.* 700–586 B.C.)," in *The Cambridge Ancient History III, Part 2: The Assyrian and Babylonian Empires and Other States of the Near East, from the Eighth to the Sixth Centuries B.C.* (ed. J. Boardman; Cambridge: Cambridge University Press, 1991), 380 and I. Eph'al, *The Ancient Arabs: Nomads on the Borders of the Fertile Crescent 9th–5th Centuries B.C.* (Jerusalem: Magnes, 1982); the relevant passages, from the A, B, C and G inscriptions, may be found together in Borger, *Assurbanipals*, 243–49. The tribes of the Arabian peninsula are also well-known to have had strong connections to the southern Levantine trading networks (see C. L. Crouch, *The Making of Israel: Cultural*

Fales has even suggested that the Aramaic and Akkadian have mutually influenced each other in the process of the production of these inscriptions.[21] As with the Sefire texts, the peculiarity of the "B" texts *vis-à-vis* known Akkadian material suggests the existence of a curse tradition that was sufficiently distinct from the Assyrian tradition as to contribute its own features to these texts.[22]

If Sanders is correct in seeing the ninth century Assyrian material as a significant source of the Aramaic tradition, it is noteworthy that by the later stage represented by the Sefire texts this influence has already developed into a distinguishably non-Assyrian form. The noticeable differences in style and content suggest that, even if parts of the Aramaic tradition had its roots in the Assyrian tradition—and/or *vice versa*—the manifestation of this phenomenon in Aramaic is not merely the rote import of foreign concepts but a developed local phenomenon, reflecting a tradition that had been nativized already by the middle of the eighth

---

Diversity in the Southern Levant and the Formation of Ethnic Identity in Deuteronomy [VTSup 162; Leiden: Brill, 2014], 57–59, *passim*, with further references). Both appearances of a futility curse in Akkadian repertoire, in other words, are in the context of probable West Semitic influence.

[21] See F. M. Fales, "Le double bilinguism de la statue de Tell Fekherye," *Syria* 60 (1983): 233–50 and the various studies of the Tel Fekheriye inscriptions, including A. Abu Assaf, P. Bordreuil, and A. R. Millard, *La statue de Tell Fekherye et sa bilingue assyro-araméene* (Paris: Editions Recherche sur les civilizations, 1982); Millard and Bordreuil, "Statue from Syria," 135–41; Greenfield and Shaffer, "Notes," 109–116; D. M. Gropp and T. J. Lewis, "Notes on Some Problems in the Aramaic Text of the Hadd-Yith'i Bilingual," *BASOR* 259 (1985): 45–61; Millard, "Assyrians and Arameans," 104–107.

[22] Most discussions of these distinctions speak in terms of an "Assyrian" and a "West Semitic" or "Aramaic" tradition, but it should be borne in mind the likely diversity also within these broader categories—even if the evidence enabling us to further nuance our own understanding of this diversity is currently inadequate. Suggesting that localization could occur even within Assyria's Akkadian-speaking territories is a document dealing with Assurbanipal's relations with the Babylonians that exhibits a "close affinity in content and vocabulary" with VTE (paraphrasing without directly replicating it) but that varies the deities referenced in the curse section in order to bring the specifically Babylonian deities to the fore (A. K. Grayson, "Akkadian Treaties of the Seventh Century B.C.," *JCS* 39 [1987]: 127–60); note also the adaptability of the Akkadian versions of treaties and loyalty oaths that is reflected in the god list of Esarhaddon's treaty with Baal of Tyre (SAA 2 5), in which several of the Tyrian gods are included.

century.[23] Both the Sefire and the Tel Fekheriye texts also support the contention that treaty and related traditions of the ancient Near East, whatever their ultimate origins, were not monolithic: elements were shared as areas came into contact with one another and were eventually nativized into local usage. If parts of the Aramaic Sefire and Tel Fekheriye material originated with Assyria, as Sanders contends, significant elements of this material were no longer recognizably Assyrian by the seventh century.[24]

Ultimately, the existence of treaty, loyalty oath, and curse traditions moving around the ancient Near East in response to the tides of political and cultural power is almost impossible to deny: there are numerous other witnesses that provide evidence in favor of their existence. Treaties, oaths, and curse texts occur in half a dozen languages from all over the ancient Near East; evidence for them dates from as early as the late third millennium, in the form of treaties between Ebla and Abarsal and between Lagash and Umma, and persists for at least two millennia.[25]

---

[23] Note, too, Weeks' observation that, though "the centres which develop the [common ancient Near Eastern] inheritance more slowly or less obviously may be stimulated from outside and may for a time borrow ... the native tradition tends to more enduring than borrowings" (N. Weeks, *Admonition and Curse: The Ancient Near Eastern Treaty/Covenant Form as a Problem in Inter-Cultural Relationships* [JSOTSup 407; London: T&T Clark, 2004], 181).

[24] Observing the mixed heritage of even the "Assyrian" tradition, Malbran-Labat concludes that "these *adê* represent a literary genre which illustrates the plurality of elements present in Neo-Assyrian culture: the form of power which they constitute probably found its origin in the mode of government of the Hittite empire. The word *adê*, very likely borrowed from Aramaic, testifies to the profound aramaisation of Assyria during the eighth century BC" (F. Malbran-Labat, review of A. Lemaire and J.-M. Durand, *Les inscriptions araméennes de Sfiré et l'Assyrie de Shamshi-ilu," RHR* 204 [1987]: 86 ["ces *adê* représentent un genre littéraire qui illustre la pluralité des éléments présents dans la culture néo-assyrienne: la forme de pouvoir qu'ils constituent trouve probablement son origine dans le mode de gouvernement de l'Empire hittite. Le mot *adê*, très vraisemblablement emprunté à l'araméen, témoigne de la profonde araméisation de l'Assyrie dès le VIIIᵉ siècle av. J.-C."]). On Akkadian *adê* as a West Semitic loan word see D. Pardee, review of J. C. L. Gibson, *Textbook of Syrian Semitic Inscriptions, Vol. 2, Aramaic Inscriptions, Including Inscriptions in the Dialect of Zenjirli, JNES* 37 (1978): 196; note Parpola's emphasis that the adoption of the term reflects the ebb and flow of international relations rather than an adoption of a specific treaty form (although his conclusion from this—"that the alleged Aramaic treaty tradition largely is a myth"—is a *non sequitur*) (S. Parpola, "Neo-Assyrian Treaties from the Royal Archives of Nineveh," *JCS* 39 [1987]: 180–83).

[25] A. H. Podany, *Brotherhood of Kings: How International Relations Shaped the Ancient Near East* (Oxford: Oxford University Press, 2010) identifies the Ebla-Abarsal

This tradition is witnessed by the treaties and oaths themselves as well as secondary references to such agreements and to their betrayal; they involve regions and peoples as far flung as the Sumerians and Amorites of Lagash, Akkad, Elam, Mari, and Alalakh; the dozens of Hittite treaties from Boghazköy, one involving Ramesses II witnessed also at Karnak; an indeterminate number from Ugarit; and Egypt (including a loyalty oath involving the population of Megiddo).[26] There are, of course, the texts from Fekheriye and Sefire as well as the material preserved by the Assyrians. Curses appear in these numerous treaties and loyalty oaths as well as in legal codes, epic texts and myths, letters, and inscriptions.[27]

While the seventh century experience of Judah in the context of an Assyrian empire would no doubt have colored its experience of treaties with a particularly Assyrian shading, treaties and oaths in the ancient Near East were thus very far from an exclusively Assyrian phenomenon.

---

treaty as the earliest; K. A. Kitchen and P. J. N. Lawrence, *Part 1: The Texts* (vol. 1 of *Treaty, Law and Covenant in the Ancient Near East*; Wiesbaden: Harrassowitz, 2012) precedes it with the Lagash-Umma text. For a description and discussion of all the ancient Near Eastern treaty and related texts see Weeks, *Admonition and Curse*. After two millennia of ancient Near Eastern dominance the Greeks and others take over the tradition, but this extends beyond the current remit; for one take on the intersection of the ancient Near Eastern material with the Greek see M. L. Barré, *The God-list in the Treaty between Hannibal and Philip V of Macedonia: A Study in Light of the Ancient Near Eastern Treaty Tradition* (Baltimore, Md.: Johns Hopkins University Press, 1983).

[26] The compendium of related material in K. A. Kitchen and P. J. N. Lawrence, *Treaty, Law and Covenant in the Ancient Near East* (3 vols.; Wiesbaden: Harrassowitz, 2012) brings together material published variously elsewhere; the second millennium Hittite material may be found in Beckman, *Hittite Diplomatic Texts*, while Fitzmyer, *Aramaic Inscriptions* and Parpola and Watanabe, *Neo-Assyrian Treaties* cover the major first millennium material (some of the same material as well as additional may be found also in W. W. Hallo and K. L. Younger, Jr., eds., *Monumental Inscriptions from the Biblical World* [vol. 2 of *Context of Scripture*; Leiden: Brill, 2000]). It perhaps also ought to be recalled that the vagaries of climate, combined with local traditions regarding inscriptional materials, have likely resulted in the loss of a larger proportion of the non-Akkadian sources; unlike other ancient Near Eastern scripts, the production of Akkadian was dictated by its three-dimensional character, resulting in the widespread use of a more durable media—clay tablets—than for scripts that could be produced, in (perishable) inks, on flat (and perishable) surfaces.

[27] Curses may be found across a wide range of texts, including treaties and loyalty oaths but also legal and epic material; for these see, for example, M. T. Roth, *Law Collections from Mesopotamia and Asia Minor* (2d ed.; SBLWAW 6; Atlanta, Ga.: Scholars Press, 1997) and W. W. Hallo and K. L. Younger, Jr., eds., *Canonical Compositions from the Biblical World* (vol. 1 of *Context of Scripture*. Leiden: Brill, 1997) and the discussion below.

Interaction between Mesopotamian and West Semitic treaty traditions is likely to have occurred already from a very early period, witnessed in a small way by the Akkadian word for these oaths, *adê*, which is probably a loan from Aramaic. More fundamentally, the existence of multiple states and polities inevitably results in international relations; international relations, in turn, require treaties. To speak of an exclusively Mesopotamian tradition or to insist on discrete "Mesopotamian" and "West Semitic" traditions is attempting more than common sense can bear: the nature of the genre means that it would have been used, reused, adopted, and adapted across the ancient Near East as its inhabitants came into contact with each other over the course of several centuries. As an independent state until the last third of the eighth century and engaged in political alliances and international affairs until its own demise, Judah would have had its own treaty tradition as part of this wider ancient Near Eastern political context.

The use of a loyalty oath or treaty form by Deuteronomy must be interpreted in this wider perspective. Merely using such material is not itself sufficient to signal an intended relationship with the Assyrian forms; a signal intended to indicate such a relationship will have needed to be more precisely tied to a specifically Assyrian manifestation of the treaty and loyalty oath tradition.

Deuteronomy's Relationship with the Assyrian Tradition

The following will therefore explore the possibility of an adaptive relationship between Deuteronomy and an Assyrian tradition of treaties and loyalty oaths. If Deuteronomy does not use material specific and distinctive to the Assyrian form of the wider tradition, prompting its audience to read it as an adaptation of the Assyrian material, an audience familiar with the wider ancient Near Eastern tradition will have understood Deuteronomy in the context of the latter.

Deuteronomy 28

Though the extent of the non-Assyrian material available for comparison to the curses in Deut 28 is frustratingly limited, the evidence that is available—from Sefire, Fekheriye, Ugarit, and Bukan—suggests that these curses would not have inherently conjured the image of an Assyrian treaty in the minds of its audience. The critical point is that the curses contained in Deut 28:20–44 are not distinctively Assyrian in their content: they share features with other ancient Near Eastern curse texts as well as other biblical curse materials. To the latter we will turn in chapter four; here the focus is on the relationship of Deut 28 to the non-Assyrian ancient Near Eastern traditions and, more importantly, whether the Deuteronomy material is recognizable, against this background, as having a particular relationship with the Assyrian material.

DEUT 28:23–24

²³The sky over your head shall be bronze, and the earth under you iron. ²⁴YHWH will change the rain of your land into powder, and only dust shall come down upon you from the sky until you are destroyed.[28]

The logic of Deut 28:23–24 is based on the existential danger of the disruption of normal precipitation patterns. It is one of several similar curses in which agricultural disaster is achieved by the deity(ies) as punishment for transgression of treaty or other stipulations, either by withholding the expected rain or by delivery of one or more unfertile alternatives in its stead. Withholding of rain and other forms of the water necessary to agricultural fertility appears in the Ugaritic epic of Aqhat,[29] while the sending of hailstones may appear also in Sefire I.[30] Though the latter text is fragmentary and the reading uncertain, the curses that follow are in keeping with a theme of agricultural devastation: the destruction wrought by locusts and other pests and the failure of grass and other vegetation to thrive.[31] This conceptual combination is also evident in the Deuteronomy material, if Deut 28:23–24 is read in the context of the preceding verses: "YHWH will make the pestilence cling to you ... YHWH will afflict you with consumption, fever, inflammation, with fiery heat and drought, and with blight and mildew; they shall pursue you until you perish" (Deut 28:21a, 22).[32]

---

[28] והיו שמיך על ראשך נחשת והארץ אשר תחתיך ברזל: יתן יהוה את מטר ארצך אבק ועפר מן השמים ירד עליך עד השמדך:

[29] KTU 1.19 i 42–46.

[30] Sef I A 26.

[31] Sef I A 27–29. B. Margalit, *The Ugaritic Poem of AQHT* (BZAW 182; Berlin: de Gruyter, 1989), 164, 416–17 also interprets the third curse of Dan'el against the locales (KTU 1.19 iv 5), against *ablm*, as a curse of dryness or "dessication," but the literal terminology involves blindness, not drought. The second curse is a curse of non-fertility that uses agricultural imagery (KTU 1.19 iii 53–54); interpreted literally it may be noted alongside Deut 28:23–24 or, interpreted as a curse on the human occupants of *mrrt-tgll-bnr*, in connection with Deut 28:32, 41.

[32] ידבק יהוה בך את הדבר...יככה יהוה בשחפת ובקדחת ובדלקת ובחרחר ובחרב ושדפון ובירקון ורדפוך עד אבדך

Seeing in these and the biblical text the language of storm and rain that is closely associated with storm deities such as Baal, Adad, and YHWH—and the implicit threats against fertility, which these have the power to grant or withhold—Koch has argued that the imagery of Deut 28:23–24 should be understood against the background of the (West Semitic) storm god rather than as an adaptation of the Assyrian material represented by VTE.[33] He also observes a number of instances in which the heavens and the earth are described in texts from the west with reference to metals, contrasting this with the exceptional appearance of this idea, as far as Akkadian texts are concerned, in VTE; he suggests that VTE has itself imported the idea from Aramaic texts.[34] The use of earth and sky as a word pair is—unsurprisingly—attested across a wide chronological, geographical, and generic range, rendering it a poor marker of a specific relationship with Assyrian language or concepts.

DEUT 28:25
YHWH will cause you to be defeated before your enemies; you shall go out against them one way and flee before them seven ways. You shall become an object of horror to all the kingdoms of the earth.[35]

In the wider ancient Near Eastern repertoire of curse material this curse is unusual. The nearest analogies are the curses by sevens found in Sefire[36] and in Bukan.[37] It seems most likely, therefore, to be a native

---

[33] Koch, *Vertrag*, 209–12.

[34] Ibid., 212–13. Koch notes a number of aspects of Deut 28 that suggest that they draw upon a wider ancient Near East tradition; ultimately, however, he identifies Deut 28:25–36 as a palindromic manipulation of an Assyrian deity sequence to which the author had been exposed through the medium of one or more vassal treaties between Judah and Assyria (ibid., 244–247). Ironically, his persistence in identifying a specifically Assyrian palindrome seems to reinforce the association between Deuteronomy and the Assyrian material that he is keen to avoid. In this chapter and the following the likelihood that Deuteronomy's audience would have recognized such a sequence is in any case drawn into question. Koch's original Deut 28, it may be noted, comprises Deut 28:1–6*, 15–19, 20–44*, and Koch clearly considers Deut 28:1–6*, 15–19 to be his strongest evidence for influences other than VTE on Deut 28. Along with Zehnder (M. Zehnder, "Building on Stone? Deuteronomy and Esarhaddon's Loyalty Oaths (Part 2): Some Additional Observations," *BBR* 19 [2009]: 511–35), he provides some of the most extensive existing discussion of the relationship of Deuteronomy material to the wider ancient Near Eastern traditions; what follows is inevitably indebted to their investigations.

[35] יתנך יהוה נגף לפני איביך בדרך אחד תצא אליו ובשבעה דרכים תנוס לפניו והיית לזעוה לכל ממלכות הארץ

[36] Sef I A 21–24, 27–28; II A 1–3a, 5–6.

formulation of the idea of military defeat (itself a very common curse concept), influenced perhaps by a West Semitic tendency to formulate curses using numbers, especially sevens and especially in the context of futility curses.

DEUT 28:26
Your corpses shall be food for every bird of the air and animal of the earth, and there shall be no one to frighten them away.[38]

Non-burial (especially anti-burial, to use the language of Hays) was perceived in negative terms across the ancient Near East, from Egypt and the Levant to Anatolia and Mesopotamia.[39] Conceptually, therefore, Deut 28:26 resides firmly in a common ancient Near Eastern framework of beliefs about the dead and the afterlife. The particular danger of carrion animals in this respect materializes in the Aqhat epic as Dan'el threatens the birds who might disturb Aqhat, his deceased son: "May Ba'lu break the wings of the hawks, may Ba'lu break their pinions, If they fly over the grave of my son, if they do him harm as he sleeps."[40] This comes on the heels of Dan'el's efforts to recover the remains of Aqhat from the innards of these birds; in each case, his express wish is to be able to bury his son: "So that I may weep, so that I may bury him, so that I may put (him) in a grave (with) the gods of the earth"[41]; when he at last locates his

---

[37] Bukan 5′–8′. The *editio princeps* of the Bukan text may be found in A. Lemaire, "Une inscription araméenne du VIIe siècle avant J.-C. trouvée à Bukân," *Studia Iranica* 27 (1998): 15–30 (more recently see H. Donner and W. Röllig, eds., *Kanaanäische und aramäische Inschriften* [vol. 1; 5th ed.; Wiesbaden: Harrassowitz, 2002], no. 320). Lemaire explicitly excludes the possibility that this text represents an Assyrian vassal treaty with the Mannaeans, despite the similarities between this text and both the Sefire and Tel Fekheriye material—the former of which, it will be recalled, he and Durand concluded was the Aramaic version of an Assyrian text (Lemaire, "Une inscription araméenne," 29). The geographical origin of this text reiterates the mobility of curse formulae across the ancient Near East.

[38] והיתה נבלתך למאכל לכל עוף השמים ולבהמת הארץ ואין מחריד

[39] C. B. Hays, *Death in the Iron Age II and in First Isaiah* (FAT 79; Tübingen: Mohr Siebeck, 2011), 11–132, 161; F. Stavrakopoulou, "Gog's Grave and the Use and Abuse of Corpses in Ezekiel 39:11–20," *JBL* 129 (2010): 67–76.

[40] *knp . nšrm b'l . yṯbr . b'l . yṯbr . diy hmt . hm . t'pn . 'l . qbr . bny tšḥṭ{.}nn . b šnth* (KTU 1.19 iii 42–45; COS 1.103 iii 148–51). Translations of the Ugaritic material are according to COS 1.103 unless otherwise noted.

[41] *ab[[p]]ky . w . aqbrnh ašt . b ḫrt . ilm . art* (KTU 1.19 iii 5–6; COS 1.103 ii 105–iii 145).

remains, his immediate response is to bury them.[42] Ramesses II's (rather overblown) account of his meeting with Muwatallis II of Hatti describes his success in terms of the overwhelming number of corpses left exposed across the countryside—shortly, interestingly, after describing his acts as like the destruction of the falcon.[43] Curses on anyone who dares to disturb the interments of the dead occur across the ancient Near East.[44] In threatening its audience with the abandonment and desecration of their bodies after death, therefore, Deut 28:26 draws on a widespread perception of the importance of proper burial after death, variant in its individual manifestations but common in its shared concern for the protection of the body from desecration, whether by human or animal perpetrators. There is nothing distinctively Assyrian in the formulation of Deut 28:26 that would signal its intention to be read as an adaptation of a specifically Assyrian source or in relation to the ideas of such a source.

DEUT 28:27
YHWH will afflict you with the boils of Egypt, with ulcers, scurvy, and itch, of which you cannot be healed.[45]

Cursing by illness appears already in the Aqhat material from Ugarit, in the first of a series of three curses called down by Dan'el on the three locales unfortunate enough to be connected with Aqhat's death.[46] The translation of the first curse has been the subject of some dispute, with the absence of word dividers in the text allowing for a multiplicity of interpretations of the critical sequence of consonants (*grbtil*). Thus Wright, following Margalit and Gaster, reads "(You shall) always (be) an alien in Il's house!" (*gr bt il*), suggesting that it might be some kind of cult-orientated curse and pointing to Deut 23:2–9, where certain persons are not allowed into the sanctuary.[47] As Hillers already pointed out, however, to be a *ger* in the house of the deity ought to be a good thing,

---

[42] KTU 1.19 iii 38–41; COS 1.103 iii 144–47.

[43] COS 2.5A 214–223, 224–250.

[44] See Hays, *Death in the Iron Age II*, especially 80, 151, 248.

[45] יככה יהוה בשחין מצרים ובעפלים ובגרב ובחרס אשר לא תוכל להרפא

[46] KTU 1.19 iii 45–47. For a discussion of these curses see D. P. Wright, *Ritual in Narrative: The Dynamics of Feasting, Mourning, and Retaliation Rites in the Ugaritic Tale of Aqhat* (Winona Lake, Ind.: Eisenbrauns, 2001), 182–90.

[47] Ibid., 182, 182 n. 4; cf. Margalit, *The Ugaritic Poem of AQHT*, 163; T. H. Gaster, *Thespis: Ritual, Myth and Drama in the Ancient Near East* (Garden City, N.Y.: Doubleday, 1961), 365–66. Note also that Deut 23:2–9 more probably refers to the Israelite community more generally (the terminology is קהל יהוה) rather than the sanctuary specifically.

rather than a curse; both he and Renfroe thus argue in favor of interpretations which see in *grbtil* a reference to skin disease, *grb*, a term commonly attested in Semitic languages, including Deut 28:27 (גרב). The former divides *grbt il* and reads "the leprosy of El," as an association between a particular disease and a particular deity; based on similar curses elsewhere, he suggests that the first word of the line, *amd*, should be understood in terms of clothing and thus reads "May you be *clothed* with leprosy of El!"[48] The latter divides *grb til*, reading the second word as a verb meaning "to seek refuge, flee, look for protection" and interprets overall as "May you always be seeking asylum as a leper."[49] Either way a reference to skin disease "makes a good deal more sense as a curse."[50] Not in dispute is that the curse concludes with a clause making it perpetual—"now, for a long time, and forever more / now and for all generations"—resembling the emphasis in Deut 28:27 on the perpetuity of the curse and the absence of anyone who might alleviate its consequences.[51]

DEUT 28:28–29
[28]YHWH will afflict you with madness, blindness, and confusion of mind; [29]you shall grope about at noon as blind people grope in darkness, but you shall be unable to find your way; and you shall be continually abused and robbed, without anyone to help.[52]

The curse of blindness appears already in Aqhat, with Dan'el proclaiming over *ablm* "May Ba'lu make you blind, at this very moment and forever more, now and for all generations."[53] Here too the emphasis

---

[48] D. R. Hillers, "A Difficult Curse in Aqht (19 [1 Aqht] 3.152–154)," in *Biblical and Related Studies Presented to Samuel Iwry* (ed. A. Kort and S. Morschauser; Winona Lake, Ind.: Eisenbrauns, 1985), 106–107; similarly M. S. Smith and S. B. Parker, *Ugaritic Narrative Poetry* (SBLWAW 9; Atlanta, Ga.: Scholars Press, 1997), 74. The analogies to which Hillers points are themselves (Neo-)Assyrian; if the Ugaritic passages are organically related to the Assyrian material's antecedents—not improbable in the Ugaritic context—this is again witness to the nativization of this type of material in the process of transmission.

[49] F. Renfroe, "*QR–MYM*'s Comeuppance," *UF* 18 (1986): 457.

[50] Ibid., 457.

[51] The exact rendering of the first of these two lines is unclear, but the perpetual nature of the intent is not. See COS 1.103 n. 118 for discussion.

[52] יככה יהוה בשגעון ובעורון ובתמהון לבב: והיית ממשש בצהרים כאשר ימשש העור באפלה ולא תצליח את דרכיך והיית אך עשוק וגזול כל הימים ואין מושיע:

[53] *'wrt . yštk . b'l . l ht w* [[x]]*'lmh . l 'nt . p dr . dr* (KTU 1.19 iv 5–6; COS 1.103 iv 151–168). Margalit, *The Ugaritic Poem of AQHT*, 164, 416–17 reads this curse as to do

is on the perpetuity of the curse, as throughout the three curses that Dan'el pronounces: each begins with the rationale for the curse, linking it to the death of Aqhat, before the pronouncement of the specific curse and a clause making the curse perpetual.[54]

This emphasis on perpetuity in Dan'el's curses attracts attention to a concentration of similarities between the curses in Aqhat and the curses in Deut 28:23–29. In addition to the overall emphasis on perpetuity, evident in Deuteronomy but already observed to be quite different from the VTE material, the more specific content of the Aqhat curses overlaps with almost all of the verses in this section.[55] Deuteronomy 28:23–24, with its focus on the withholding of the rains unto destruction, is akin to the imagery of the failed agriculture[56]; Deut 28:26 articulates concerns regarding the consumption of the dead body by carrion birds and the attendant disruption of the deceased's afterlife[57]; Deut 28:27 echoes the curse of skin disease(s)[58]; and Deut 28:28–29 involves blindness.[59] This is not, it should be emphasized, a suggestion that the Deuteronomy curses have been based on—never mind intend to allude to—the Aqhat curses; these texts also fail the criteria of specificity, frequency, and distinctiveness that would require satisfaction in order for such a claim to be substantiated. The common ground of their content, however, reiterates that the Deuteronomy material is at home in the environment of West Semitic curse traditions, with the emphasis on perpetuity an especially noteworthy element.

DEUT 28:30–33
[30]You shall become engaged to a woman, but another man shall lie with her. You shall build a house, but not live in it. You shall plant a

---

with drought—"May Baal stop up thy well-spring(s)"—but this is based on an overall interpretation of these curses in terms of damming up the Sea of Galilee and related imagery.

[54] On the structure of the curses see Renfroe, "QR–MYM's Comeuppance," 455.

[55] The one exception is Deut 28:25 ("YHWH will cause you to be defeated before your enemies; you shall go out against them one way and flee before them seven ways"); as noted already above, this curse is broadly in line with the curses by sevens in Sefire and Bukan but is ultimately quite unusual in its use of the stereotyped number. In the immediately following scene of Aqhat (as elsewhere in the epic) the number turns up as the number of years for which Dan'el mourns, but other than a general affirmation of the number's common significance this should not be given additional weight.

[56] KTU 1.19 iii 53–54; cf. KTU 1.19 i 42–46.

[57] KTU 1.19 iii 148–151.

[58] KTU 1.19 iii 45–47.

[59] KTU 1.19 iv 5.

vineyard, but not enjoy its fruit. [31]Your ox shall be butchered before your eyes, but you shall not eat of it. Your donkey shall be stolen in front of you, and shall not be restored to you. Your sheep shall be given to your enemies, without anyone to help you. [32]Your sons and daughters shall be given to another people, while you look on; you will strain your eyes looking for them all day but be powerless to do anything. [33]A people whom you do not know shall eat up the fruit of your ground and of all your labors; you shall be continually abused and crushed.[60]

The futility aspect of Deut 28:30–33 is probably most famously compared to the futility curses of Sefire, though the latter are characterized by a fondness for sevens that the Deuteronomy curses do not reflect in this section (though cf. Deut 28:25).[61] Futility curses also appear in the "B" texts of the Tel Fekheriye inscription, where the relationship between the Aramaic and the Akkadian suggests that these reflect a tradition native to the former.[62] Ramos has recently argued that the numeric versions of such curses reflect a common Northwest Semitic pattern of formulaic curse language and ought to be understood in that context.[63]

The collocation of the woman, house, agriculture, and livestock occurs in numerous variations, especially in the preserved Hittite treaties. The treaty between Suppiluliuma I of Hatti and Huqqana of Hayasa warns the latter that if they do not honor their treaty oath then they, along with their wives, sons, brothers, sisters, families, households, fields, vineyards, threshing floors, cattle, sheep, and other possessions will be destroyed[64]; the treaty between Muwattalli II of Hatti and Alaksandu of Wilusa lists the latter's wife, sons, lands, cities, vineyard,

---

[60] אשה תארש ואיש אחר ישגלנה בית תבנה ולא תשב בו כרם תטע ולא תחללנו: שורך טבוח לעיניך ולא תאכל ממנו חמרך גזול מלפניך ולא ישוב לך צאנך נתנות לאיביך ואין לך מושיע: בניך ובנתיך נתנים לעם אחר ועיניך ראות וכלות אליהם כל היום ואין לאל ידך: פרי אדמתך וכל יגיעך יאכל עם אשר לא ידעת והיית רק עשוק ורצוץ כל הימים: Again, the redactional status of Deut 28:33 has little bearing on the overall conclusions.

[61] Sef I A 21–26; II A 1–9; thus H. Tawil, "A Curse Concerning Crop-Consuming Insects in the Sefire Treaty and in Akkadian: A New Interpretation," *BASOR* 225 (1977): 59–62.

[62] Note also the two appearances of futility curses in Akkadian texts with probable West Semitic influences, discussed above.

[63] M. Ramos, "Malediction and Oath: The Curses of the Sefire Treaties and Deuteronomy 28" (paper presented at the annual meeting of the Society of Biblical Literature, Baltimore, Md., 23 November 2013).

[64] Beckman, *Hittite Diplomatic Texts*, 3 A iv 50'–59'.

threshing floor, field, cattle, sheep, and possessions.[65] Numerous others include similar lists of greater or lesser exhaustiveness.[66] The similarities between these lists and those in Deut 28:30–33 seem unlikely to be the consequence of a direct line of inheritance from the Hittite material to the biblical so much as a reiteration that the persons and possessions included in these lists represent the range of targets through which the signatories to treaties and oaths might be punished: family members—the destruction of whom is sometimes explicitly linked to the destruction of the oath-takers' prospects of progeny—and property of both the animate (cattle, sheep) and inanimate (fields, vineyards, houses, etc.) variety.[67] The mundane character of each of these elements renders their inclusion in curses unsurprising as well as largely indistinguishable, barring additional and more distinctive content.

In addition to the Deuteronomy curse material most usually associated with an Assyrian source, several other curses reiterate that Deut 28:20–44 is comfortably at home in a wider ancient Near Eastern curse tradition. The process of desertification which drives the logic of Deut 28:21–24 is a similar combination of concepts to the curses in Sefire I[68] as well the material in Aqhat.[69] The locust, worm, and cicada of Deut 28:38, 39, 42 have often been linked to the locust, worm, and unidentified *twy* of Sefire I[70]; Koch notes the similar sense of futility with respect to agricultural production in the "B" texts of Tel Fekheriye.[71] The inversions

---

[65] Ibid., 13 A iv 31–46.

[66] Ibid., 1 obv. 12–18, 19–22; 5 A rev. 12′–16′; 6A A rev. 58–69; 6B rev. 40–62; 7 A iv 44′–57′; 8 A iv 21–26; 18B rev. 5–7. The inevitably cross-cultural nature of treaties is reiterated by 6A and 6B, both extant—at least in part—in both Hittite and Akkadian and representing the two sides of the agreement. Note also that there is substantial scope for variations in these multiple renderings of the same agreement.

[67] See also A. M. Kitz, "Curses and Cursing in the Ancient Near East," *Religion Compass* 1 (2007): 621.

[68] Sef I A 26–29, 32.

[69] KTU 1.19 i 42–46.

[70] Sef I A 27–28.

[71] Koch, *Vertrag*, 235. Koch also links the Deuteronomy pests, the pests in Sef I A 31–32, and the lexical series ur₅-ra = *ḫubullu* XIV to suggest that they indicate a shared scribal culture mediated by Aramaean scribes (ibid., 284–286). Given that the Sefire material resembles initially the Deuteronomy material, then a curse buried in the depths of VTE, then the lexical series (which does also include similar names of pests to the Deuteronomy list, in the same order—but scattered over a hundred lines [ll. 227, 271–273, 359]), it seems rather unlikely that these may be construed as deliberate allusions. At most they may reflect a semi-stereotyped list; more likely they simply represent common agricultural pests and therefore pests liable to turn up in curses against agricultural productivity. In the context of these curses the association

that dictate the curse function of Deut 28:43–44 ("Aliens residing among you shall ascend above you higher and higher, while you shall descend lower and lower; they shall lend to you but you shall not lend to them; they shall be the head and you shall be the tail"[72]) are mirrored by the inversions that comprise the final curse section of Sefire I: "may the gods overturn th[at m]an and his house and all that (is) in it; may they make its lower part its upper part!"[73] Like the curses of Deut 28:23–24, (25,) 26–33, this material locates Deuteronomy in a conceptual world that is broadly ancient Near Eastern rather than distinctively Assyrian.

DEUTERONOMY 13

The exclusivity of Deut 13's relationship with the Assyrian treaty, loyalty oath, and curse materials is similarly questionable; its concerns and concepts are common to much of the ancient Near Eastern tradition. Pakkala, Koch, and Zehnder have been particularly prominent in this quarter of late, with the first and last focusing especially on Deut 13. Koch's arguments regarding Deut 13 are aimed at dismantling the supposedly exclusive use of VTE by Deuteronomy by suggesting that Deut 13 contains equal if not better connections with other ancient Near Eastern treaty and oath material; the breadth of the material he identifies in this regard contributes to the dilution of Deut 13's specific association with distinctively Assyrian ideas.[74] Zehnder's catalogues of both Deuteronomy's and VTE's continuities with wider ancient Near Eastern traditions likewise serves to diffuse the exclusivity of the relationship between Deuteronomy and Assyrian traditions necessary to the subversion argument, though this is not his explicit aim.[75] Pakkala's

---

between locust plagues and warfare noted by Wright may also be of interest (J. L. Wright, "Warfare and Wanton Destruction: A Reexamination of Deuteronomy 20:19–20 in Relation to Ancient Siegecraft," *JBL* 127 [2008]: 429). Koch also compares the contents of Deut 28:38–42 to curses in the treaty of Assur-nerari (SAA 2 2 iv 14–16) and the treaty with Baal of Tyre (SAA 2 5 iv 16′–17′); with regard to the latter we might wish to note that the curse in question is attributed to the Tyrian deities, Melqart and Eshmun (Koch, *Vertrag*, 233).

[72] הגר אשר בקרבך יעלה מעלה מעלה ואתה תרד מטה מטה: הוא ילוך ואתה לא תלונו הוא יהיה לראש ואתה תהיה לזנב

[73] יהפכו אלהן אש[א ה]א וביתה וכל זי [ב]ה וישמו תחתיתה [ל][ע]ליתה (Sef I C 21–24). Transcriptions and translations of the Sefire material are according to Fitzmyer, *The Aramaic Inscriptions*.

[74] Koch, *Vertrag*, 151–68.

[75] Zehnder, "Building on Stone ... (Part 2)," 511–35.

underlying motivation for rejecting a connection between Deut 13 and the Assyrian tradition is linked to his conviction that the entirety of Deuteronomy derives from the exilic period and later; nevertheless, he highlights the extent to which the elements of Deuteronomy taken to indicate its adaptation of VTE are equally if not more characteristic of other, non-Assyrian manifestations of the treaty and loyalty oath tradition.[76] The following discussion will draw particular attention to the issue of loyalty as well as to some of the more specific components of Deut 13.

It would not be an exaggeration to suggest that loyalty is an obsession of the extant treaty and loyalty oath materials; both loyalty and its opposite, sedition, are extremely common throughout. This is hardly surprising; the nature of a treaty or loyalty oath is to delineate the relationship between two persons and the states or peoples they represent and, more to the point, to differentiate this relationship from other relationships by virtue of the special obligations that the treaty partners have to each other and not to others. Exclusivity of commitments is therefore a naturally prominent feature of this genre, often expressed in terms of the special responsibilities of treaty partners to come to each other's aid in times of crisis, support for each other's royal successions, and the like. It is hardly surprising to see scholars such as Dion—undermining his own claims for Deut 13's basis in VTE—concluding from this material that suppression of political subversion is richly documented across the ancient Near East.[77]

Perhaps the most interesting category of these materials' concerns about loyalty for the current purposes is the material that warns about allowing verbal expressions of disloyalty—"sedition," in the more usual terminology of the VTE and Deuteronomy discussion—to occur without consequence in the presence of the treaty partner. Instructions to reveal or hand over the speaker of seditious sentiments, as well as a corollary emphasis on not concealing or supporting such persons, are common in these texts, much as Deut 13 warns against those who "speak treason." Some variation of this issue, for example, appears in almost every single one of the Hittite treaty texts. In his treaty with the men of Ismerika, Arnuwanda I warns as follows:

---

[76] Pakkala, "Deuteronomium 13."

[77] P. E. Dion, "Deuteronomy 13: The Suppression of Alien Religious Propaganda in Israel during the Late Monarchical Era," in *Law and Ideology in Monarchic Israel* (ed. B. Halpern and D. W. Hobson; JSOTSup 124; Sheffield: JSOT, 1991), 201, 203; cf. Zehnder, "Building on Stone ... (Part 2)," 511–18.

If someone speaks an evil word before you—whether he is a governor of a border province, [or he is a nobleman], or he is one of modest rank; or if he is a Hittite, or he is a Kizzuwatnaean, [...]; or if he is some person's father, mother, brother, sister, or his child or [his] relative by marriage— [...] No one shall conceal the one who speaks an (evil) word, but shall rather seize him and make him known.[78]

The treaty between Mursili II and Tuppi-Teshshup of Amurru instructs the latter that "[i]f someone should bring up before you, Tuppi-Teshshup, evil matters against the King or against Hatti, you shall not conceal him from the King"[79]; his treaty with Kupanta-Kurunta of Mira-Kuwaliya declares that "if you hear in advance about some evil plan to revolt, and either some Hittite or some man of Arzawa carries out the revolt ... but you do not quickly send word in advance to my Majesty," then the latter will have transgressed his responsibilities of loyalty to the Hittite king.[80] Similarly Suppiluliuma I, in his treaty with Aziru of Amurru, warns that "[if] someone speaks about [evil matters concerning] My Majesty before you, Aziru, whether [a Hittite] or your own subject, and you, [Aziru], do not seize him and send him to the [King] of Hatti, you will have transgressed the oath."[81] In his treaty with Huqqana of Hayasa Suppiluliuma returns to this issue repeatedly: "if you ever hear evil concerning My Majesty from someone and conceal it from me, and do not speak of it to me, and do not point out that person but even hide him, you will transgress the oath"[82] and, at length:

---

[78] Beckman, *Hittite Diplomatic Texts*, 1A obv. 21'–24'. On similarities between Deut 13 and Ismerika see also J. Berman, "CTH 133 and the Hittite Provenance of Deuteronomy 13," *JBL* 131 (2011): 25–44; note the subsequent discussion between Berman, Levinson, and Stackert in B. M. Levinson and J. Stackert, "Between the Covenant Code and Esarhaddon's Succession Treaty: Deuteronomy 13 and the Composition of Deuteronomy," *JAJ* 3 (2012): 133–136; J. Berman, "Historicism and Its Limits: A Response to Bernard M. Levinson and Jeffrey Stackert," *JAJ* 4 (2013): 297–309; B. M. Levinson and J. Stackert, "The Limitations of »Resonance«: A Response to Joshua Berman on Historical and Comparative Method," *JAJ* 4 (2013): 310–33.

[79] Beckman, *Hittite Diplomatic Texts*, 8 A ii 46'–iii 11.

[80] Ibid., 11 C iii 22–28; 11 D iii 47–66; 11 B iii 27'–30'; cf. ibid., 10 obv. 10'–17' and the warnings about rumors and murmurings towards insurrection in ibid., 10 obv. 28'–34'; 11 D iv 19'–34'. Zehnder, "Building on Stone ... (Part 2)," 514–15 notes several of the Hittite texts in connection with the report of an appropriate response to disloyal conspirators.

[81] Beckman, *Hittite Diplomatic Texts*, 5 iii 29'–34'.

[82] Ibid., 3 A i 22–30.

if some Hittite undertakes evil against me, whatever sort of person he might be—if you hear about him and do not tell me about him at that moment ... if [you think] such [a thought and] do not report the evil person [to My Majesty immediately], but you [even ...] proceed to go over to his side, [these] oath gods shall destroy [you, Huqqana] ... whatsoever [evil] matter you hear of— [if] you conceal it from me and do not report it to me, [or] conceal that person [from me] and do [not report] him to me, but even hide him—we [have placed] such matters as these under oath for you. If you do not observe it but transgress it, then these oath gods shall destroy you ... if [you hear of] an evil deed, whatever sort of deed, and if [you do not come] to me [immediately]...[83]

Nearer to Deuteronomy both chronologically and geographically, both Sefire III and Sefire I exhibit similar concerns. Much of Sefire I B reflects a nexus of ideas involving speech, loyalty, and action for or against the treaty partner; the opening of Sefire III instructs that

[... And whoever will come to you] or to your son or to your offspring or to one of the kings of Arpad and will s[pea]k [ag]ainst me or against my son or against my grandson or against my offspring, *indeed*, any man who *rants* and utters evil words against me, [you] must [not] accept such words from him. You must hand them (i.e., the men) over into my hands, and your son must hand (them) over to my son, and your offspring must hand (them) over to my offspring, and the offspring of [any of the ki]ngs of Arpad must hand (them) over to me. Whatever is good in my sight, I will do to them.[84]

Given the attention paid to the phrase דבר סרה, it is worth emphasizing the frequency with which these issues are articulated in terms of false speech: someone who "speaks an evil word" or "speaks about evil matters," someone who brings up of "evil matters", "any man who rants and utters evil words."[85] Koch is particularly attentive to Sefire III in connection with the language in Deut 13 about listening to the inciting individual, but the focus on the dangers posed by the treaty partner who

---

[83] Ibid., 3 A ii 32–B obv. 8′–12′.

[84] או אל ברך או אל עקרך או אל חד מלכי ארפד וי[מל]ל [ע]לי או על ברי או על בר ברי או על עקרי כים כל גבר זי יבעה רוח אפוה וימלל מלן לחית לעלי [את ל]תקה מליא מן ידה הסכר תהסכרהם בידי ברך יהסכר לברי ועקרך יסכר לעקרי ועקר [חד מ]לכי ארפד יהסכרן לי מה טב בעיני אעבד להם (Sef III 1–3). In the interests of Deut 13 one might also note, in the immediately following instructions regarding fugitives, the listing of "me, one of my officials, or one of my brothers, or one of my courtiers, or one of the people who are under my control" (Sef III 4b–5a).

[85] Beckman, *Hittite Diplomatic Texts*, 1A obv. 21′–24′; 5 iii 29′–34′; 8 A ii 46′–iii 11; Sef III 2.

hears but fails to report disloyal speech and instead follows the insurrectionist's lead against the authority of the other treaty partner recurs across the entire tradition: as would be expected, given the purpose of the genre.[86] Indeed, such a focus is hardly surprising in a context in which the major point under issue is the preservation of loyalty between two parties and the implications of that loyalty for the elimination of potential threats to one or both parties' authority.

Several scholars have noted analogies in the wider ancient Near Eastern repertoire to the potential avenues of insurrection on which Deut 13 is focused.[87] The risk from an entire city in Deut 13:13–19, as an idea that is not apparent in the Assyrian material, has drawn particular attention; Sefire III instructs that "you must come and avenge my blood ... If it is a city, you must strike it with a sword,"[88] while the possibility of insurrection by and consequent punishment of a city, as well as a household or an individual, is also imagined in the treaties between Arnuwanda I of Hatti and the men of Ismerika[89] and between Tudhaliya II of Hatti and Sunashshura of Kizzuwatna.[90]

The Sefire III instructions regarding the destruction of an offending city are followed by a list of other potential offenders: "one of my brothers or one of my slaves or [one] of my officials or one of the people who are under my control."[91] This list echoes and is echoed by the many other lists of persons whose danger to the treaty partner(s) is perceived by the authors of these treaties.[92] Some of these are brief, others exhaustive; all resemble the persons enumerated by Deut 13, as it makes its own attempt to anticipate the innumerable directions from which loyalty to YHWH might face challenge. Among these Koch draws particular attention to the Arnuwanda I-Ismerika treaty, which in some respects resembles the list of persons in Deut 13:7 ("your brother, your mother's son, or your son or daughter, or the wife you embrace, or your most intimate friend"). The list of potential insurrectionists envisioned by the Arnuwanda I-Ismerika treaty includes the one who is "governor of a border province, [or he is a nobleman], or he is one of modest rank;

---

[86] Koch, *Vertrag*, 158–59.

[87] Pakkala, "Deuteronomium 13," 129; Koch, *Vertrag*, 154–55, 158–59; Zehnder, "Building on Stone ... (Part 2)," 514.

[88] את תאתה ותקם דמי...והן קריה הא נכה תכוה בחרב (Sef III 11–13).

[89] Beckman, *Hittite Diplomatic Texts*, 1A obv. 25′–28′.

[90] Ibid., 2 A ii 16–18.

[91] חד אחי הא או חד עבדי או [חד] פקדי או חד עמא זי בידי (Sef III 13).

[92] Beckman, *Hittite Diplomatic Texts*, 1A obv. 21′–24′; 3 A ii 32–38; 5 iii 29′–34′; 11 C iii 22–28, D iii 47–66, B iii 27′–30′, among others.

or if he is a Hittite, or he is a Kizzuwatnaean, […]; or if he is some person's father, mother, brother, sister, or his child or [his] relative by marriage."[93] As with the VTE list, however, the significance of these similarities is deceptive: they again comprise no more than variant permutations of lists involving common family members.

Of final note in this discussion of Deuteronomy's relationship with the wider ancient Near Eastern tradition is the non-alteration clause in Deut 13:1, which Levinson suggested might be linked to VTE. This is a common trope in the ancient Near Eastern treaty and loyalty oath texts, appearing in the "A" texts of Tel Fekheriye (again, an overt example of interaction in this genre across languages) as well as much earlier, in treaties between Mursili II of Hatti and Manapa-Tarhunta of the Land of the Seha River, and between Hattusili III of Hatti and Ulmi-Teshshup of Tarhuntassa, in which the Hittite kings warn their treaty partners that the curses contained in the treaty will be invoked should "you alter the words of this tablet."[94] An invocation of curses on anyone who "will say, 'I shall efface some of its words,'" appears in Sefire I[95]; a more expansive expression of the same occurs in Sefire II:

> [and whoever will] give orders to efface [th]ese inscriptions from the bethels, where they are [wr]itten, and [will] say, "I shall destroy the inscript[ion]s and *with impunity* shall I destroy KTK and its king," should that (man) be frightened from effacing the inscript[ion]s from the bethels and say to someone who does not understand, "I shall engage (you) indeed," and (then) order (him), "Efface these inscriptions from the bethels," may [he] and his son die in oppressive torment.[96]

Again, the idea that oaths of loyalty might be put in jeopardy through the alteration of the record of the oath is recurrent throughout the tradition.[97]

Quite obviously the chronological separation between many of these texts—those from Hittite Anatolia being the most apparent—and Deuteronomy makes the latter's direct dependence on them highly

---

[93] Ibid., 1A obv. 21'–24'; Koch, *Vertrag*, 154.

[94] Beckman, *Hittite Diplomatic Texts*, 12 A iv 29'–39'; 18B rev. 5–7.

[95] ויאמר אהלד מן מלוה (Sef I C 18–19).

[96] ‏[ומן י]אמר להלדת ספריא [א]לן מן בתי אלהיא אן זי י[ר]שמן ו[י]אמר אהאבד ספר[י]א ולמ[ג]ן‏
‏אהבד אית כתך ואית מלכה ויחל הא מן לד ספר[י]א מן בתי אלהיא ויאמר לזי לידע אנה אגר אגר‏
‏וברה [מת הא] י‏ ו[י]אמר לד [ספ]ריא אלן מן בתי [א]להיא ובלחץ עלב י (Sef II C 1–11).

[97] Note, however, that the evidence for the multiplicity of texts recording the same agreement suggests that this concern refers to the theoretical potential rather than being aimed at actually eliminating the possibility of variant renderings of a particular oath.

unlikely (efforts to associate the book with Moses not withstanding). Nevertheless, the ability to see equally if not more compelling similarities between Deuteronomy and such material demonstrates the extremely limited extent to which any of the material in Deuteronomy may be understood in specifically Assyrian terms. These similarities also support the case for a widespread ancient Near Eastern treaty and loyalty oath tradition that, though manifest in numerous particular forms in different times and places, exhibited also a significant degree of continuity across both. At the crossroads of the southern Levant and intimately caught up in centuries of local and regional struggles for power, Judah can hardly have been ignorant of this tradition.

Deuteronomy 13's continuities with a variety of ancient Near Eastern traditions suggest that its affinities with the Assyrian traditions reflect little more than their place in a more widely known common tradition. This casts into doubt Deuteronomy's ability or intent to signal an interpretive relationship with a specifically Assyrian tradition, given the general material it contains. Considering the breadth and depth of the treaty and loyalty oath traditions circulating in the ancient Near East, any attempt to signal a relationship with a specifically Assyrian form of the tradition would have been obliged to signal quite specifically to the elements of the tradition's Assyrian manifestation, in order to distinguish it from this wider morass. As was the case in the discussion of Deuteronomy's ability to signal a relationship with VTE, however, there has been nothing to suggest that Deut 13 intends to signal a relationship with the Assyrian form of this tradition, as distinct from a more general ancient Near Eastern one. It therefore becomes difficult to imagine that Deuteronomy's use of treaty and oath material would have been construed as reflecting Assyrian material and ideology only. Instead, Deut 13's location in the midst of the wider tradition continues to diminish the likelihood that its audience would have been inclined to look to Assyria for its interpretation in the first place. While the author of the Deuteronomy material was undoubtedly aware that the loyalty oath and the vassal treaty were genres often used by the Assyrian empire to formalize relations both within and beyond its borders, these forms cannot be understood to be exclusively Assyrian in connotation or context.

CONCLUSIONS

The preceding textual study of the similarities between Deuteronomy and other ancient Near Eastern texts shows that it is difficult, perhaps impossible, to demonstrate that a specifically Assyrian tradition was the source of and referent for the Deuteronomy material, as well as how problematic it is to suggest that Deuteronomy's use of these generalized concepts would have evoked only Assyrian precedents. While clearly related to wider ancient Near Eastern treaty, loyalty oath, and curse traditions, neither Deut 13 nor 28 use Assyrian ideas or concepts in a way which renders this material recognizable as the referent of deliberate signaling on the part of Deuteronomy.

Once the Assyrian manifestation of the treaty, loyalty oath, and curse traditions is stripped of its status as the specific referent of the Deuteronomy texts, it becomes all but impossible to contend that Deuteronomy's use of these traditions intended to signal a relationship with the Assyrian material. In turn, this undermines the suggestion that Deuteronomy intended to subvert Assyrian ideology, as the lack of a distinctive and recognizable signal of Deuteronomy's relationship with the Assyrian tradition in particular means that Deuteronomy could not be experienced by its audience in relation to the Assyrian material. Without the recognition of the new material as an adaptation of an older source, the intent to alter or replace the source—to subvert it—becomes invisible. The intention of Deuteronomy's author in using the enforcing power of curses and in articulating Israel's loyalty to YHWH in terms of loyalty to the sovereign (and betrayal thereof in terms of sedition) cannot, without a clear signal to the Assyrian tradition as the framework for interpretation, be understood in terms of a polemical relationship with Assyrian ideology.

4

DEUTERONOMY AND THE BIBLICAL TRADITION

Chapters two and three have considered the issue of Deuteronomy's subversive intent from the point of view of the text and its source, whether the latter is conceived as an individual source text or a source tradition. In the background of these chapters was the question of audience knowledge, noted briefly by the acknowledgment in chapter three that, if Deuteronomy's audience only knows Assyrian treaties and loyalty oaths (or only knows VTE), it will most naturally interpret Deuteronomy in Assyrian terms, even if the signal to the Assyrian form of the tradition was weak. There is the possibility, in other words, that a non-specific or non-distinctive signal might have the effect of specificity and distinctiveness (or, rather, be successful despite its lack of these), as a result of either the ignorance of the audience or the dominance of a specific form of the tradition in the audience's memory. In the case of Deuteronomy, the question is whether a non-specific and non-distinctive signal to the treaty and loyalty oath tradition could have the effect of a much more precise signal to an Assyrian manifestation of that tradition, by virtue of the audience's ignorance regarding the existence of other forms of this tradition or the dominance of this particular form in the audience's memory.

Though essential to the ability of an audience to recognize a work's use of a particular source—whether text or tradition—the skill of the author in producing allusions that are sufficiently frequent and sufficiently distinctive as to be recognizable is thus not the entirety of the subversive project. In addition to authorial ability, the successful subversion of a source text depends on the new text's audience having the kind of knowledge necessary for subversion. This relates to the audience's knowledge of the source with which the author intends to signal a relationship: if the audience is not aware of the source, it cannot identify it and will not, therefore, be able to interpret the new work within the framework established by the older material. In other words, subversion requires not only an author sufficiently versed in the source text as to be capable of subverting it, but demands also an audience familiar enough with the source to be able to recognize the author's subversive efforts.[1] Hutton observes that,

> No matter the author's intention or skill, the actualization of the allusion on the part of the reader is by no means guaranteed. The marking text's effectiveness requires the reader's sufficient competence to actualize the allusion to the earlier work. Without prior knowledge of the marked text, the allusion can only remain unactualized by the reader.[2]

To recall Hutcheon: "To experience [a text] *as an adaptation* … we need to recognize it as such and to know its adapted text, thus allowing the latter to oscillate in our memories with what we are experiencing."[3]

The next two chapters will therefore consider the audience more explicitly, asking what sort of knowledge Deuteronomy's audience might have had regarding treaties, loyalty oaths, and curses and whether, in light of this, Deuteronomy is likely to have been understood by this audience in relation to an Assyrian treaty, loyalty oath, and curse tradition. Whether the audience of Deuteronomy would have been sufficiently familiar with either VTE or another Assyrian-Judahite treaty or loyalty oath as to recognize an allusion to it, if such were intended, will be discussed in chapter five. In addition to this, however, there is another aspect of audience knowledge that is relevant—namely, what else the audience knows—and which might affect its interpretation of the new work. Hutcheon speaks of the "differently knowing" audience; the question here concerns the wider knowledge of Deuteronomy's audience about treaties, loyalty oaths, and curses, insofar as this constitutes the framework in which this material in Deuteronomy would have been

---

[1] Subversion as mere intellectual exercise is, of course, conceivable, but one would wonder why an author would risk the consequences of subversive activities with no possibility of gain.

[2] J. M. Hutton, "Isaiah 51:9–11 and the Rhetorical Appropriation and Subversion of Hostile Theologies," *JBL* 126 (2007): 277.

[3] L. Hutcheon, *Theory of Adaptation* (New York, N.Y.: Routledge, 2006), 120–21.

understood and interpreted.[4] This chapter will thus consider the language and ideas of Deut 13 and 28 with reference to other biblical texts, using these materials to estimate Deuteronomy's audience's knowledge of treaty, loyalty oath, and curse traditions.

There are two questions to be answered from this exercise. The first is whether Deuteronomy's audience would have understood all treaty, loyalty oath, and curse material in Assyrian terms. If the biblical material suggests that the only context in which Deuteronomy's audience might have encountered treaty, loyalty oath, or curse material was in conjunction with Assyrian activities and personnel, then it would be reasonable to conclude that any use of such material by Deuteronomy would have been understood in similar terms. If, however, there are regular references to treaty, loyalty oath, and curse material in non-Assyrian terms, then it is reasonable to suppose that Deuteronomy's audience had a more general familiarity with this type of material. This, in turn, would mean that if Deuteronomy intended to signal a relationship with the Assyrian material in particular, its signaling efforts would need to distinguish a specifically Assyrian point of reference rather than relying on its audience's ignorance to equate all treaties, loyalty oaths, and curses with Assyria.

That the latter is the case is quite readily apparent, and this leads to the second question to be considered by this chapter: against a background of generalized familiarity with treaty, loyalty oath, and curse traditions, is there anything in Deuteronomy's rendering of these materials that would have been sufficiently unfamiliar to its audience as to have triggered the suspicion that the text intended to allude to some other source, rather than drawing on this general reservoir of tradition?

TREATIES, LOYALTY, AND CURSES IN THE BIBLICAL TRADITION

The answer to the first of these questions is straightforward. That treaty, loyalty oath, and curse traditions were well known in Judah is clearly indicated by the preponderance of references and allusions to treaties, loyalty oaths, and curses across the biblical corpus, appearing in texts as diverse as Genesis, Samuel, Micah, Isaiah, Jeremiah, Psalms, Amos, Nahum, Exodus, Ezekiel, Judges, Job, and Kings.[5] 1 Kings 15 describes

---

[4] Ibid., 125.

[5] The classic catalogue is D. R. Hillers, *Treaty-Curses and the Old Testament Prophets* (BibOr 16; Rome: Pontifical Biblical Institute, 1964), 43–78, appearing on the heels of D. J. McCarthy, *Treaty and Covenant: A Study in Form in the Ancient Oriental*

shifting power relations between Judah, Israel, and Aram in which the king of Judah negotiates with the king of Aram to abandon his alliance with the northern kingdom in favor of one with the south; Isa 7 presupposes a similar system of alliances among the western kingdoms as the pretext for Ahaz's appeal to the Assyrian king for support. Joshua 9–10 recounts the infamous story of a treaty agreement between the Israelites and the Gibeonites, which resurfaces in 2 Sam 21:1–14 with an account of the punishment meted out upon Saul's sons as a consequence of his failure to respect this agreement. Similar condemnation for transgression of treaty relationships appears in Amos 1:11 as well as the oracles against the nations in Amos 1–2 more broadly and in Ezek 17:12–13.[6] Prophetic and poetic imagery that relies for its power on expectations of punishment for those who betray an alliance includes Ps

---

Documents and in the Old Testament (AnBib 21A; Rome: Pontifical Biblical Institute, 1978). Among numerous studies of individual texts see also J. Ben-Dov, "The Poor's Curse: Exodus XXII 20–26 and Curse Literature in the Ancient World," VT 56 (2006): 447–50; K. J. Cathcart, "Treaty-curses and the Book of Nahum," CBQ 34 (1973): 179–87; T. J. Lewis, "The Identity and Function of El/Baal Berith," JBL 115 (1996): 401–23; K. A. Kitchen and P. J. N. Lawrence, Part 1: The Texts (vol. 1 of Treaty, Law and Covenant in the Ancient Near East; Wiesbaden: Harrassowitz, 2012); M. Tsevat, "The Neo-Assyrian and Neo-Babylonian Vassal Oaths and the Prophet Ezekiel," JBL 78 (1959): 199–204; D. L. Magnetti, "The Function of the Oath in the Ancient Near Eastern International Treaty," American Journal of International Law 72 (1978): 824–29; T. Wittstruck, "The Influence of Treaty Curse Imagery on the Beast Imagery of Daniel 7," JBL 97 (1978): 100–102 (who mentions various texts, but whose argument regarding Dan 7 specifically is countered by J. Rimbach, "Bears or Bees? Sefire I A 31 and Daniel 7," JBL 97 [1978]: 565–66); cf. also M. Weinfeld, "Ancient Near Eastern Patterns in Prophetic Literature," VT 27 (1977): 178–95; and the discussions referenced more specifically below. Sweeping visions of treaty terminology in the Hebrew Bible have been articulated by H. B. Huffmon, "The Treaty Background of Hebrew Yāda'," BASOR 181 (1966): 31–37; H. B. Huffmon and S. B. Parker, "A Further Note on the Treaty Background of Hebrew Yāda'," BASOR 184 (1966): 36–38; J. C. Greenfield, "Some Aspects of the Treaty Terminology of the Bible," in Fourth World Congress of Jewish Studies: Papers (Jerusalem: World Union of Jewish Studies, 1967), 117–119; J. S. Holladay, Jr., "Assyrian Statecraft and the Prophets of Israel," HTR 63 (1970): 29–51. Note, however, Nicholson's warning against the over-interpretation of biblical texts in treaty terms and especially his observation that much of the curse material in particular should be understood in terms of a more general curse tradition (E. W. Nicholson, God and His People: Covenant and Theology in the Old Testament [Oxford: Oxford University Press, 2002], 68–82, especially 77–78).

    [6] On Amos see M. L. Barré, "The Meaning of l' 'šybnw in Amos 1:3–2:6," JBL 105 (1986): 617–20, with further references.

109, Jer 34, Mic 6, and Hag 1, among the many other passages that will be considered more closely below.[7]

The generic and chronological range of these texts, in addition to their sheer quantity, suggests that Judah was quite at home in the ancient Near Eastern world of treaties, loyalty oaths, and their associated curses. There is therefore no reason to think that the treaties employed by the Assyrians would have been perceived as out of the ordinary to a Judahite audience; there is also no reason to think that, for Deuteronomy's audience, all treaties had become Assyrian treaties. Merely the fact of Deuteronomy's use of treaty and loyalty oath concepts and curses would not have been enough to suggest to its audience that its target was Assyrian treaty or loyalty oath ideologies in particular.

DEUTERONOMY'S RELATIONSHIP WITH THE BIBLICAL TRADITION

Having established that the genre alone is unlikely to have signaled "Assyrian" to Deuteronomy's audience, it is necessary to consider the content of Deut 13 and 28 in more detail. The question here is: how might Deuteronomy's audience have reacted to this material, given a general knowledge of the genre? More exactly: is there anything about this material in Deuteronomy that would have struck its audience as odd—such that the possibility of Deuteronomy's use of some other source might have occurred? This returns us to the idea of distinctiveness, from a slightly different perspective: if a word, phrase, or concept is distinctively Assyrian, such that it might function as an effective signal to the Assyrian tradition, it will be noticeably alien to the native traditions of Deuteronomy's audience. As suggested by the types of signals discussed above, the focus in what follows will be on the relationship of Deuteronomy's vocabulary and concepts—its words,

---

[7] A. M. Kitz, "An Oath, Its Curse and Anointing Ritual," *JAOS* 124 (2004): 315–21 examines the language of being "clothed" in a curse in Ps 109:18 in the context of Hittite and Akkadian curse texts, noting also the curses of Pss 35; 40; 55; 129; 137. J. A. Hackett and J. Huehnergard, "On Breaking Teeth," *HTR* 77 (1984): 259–75 discuss the punitive legal clauses behind curses invoked in Ps 3 and in Job; similarly Ben-Dov, "The Poor's Curse," 447–50, who focuses on the use of curses as a form of reinforcing justice (cf. J. Assmann, "When Justice Fails: Jurisdiction and Imprecation in Ancient Egypt and the Near East," *JEA* 78 [1992]: 149–62). On Micah see H. G. M. Williamson, "Marginalia in Micah," *VT* 47 (1997): 367.

phrases, and ideas—to those of its audience, insofar as that may be estimated from other biblical texts.[8]

DEUTERONOMY 28

Though most of the attention granted the curse material in Deut 28 has focused on the verses with ostensibly Assyrian pedigrees, it is worth taking a slightly wider view here.[9] Beginning at Deut 28:20, that verse declares that YHWH will send "disaster, panic, and frustration" (מארה, מהומה ,מגערת) on Deuteronomy's audience if it fails to obey its commands. What might Deuteronomy's audience have made of such a threat? "Disaster" and "panic" are familiar terms, attested in other texts; the second is especially common in the context of other descriptions of military chaos.[10] The third, "frustration," is *hapax* within the extant corpus (though the root from which it derives is common enough). It might therefore be of interest because unusual, but neither this nor the others are loan words or otherwise suggestive of an intention to signal beyond a general tradition of threatened disaster to something as specific as the Assyrian tradition.[11] Threat of destruction is, as evident from the above, a generic component of the curse tradition as a whole. Already in the early years of study of the biblical curse material in its ancient Near

---

[8] The location of Deuteronomy (in some form) on the early end of the chronological span of the biblical collection makes the contextualization of its vocabulary and imagery more difficult than if there was a substantial corpus of earlier material with which to compare it. As it stands, we are obliged to use the biblical material as a type of general guidance regarding the kind of language that would have likely been familiar to Deuteronomy's audience, weighting more heavily material that seems likely to be older, discounting material that is obviously derived from Deuteronomy itself, and so on. The science is hardly exact; however, as the criterion of distinctiveness itself suggests, the greater the preponderance of the evidence that suggests the widespread use of particular terms, phrases, and ideas, the correspondingly greater the likelihood that Deuteronomy's audience would have been familiar with such material and disinclined to look beyond common knowledge to understand and interpret it.

[9] On the affinities of the material in Deut 28:1–6*, 15–19 see C. Koch, *Vertrag, Treueid und Bund: Studien zur Rezeption des altorientalischen Vertragsrechts im Deuteronomium und zur Ausbildung der Bundestheologie im alten Testament* (BZAW 383; Berlin: de Gruyter, 2008), 204–209. Note that here, as with Deut 13, the necessary course is to err on the side of generosity in redactional conclusions.

[10] מארה: Prov 3:33; 28:27; Mal 2:2; 3:9; מהומה: Deut 7:23; 1 Sam 5:9, 11; 14:20; 2 Chr 15:5; Prov 15:16; Isa 22:5; Ezek 7:7; 22:5; Amos 3:9; Zech 14:13; HALOT 2:541, 552; Ges[18] 3:623, 637.

[11] HALOT 2:546; Ges[18] 3:629.

Eastern context, Hillers observed that such general pronouncements were so common as to be pointless to catalogue.[12] Neither the ideas expressed by these terms, nor the terms themselves, are likely to have attracted attention from Deuteronomy's audience.

Deuteronomy 28:21 threatens pestilence (דבר), common throughout biblical literature and similarly unremarkable.[13] More unusual are a number of the elements of Deut 28:22: "consumption, fever, inflammation ... fiery heat and drought ... blight and mildew," according to the NRSV (ירקון, שדפון, חרב, חרחר, דלקת, קדחת, שחפת). The first four are nearly unique, with שחפת and קדחת appearing otherwise only in Lev 26:16 and חרחר in Sir 40:9; like מגערת, however, they are quite clearly West Semitic and unlikely to have evoked an Akkadian referent for the curse.[14] חרב is altogether common, while שדפון and ירקון appear together in four other biblical curse passages: 1 Kgs 8:37 // 2 Chr 6:28, where they are listed alongside famine (רעב), plague (דבר, as in Deut 28:21), the locust (ארבה), and the grasshopper or caterpillar (חסיל); in Amos 4:9; and in Hag 2:17, where they are joined by hail (ברד).[15] The overall conceptual content of Deut 28:21–22—illnesses and agricultural devastation—is similarly mundane, as even the most basic survey of references to plague and famine bear out: they are common natural disasters that therefore form a natural component of descriptions or threats of divine punishment. Given that this material appears to be quite comfortably at home in this wider context, there is no reason to suppose that it would have prompted Deuteronomy's audience to suspect its intention of signaling a relationship with an Assyrian source.

That most famous of curses, Deut 28:23, promises the advent of a brazen sky and iron earth. Read together with Deut 28:24, this curse appeared at first inspection remarkably similar to VTE §§63–64, even sharing several items of vocabulary (earth, sky, iron, bronze, rain). Read against its own tradition, however, this terminology fails the distinctiveness criterion: though shared terminology may provide good evidence for a case of allusion, the viability of the allusion depends on the distinctiveness of the vocabulary involved. The items of vocabulary that VTE and Deut 28:23–24 share are all extremely common: bronze, iron, earth, and heaven are all everyday items, and each appears dozens

---

[12] Hillers, *Treaty-Curses*, 43.

[13] HALOT 1:212; Ges[18] 2:240-41.

[14] HALOT 4:1465 (שחפת), 3:1067 (קדחת), 1:223 (דלקת), 1:352 (חרחר); Ges[18] 6:1341 (שחפת), 5:1147 (קדחת), 2:252 (דלקת), 2:396 (חרחר).

[15] HALOT 1:350 (חרב), 4:1423 (שדפון), 2:440–41 (ירקון); Ges[18] 2:393 (חרב), 6:1326 (שדפון), 2:500 (ירקון).

or hundreds of times in other texts.[16] Even clustered together, they are not unusual. Iron and bronze are paired in dozens of passages and heaven and earth appear together on hundreds of occasions.[17] Even all four terms together are not unique to Deut 28:23: the quartet appears also in Lev 26:19 (cf. Dan 4:12 [ET 4:15], in Aramaic; Mic 4:13; Job 28:2). Though these are probably all later than the Deuteronomy text, the overwhelming commonality of all of the individual terms as well as their frequent occurrence in pairs work against the suggestion that their combination in Deut 28:23 is meant to evoke the audience's knowledge of an Assyrian treaty or loyalty oath text; there is nothing in these terms that would prompt its audience to enquire as to their origins in the first place.

Similarly, the idea of withheld rain and the replacement of normal precipitation with "powder" (אבק) and "dust" (עפר) sits comfortably within the biblical tradition. The overarching concept, in which rain (or its replacement) descends from the heavens as part of the divine blessing or cursing of the land, is witnessed in a diverse range of texts (Exod 9:23, 33; Deut 11:11, 14, 17; 28:12; 2 Chr 6:26–27; 7:13; Job 5:10; 37:6; Pss 72:6; 78:24; 135:7; 147:8; Jer 10:13; 51:16; 1 Kgs 8:35–36; Isa 5:6). Powder appears frequently in texts detailing the threat or manifestation of military-related destruction (Exod 9:9; Isa 5:24; 29:5; Ezek 26:10; Nah 1:3) and dust is so ordinary as to hardly merit a second thought.[18] Again, there is nothing in these two verses that might have struck Deuteronomy's audience as in need of external explanation, nor anything that might be considered distinctively Assyrian.

Deuteronomy 28:25 opens with a general threat of military defeat before using the more specific phraseology of going out one way and fleeing by seven. The apparent particularity of the number seven is illusory; the number is well known for its prominence in biblical material and appears in everything from the number of days of creation to the number of pairs of clean animals to be preserved by Noah; from the number of years of service by Jacob for his wives to the enumeration of symbols in Joseph's dreams; from the calculations for Passover, Weeks,

---

[16] HALOT 2:691 (נחשת), 1:155–56 (ברזל), 1:90–91 (ארץ), 4:1559–62 (שמים); Ges[18] 4:807–808 (נחשת), 1:174 (ברזל), 1:101–102 (ארץ), 6:1378–79 (שמים).

[17] M. Delcor, "Les attaches litteraires, l'origine et la signification de l'expression biblique 'Prendre a temoin le ciel et la terre'," *VT* 16 (1966): 8–25 has suggested that in some of these latter cases the pair may be invoked as witnesses to treaty and oath agreements. In light of the phrasing in Deut 28:23 this seems unlikely here, though it may elsewhere constitute further evidence of the biblical materials' comfortable location in an ancient Near Eastern tradition.

[18] HALOT 1:9 (אבק), 2:861–62 (עפר); Ges[18] 1: 10 (אבק), 4:996 (עפר).

and Booths to the dozens of prescriptions relating to worship of YHWH in Exodus, Leviticus, and Numbers; from the provisions for the conquest of Jericho to Delilah's efforts to entrap Samson; from the number of sons of Jesse and of Saul to the number of nights Job's friends keep vigil; from the visions of the prophets to their calculations of punishment. Punishment by sevens is perhaps most famous in the boast of Lamech in Gen 4:24, but it appears also on the lips of the psalmist in a plea for punishment in Ps 79:12, in the description of the fate that awaits Jerusalem in Isa 4:1, and in Prov 6:31. Though at first glance it seems quite specific, the imagery here is a stereotype that would have attracted little attention.

The curse of non-burial and consumption of the corpse by carrion animals in Deut 28:26 was noted to differ from VTE especially with respect to its specification of both the carrion bird and the carrion animal. The pairing of the "bird of the air" (עוֹף הַשָּׁמִים) with permutations of "animal of the earth" (בהמת הארץ in Deut 28:26, variously also חית הארץ, חית השדה), however, is common in biblical literature, especially as a merism for all living creatures (Gen 1:30; 2:19; 9:2; 2 Sam 21:10; Ps 104:12; Eccl 10:20; Jer 4:25; 15:3; Ezek 31:6, 13; 32:4; Hos 2:20; cf. their appearance in the longer lists of Gen 6:7; 7:23; Zeph 1:3). One or both of these elements occur especially frequently in descriptions of corpse desecration akin to that envisioned by the Deuteronomy text (2 Sam 21:10; Pss 79:2; 83:11; 104:12; Eccl 10:20; Jer 4:25; 7:33; 15:3; 16:4; 19:7; 34:20; Ezek 32:4; 39:17–20; in these cases the appearance of dogs, כלבים, as the terrestrial antagonist is also common, as in 1 Kgs 14:11; 16:4; 21:24; Jer 7:33; 15:3; cf. also Isa 18:6).[19] The underlying aversion to non- (or anti-) burial and corpse desecration is well-attested and unlikely to have stood out as exceptional to Deuteronomy's audience.[20] Again, there is nothing that would provoke Deuteronomy's audience to seek an outside source for the language or the imagery used to articulate this threat.

The skin diseases of Deut 28:27 are obscure, but none can make a convincing case for being a loan word of Akkadian origin, of the sort that might be expected in the case of a culture-specific item derived from an Akkadian source. חרס is *hapax* with West Semitic cognates[21]; גרב appears

---

[19] Some of these are noted by Hillers, *Treaty-Curses*, 68–69.

[20] C. B. Hays, *Death in the Iron Age II and in First Isaiah* (FAT 79; Tübingen: Mohr Siebeck, 2011), 133–201; F. Stavrakopoulou, "Gog's Grave and the Use and Abuse of Corpses in Ezekiel 39:11–20," *JBL* 129 (2010): 67–76; S. A. Marzouk, "Not a Lion but a Dragon: The Monstrification of Egypt in the Book of Ezekiel" (Ph.D. diss., Princeton Theological Seminary, 2012).

[21] HALOT 1:355; Ges[18] 2:399.

twice in Leviticus as well as across a full range of Semitic languages.[22] שחין materializes in Leviticus as well as Job; there is no parallel for the attribution of these to Egypt specifically, but in the current context it would be most likely to evoke the exodus tradition that is so central to Deuteronomy rather than some other source.[23] עפלים is unusual, but it appears in several other West Semitic vocabularies.[24] The danger of skin-related illnesses is unsurprisingly prominent in priestly texts but attested sufficiently elsewhere as to indicate that the imposition of such diseases as an unwelcome fate would not be unfamiliar. The image of the incurable wound, which distinguished Deut 28:27 from VTE especially, appears in various forms elsewhere, including Isa 1:5–6; Jer 30:12–13; Hos 5:13; Mic 1:9; and Nah 3:19.[25] Skin disease in conjunction with the idea of perpetuity appears in the curse pronounced on Joab and his house in 2 Sam 3:29: "may the house of Joab never be without one who has a discharge, or who is leprous, or who holds a spindle, or who falls by the sword, or who lacks food."[26]

The madness of Deut 28:28 is unusual as a noun but derives from a verb (שגע) attested several times elsewhere.[27] The concept is further attested by derivations of הלל.[28] Blindness (from עור) is well attested in both noun and verb forms[29]; confusion (from תמה) occurs several times across a diverse range of texts as well as being attested in derivations from המה, הום, and המם.[30] That blindness was an accursed fate is witnessed by other biblical passages (Gen 19:11; Deut 15:21; 2 Kgs 6:18; Zech 12:4). Various forms of confusion also occur as a threatened punishment (Exod 23:27; Isa 19:4; 22:5; 34:11; 45:16; Mic 7:4; Pss 35:26; 40:14; 70:2). Groping about (משש, Deut 28:29) as something done in darkness is attested by Exod 10:21 and Job 5:14; 12:25; the latter references use similar imagery of the inversion of such behavior from

---

[22] Lev 21:20; 22:22; see HALOT 1:201; Ges[18] 1:227–28.

[23] Lev 13:20; Job 2:7; see HALOT 4:1460; Ges[18] 6:1341.

[24] See HALOT 2:861; Ges[18] 4:995.

[25] Hillers, *Treaty-Curses*, 65–66.

[26] אל יכרת מבית יואב זב ומצרע ומחזיק בפלך ונפל בחרב וחסר לחם On the meaning of the third of these see S. W. Holloway, "Distaff, Crutch or Chain Gang: The Curse of the House of Joab in 2 Samuel III 29," *VT* 37 (1987): 370–75.

[27] HALOT 4:1415; Ges[18] 6:1323–24.

[28] HALOT 1:249; Ges[18] 2:279.

[29] HALOT 2:802-804; Ges[18] 4:938 (עור), 4:940 (עורון).

[30] HALOT 4:1745 (תמהון), 1:250 (המה), 1:242 (הום), 1:251 (המם); Ges[18] 6:1442 (תמהון), 2:280 (המה), 2:271 (הום), 2:281 (המם).

night to day.[31] Accusations of abuse and robbery (from עשק and גזל) are common terminology relating to justice and failures thereof, occurring dozens of times individually as well as together on several other occasions (Eccl 5:7; Ezek 18:18; 22:29; Jer 21:12; Lev 5:21, 23; 19:13; Mic 2:2; Ps 62:11).[32]

The curses that follow are of the futility type, in which the cursed person's efforts in a particular venture will be doomed to failure; the particular prominence of this type of curse in West Semitic contexts has been noted already above. The first three, in Deut 28:30, echo the caveats for military personnel in Deut 20:5–7 and appear to reflect a semi-stereotyped set of concerns about male achievement: acquisition of a wife, construction of a home, and provision of sustenance through agriculture. Concerns regarding the latter two are reflected similarly elsewhere (Jer 29:4–6; Isa 65:18–23; Ezek 28:26; Amos 9:14; Mic 6:15), while the betrothal stage of a relationship seems particularly, albeit not exclusively, characteristic of Deuteronomy (Deut 20:7; 22:23, 25, 27–28; 28:30; also Exod 22:15; 2 Sam 3:14; Hos 2:21–22). The commonality of each of the components of this curse, both individually and in various pairs and triads, establishes a natural interpretive framework for this material in the native tradition of Deuteronomy's audience and reduces the likelihood that it would have prompted this audience to look elsewhere for contextualization.

Although Smoak has suggested a background to the house and vineyard curses in Assyrian practices of siege warfare, tracing the abundant biblical material to an eighth century passage in Amos, he notes that "the relatively imprecise and vague nature of the curse's imagery allowed it to be customized and reformulated," suggesting that, if the imagery did originate in response to a (northern) experience of siege warfare, it soon took on a life of its own; the fact that the material is formulated in futility curse form seems to reiterate this process of nativization.[33] While highlighting 2 Sam 12:11; 16:20–22; and Jer 8:10 as

---

[31] On darkness as a curse see C. R. Moss and J. Stackert, "The Devastation of Darkness: Disability in Exodus 10:21–23, 27, and Intensification in the Plagues," *JR* 92 (2012): 362–72.

[32] HALOT 2:897 (עשק), 1:186 (גזל); Ges[18] 4:1025 (עשק), 1:210 (גזל).

[33] J. D. Smoak, "Building Houses and Planting Vineyards: The Early Inner-Biblical Discourse on an Ancient Israelite Wartime Curse," *JBL* 127 (2008): 35. Note also Wright's recent argument against the related instructions in Deut 20:19–20 as having to do with Assyrian practice, to which we will return in chapter six (J. L. Wright, "Warfare and Wanton Destruction: A Reexamination of Deuteronomy 20:19–20 in Relation to Ancient Siegecraft," *JBL* 127 [2008]: 423–58).

indicating a common assumption that the spoils—including women—go to the victor, Koch also compares the curses as a whole to other biblical traditions utilizing the wife-house-vineyard triad—noting especially Deut 20:5*–7—and observes that Deuteronomy need hardly have relied on Assyrian curses (or, indeed, the Assyrians) to imagine that curses might invoke the loss of such properties.[34]

Regarding terminology, the deployment of חלל in the sense of "to use" is not particularly common—it occurs here, in Deut 20:6, and in Jer 31:5, all with reference to the use of the produce of vineyards—but the concept seems to be rooted in ideas about the ultimate divine ownership of the produce of the land (Lev 19:23, 25) rather than in anything alien.[35] The verb שגל to describe the fate of the betrothed is unusual (otherwise only Isa 13:16; Zech 14:2; Jer 3:2) and seems to be a loan word derived from the Akkadian šagālu, to confiscate or seize.[36] It is not used in Akkadian in this more specific sense regarding the seizure of a woman, however, nor does it appear in any known Assyrian curse material. Depending on the date of the loan the term might be a rather unusual item of vocabulary to Deuteronomy's audience, but its strength as a signal to an Assyrian curse tradition is dubious. The subsequent material in Deut 28:31, concerning livestock, and Deut 28:32, concerning children, develops the theme using unremarkable language found throughout the biblical material.

The material in Deut 28:33–37 is heavily repetitive of much of the preceding and, in its entirety or in part, is often deemed to be secondary elaborations on the material to this point. Whatever the redactional judgment laid against these verses, they are wholly ordinary in their language and phraseology, containing nothing to rouse suspicion on the part of Deuteronomy's audience with regard to their origins or referents.[37]

The futility material that resumes in Deut 28:38 is similarly unremarkable; the threat of locusts (ארבה) in Deut 28:38 is a common form of curse or plague (Exod 10:4, 12–14, 19; Lev 11:22; Judg 6:5; 7:12; 1 Kgs 8:37; 2 Chr 6:28; Job 39:20; Pss 78:46; 105:34; 109:23; Prov 30:27; Jer 46:23; Joel 1:4; 2:25; Nah 3:15, 17), while the seed, the vineyard, and the

---

[34] Koch, *Vertrag*, 223–24.

[35] HALOT 1:319; Ges[18] 2:355–66.

[36] HALOT 4:1415; Ges[18] 6:1323.

[37] The same is of course true of other words and phrases in Deut 28:20–44 that are sometimes considered secondary accretions, such as the reference to "the land that you are entering to possess" in Deut 28:21 or the phrase "all the kingdoms of the earth" in Deut 28:25, insofar as the motivation in every case is the similarity of the material to other biblical texts.

olive tree which structure Deut 28:38, 39, 40 are familiar from numerous other biblical passages—as are their produce of wheat, wine, and oil—where they effectively function as a tripartite merism for all agricultural activities (Exod 23:11; Num 18:12; Deut 11:14; 12:17; 14:23; 18:4; Judg 15:5; 1 Sam 8:14; Neh 5:11; Hos 2:8, 24; Mic 6:15; Joel 1:10; 2:19, 24; Hag 1:11). They also occur in pairs and in longer lists, using a variety of terminology. Again, there is nothing particularly distinctive about the terms or the ideas in these verses, whether the curses are taken individually or collectively, and the commonality of their content continues to work against the ability of Deuteronomy to signal with this material an intention to be understood in relation to Assyria.

The transition from futility to deprivation begins in Deut 28:41, with the final verses drawing especially on the imagery of the economically marginal *ger* that is so common to Deuteronomy. None of the vocabulary or imagery here is in any way out of the ordinary.

In sum, there is nothing in Deut 28 that suggests that its audience would have needed, or been prompted, look outside its native tradition to interpret this material. The vocabulary is overwhelmingly familiar from other biblical texts and, when less common terms or phrases do arise, there is no reason to suspect origins in the translation of culture-specific items of Assyrian provenance, such as might reflect Deuteronomy's use of an Assyrian source and signal to Deuteronomy's audience a relationship with an Assyrian text or with Assyrian ideology. Concepts are inherently weak as signals in the first place and nothing in the content of those in Deut 28 is suggestive of the starkly distinctive type that may, sometimes, act successfully as such.[38] The concepts employed by Deut 28 to threaten its audience with punitive disaster are those found elsewhere. The piling up of distinctive ideas that might render a conceptual signal recognizable is entirely absent.

---

[38] On the difficulty of identifying cases of allusion on the basis of concepts rather than specific terms and phrases see J. Leonard, "Identifying Inner-Biblical Allusions: Psalm 78 as a Test Case," *JBL* 127 (2008): 246–47; recall also the degree of distinctiveness, the level of specificity, and the overall frequency of conceptual similarities that rendered Hamori's discussion of the story of Jacob at Jabbok convincing, by contrast to O'Connell's analysis of Isa 14 (E. Hamori, "Echoes of Gilgamesh in the Jacob Story," *JBL* 130 [2011]: 625–42 and R. H. O'Connell, "Isaiah XIV 4b–23: Ironic Reversal through Concentric Structure and Mythic Allusion," *VT* 38 [1988]: 407–18).

DEUTERONOMY 13

In the context of the probable wider knowledge of Deuteronomy's audience, then, Deut 28 contains nothing sufficiently distinctive as to suggest that it might have attracted the attention of this audience, a prerequisite to acting as a signal to other source material. What, however, of Deut 13? Conceptually this chapter is of critical importance in Deuteronomy's ability to subvert Assyrian ideology, insofar as its focus on loyalty to YHWH is proposed to be an attempt to reorient Deuteronomy's audience's loyalties away from the Assyrian king.

First, it should be noted that there is nothing inherently subversive *vis-à-vis* Assyria in Deuteronomy's claim on Israelites' loyalty to YHWH.[39] The Assyrians interests in vassals' loyalties were political; theological and religious commitments, if attended to at all, were focused on provincial territories, not vassal kingdoms.[40] Deuteronomy 13 is making

---

[39] M. Zehnder, "Building on Stone? Deuteronomy and Esarhaddon's Loyalty Oaths (Part 1): Some Preliminary Observations," *BBR* 19 (2009): 370–71. Note, too, that the subversion argument, insofar as it sees Deuteronomy as replacing the human Assyrian king with a divine YHWH-king, depends on Deuteronomy actually intending to position YHWH in the role of king. This is itself questionable: YHWH is called "king" in the poetic material of Deut 33:5, but all other references to kings or ruling are to the human variety (this is not to deny that elsewhere the biblical texts reflect the idea of YHWH as king, only to emphasize that this is not prominent in Deuteronomy). For an argument that Deuteronomy does depict YHWH in royal terms see M. Nevader, *Yahweh versus David: The Monarchic Debate of Deuteronomy and Ezekiel* (OTM; Oxford: Oxford University Press, 2014). Further problematizing the relationship between YHWH's kingship and subversion, however, is that divine kingship was not perceived by the Assyrians as an exclusive attribute; Assur is king, but so too are Marduk, Ninurta, and even Ishtar (C. L. Crouch, "Ištar and the Motif of the Cosmological Warrior: Assurbanipal's Adaptation of *Enuma Elish*," in *"Thus Speaks Ishtar of Arbela": Prophecy in Israel, Assyria, and Egypt in the Neo-Assyrian Period* [ed. R. P. Gordon and H. M. Barstad; Winona Lake, Ind.: Eisenbrauns, 2013], 129–141). To characterize YHWH as king, therefore, would have challenged neither the kingship of a particular Assyrian god nor the kingship of his (or her) human counterpart.

[40] See A. Berlejung, "The Assyrians in the West: Assyrianization, Colonialism, Indifference, or Development Policy?," in *Congress Volume Helsinki 2010* (ed. M. Nissinen; VTSup 148; Leiden: Brill, 2012), 32–39; idem, "Shared Fates: Gaza and Ekron as Examples for the Assyrian Religious Policy in the West," in *Iconoclasm and Text Destruction in the Ancient Near East and Beyond* (ed. N. N. May; Oriental Institute Seminars 8; Chicago, Ill.: The Oriental Institute of the University of Chicago, 2012), 151–174; A. M. Bagg, "Palestine under Assyrian Rule: A New Look at the Assyrian Imperial Policy in the West," *JAOS* 133 (2013): 119–44; S. W. Holloway, *Aššur is King! Aššur is King!: Religion in the Exercise of Power in the Neo-Assyrian Empire* (CHANE 10; Leiden: Brill, 2001); D. R. Miller, "The Shadow of the Overlord: Revisiting the

a claim on the Israelites' theological loyalties, not on their political ones, and the equation of these depends on the presupposition of the mandatory worship of Assyrian deities as an expression of vassal loyalties.[41]

In any case, merely making a claim on Israelite loyalty would have functioned as a terrible signal of Deuteronomy's intention *vis-à-vis* Assyria, because the idea is well-attested in the traditions of Deuteronomy's audience; Deuteronomy's declarations will have been interpreted against this native background before being interpreted in reference to Assyria. There are numerous passages that reflect ideas about the importance of loyalty: loyalty in general, loyalty to a human sovereign, and loyalty to YHWH, the latter both in general terms and as the divine sovereign.[42] These passages appear in numerous literary genres and in texts from various periods.

Given the parameters of the subversion argument, ideas regarding loyalty to kings—both human and divine—are of primary interest. Psalm 101 is acutely concerned with the loyalty of those who surround the king, and its royal speaker's vow to destroy anyone who "practices deceit" or "utters lies" is particularly notable given the focus of the treaty

---

Question of Neo-Assyrian Imposition on the Judaean Cult during the Eighth-Seventh Centuries BCE," in *From Babel to Babylon: Essays on Biblical History and Literature in Honor of Brian Peckham* (ed. J. R. Wood, J. E. Harvey, and M. Leuchter; LHBOTS 455; London: T&T Clark, 2006), 146–68; M. D. Cogan, *Imperialism and Religion: Assyria, Judah and Israel in the Eighth and Seventh Centuries B.C.E.* (SBLMS 19; Missoula, Mont.: Scholars Press, 1974); idem, "Judah under Assyrian Hegemony: A Reexamination of Imperialism and Religion," *JBL* 112 (1993): 403–14.

[41] On the lack of Assyrian interest in vassal states' religious identities and practices see the previous note. Politically Deuteronomy is remarkably cautious, preferring in the main to simply ignore Judah's political existence and, when attending to it, to warn against activities that might challenge Assyrian authority. See the discussion in chapter six and C. L. Crouch, *The Making of Israel: Cultural Diversity in the Southern Levant and the Formation of Ethnic Identity in Deuteronomy* [VTSup 162; Leiden: Brill, 2014], 177–84).

[42] Much of this revolves around the language of חסד in particular; see, for example, U. Y. Kim, *Identity and Loyalty in the David Story: A Postcolonial Reading* (HBM 22; Sheffield: Sheffield Phoenix, 2008); K. D. Sakenfeld, *Faithfulness in Action: Loyalty in Biblical Perspective* (OBT 16; Philadelphia, Penn.: Fortress. 1985); N. P. Lemche, "Kings and Clients: On Loyalty between Ruler and the Ruled in Ancient Israel," *Sem* 66 (1994): 119–32. See also S. Ackerman, "The Personal is Political: Covenantal and Affectionate Love (*'āhēb, 'ahābâ*) in the Hebrew Bible," *VT* 52 (2002): 437–58; W. L. Moran, "The Ancient Near Eastern Background of the Love of God in Deuteronomy," *CBQ* 25 (1963): 77–87.

and loyalty oath traditions on those who might endanger the authority of the king through false speech (דבר שקרים, עשה רמיה; Ps 101:7). Similar concerns—explicitly in the context of military domination, with its attendant implications of political relations—appear in Ps 144:5–11, appealing to YHWH against those "whose mouths speak lies and whose right hands are false" (אשר פיהם שוא וימינם ימין שקר; Ps 144:8, 11). Psalm 7 acknowledges that disloyalty to an ally would be legitimate cause for punitive destruction.[43] Loyalty is listed alongside faithfulness and righteousness as the foundations of royal continuity in Prov 20:28, while Prov 24:21–22 instructs fear of and obedience to the sovereign. The importance of loyalty for the reign of the human king is similarly apparent in its foregrounding as part of the rhetoric of coronation in Ps 2. Psalm 72 includes in its catalogue of the accolades of the king several verses proclaiming his authority over other kings, emphasizing the expressions of their loyalty in terms of prostration before him and the presentation of tribute and gifts (Ps 72:8–11).

Many of the stories surrounding David also reflect assumptions about the loyalty due to kings: in the episode in 1 Sam 24, in which David has the opportunity to kill Saul while hidden in a cave, David's contrition at having even cut off the corner of Saul's cloak is based on the implicit threat of this action against a divinely-appointed sovereign.[44] David rejects the possibility of a direct attack on Saul in similar terms in 1 Sam 26. Later David's sovereignty is threatened by his own son, Absalom (2 Sam 15–18); here, too, the claim of the king to his subjects' loyalty is a prominent feature of the narrative. The declaration of Ittai the Gittite, when David attempts to send him back to the city, sums the sentiment up: "As the Lord lives, and as my lord the king lives, wherever my lord the king may be, whether for death or for life, there also your servant will be" (2 Sam 15:21).[45] As David's reign comes to a close, Solomon's first act as king is deeply entrenched in these same issues,

---

[43] On Ps 7:5 as reflecting an association of curses with failures of loyalty see J. H. Tigay, "Psalm 7:5 and Ancient Near Eastern Treaties," *JBL* 89 (1970): 178–86.

[44] On issues of loyalty in the stories of David see Kim, *Identity and Loyalty in the David Story*; K. D. Sakenfeld, "Loyalty and Love: The Language of Human Interconnections in the Hebrew Bible," *MQR* 22 (1983): 195–201; A. Taggar-Cohen, "Political Loyalty in the Biblical Account of 1 Samuel XX–XXII in the Light of Hittite Texts," *VT* 55 (2005): 251–68. Note also Saul's focus on the fate of his descendants in the face of David's eventual assumption of the kingship, echoing the persistent focus of loyalty oath and treaty texts on the importance of the preservation of the dynasty as one of the stipulations of such agreements.

[45] חי יהוה וחי אדני המלך כי אם במקום אשר יהיה שם אדני המלך אם למות אם לחיים כי שם יהיה עבדך

with Adonijah fearing for his life lest his previous actions be interpreted as disloyal to the new sovereign (1 Kgs 1).[46] In each of these texts, loyalty or disloyalty to the king acts as a litmus test: because the expectation of the loyalty due to the sovereign is a given, disloyal action acts as a black mark on the actor's character and evaluation. Thus Ittai the Gittite's oath to stay with David underscores his fidelity, while Absalom's rejection of the loyalty he owes to David anticipates his ultimate demise. David's own refusal to attack Saul, respecting Saul's claim as king to David's loyalty, contributes to the legitimation of David's (eventual) claim to the throne. If the assertions about loyalty to YHWH in Deuteronomy were meant and understood against a background of specifically royal claims to loyalty, this is what would have formed that background.

With this in mind it is also worth emphasizing that the conceptualization of YHWH in royal terms is unlikely to have provoked interpretation in Assyrian terms either; the idea of YHWH as Israel's sovereign king, to whom loyalty is owed, finds multiple witnesses in texts much closer to home. God as king is "the predominant relational metaphor used of God in the Bible, appearing much more frequently than metaphors such as 'God is a lover/husband' ... or 'God is a father.'"[47] The explicit description of the deity as "king" occurs repeatedly in numerous other psalms, including Pss 24; 44; 47; 93; and 95–99. Though there have been attempts to claim that the acclamation of YHWH as king occurred in reaction to the disappearance of the human king in the wake of the destruction of Judah, the theological difficulties faced by Ezekiel and Second Isaiah precisely because of YHWH's existing status as king militates against the delay of this imagery to the exilic or post-exilic periods.[48] The intimate association between loyalty and

---

[46] On 1 Kgs 1 see S. Bar-Efrat, *Narrative Art in the Bible* (JSOTSup 70; Sheffield: Sheffield Academic, 1997), 164–65.

[47] M. Z. Brettler, *God Is King: Understanding an Israelite Metaphor* (JSOTSup 76; Sheffield: Sheffield Academic, 1989), 160. For a discussion of the integration of the idea with the Zion and Jerusalem cult traditions see B. C. Ollenberger, *Zion the City of the Great King: A Theological Symbol of the Jerusalem Cult* (JSOTSup 41; Sheffield: Sheffield Academic, 1987).

[48] I have discussed the implications of this imagery for Ezekiel in C. L. Crouch, "Ezekiel's Oracles against the Nations in Light of a Royal Ideology of Warfare," *JBL* 130 (2011): 473–92 and in C. A. Strine and C. L. Crouch, "Yahweh's Battle against Chaos in Ezekiel: The Transformation of Judahite Mythology for a New Situation," *JBL* 132 (2013): 883–903. In Flynn's recent discussion of YHWH's kingship he contends that the idea of YHWH as a creator king, in contrast to an earlier conception of YHWH as a warrior king, developed in response to Assyrian imperialism (S. W. Flynn,

kingship of any kind is apparent in Ps 2, in which loyalty to the human king is closely associated with loyalty to YHWH; similar closeness is reflected in the combination of YHWH and the human king as those to whom fear and obedience are owed in Prov 24:21. The perpetual language of humans as "servants" of YHWH may be closely connected to the idea of YHWH as the divine sovereign.[49] The articulation of the attributes of YHWH as analogous to those of the human king (and *vice versa*) is apparent throughout Ps 18; a similar phenomenon is evident in Ps 89.[50] There is also the profound integration of loyalty to YHWH with

---

YHWH is King: The Development of Divine Kingship in Ancient Israel [VTSup 159; Leiden: Brill, 2013]). However, this suggestion does not take into account the close connection between YHWH's acclamation as king and his military success at creation, nor the extent to which both the creative and the military aspects of YHWH's kingship are integrated into the mythology and ideology of human kingship. Denying YHWH his multivalent role as both creator and warrior king is to remove the lynchpin of an entire mythological and ideological system: the human king is no longer a model of the divine king, his military endeavors are no longer commissioned as part of the deity's quest to maintain cosmic order, and the mythology of creation in which YHWH does battle against the sea loses its climax, the acclamation of YHWH as king. The idea of a divine king who battles with the sea is attested in the southern Levant at least as far back as second-millennium Ugarit; in the biblical material this battle is clearly associated with creation. There is no reason, therefore, to separate these into an "early" and a "late" version of YHWH's kingship or to make the association of YHWH's kingship with creation dependent on interaction with the Assyrians. In any case, the (non-)characterization of YHWH as king in Deuteronomy is, if anything, military rather than creative (although to attempt to be even that specific is difficult); even if Flynn is correct, therefore, there is no sign of an "anti-Assyrian" characterization here.

[49] E. J. Bridge, "Loyalty, Dependency and Status with YHWH: The Use of 'bd in the Psalms," *VT* 59 (2009): 360–78 has addressed the use of this language in the psalms in particular; though he tends to trace the ultimate roots of the metaphor to the master-slave relationship, he is well aware of its prevalence in articulating king-subject relations.

[50] K.-P. Adam, *Der Königliche Held: Die Entsprechung von kämpfendem Gott und kämpfendem König in Psalm 18* (WMANT 91; Neukirchen-Vluyn: Neukirchner Verlag, 2001); also C. L. Crouch, *War and Ethics in the Ancient Near East: Military Violence in Light of Cosmology and History* [BZAW 407; Berlin: de Gruyter, 2009], 29–32. On this phenomenon more broadly see Brettler, *God is King*. Gerstenberger contends that claims of dominion on the part of the divine king are unrealistic in the pre-exilic period and must, therefore, be dated to the post-exilic period (E. S. Gerstenberger, "'World Dominion' in Yahweh Kingship Psalms: Down to the Roots of Globalizing Concepts and Strategies," *HBT* 23 [2001]: 192–210). The exaggerations of reality, however, may be traced to the ideological function of such statements, namely, the conceptualization of the human and divine kings as acting in concert against the chaos and disorder represented by nations and territories not under the control of the

loyalty to the king which underpins the entirety of the aforementioned issues about loyalty in the David narratives: disloyalty to the human king is tantamount to disloyalty to YHWH.

The application to YHWH of ideas about the loyalty due the human king as a means of articulating the importance of loyalty to YHWH (and the consequences of disloyalty) would thus not have evoked the recognition of a foreign source for such concepts, never mind a specifically Assyrian one. The assumption that Deuteronomy placing YHWH in this role must be read as a statement about Assyria requires that there is no native tradition of YHWH's kingship—indeed, no tradition about kingship at all—that might have prompted such a characterization and provided the framework for its interpretation, which is untenable. Indeed, given Deuteronomy's acute interest in the importance of the Israelites' loyalty to YHWH, it ought hardly to be a surprise that its expressions of this interest might draw on the ideas about loyalty to kings that would have been familiar to its audience.

Having established that neither the invocation of the loyalty due to a sovereign nor the application of such ideas to YHWH are likely to have succeeded in signaling Deuteronomy's intention to be interpreted in relation to Assyrian ideas, the remaining question concerns whether there are any more distinctive elements of Deut 13 that might succeed in attracting sufficient attention as to point towards Assyria. In the preceding discussions we have noted two short phrases that might constitute such elements: the reference to "your brother, the son of your mother" (אחיך בן אמך) in Deut 13:7 and the phrase דבר סרה in Deut 13:6.

With regard to the reference to "your brother, the son of your mother" (אחיך בן אמך), it will be recalled that Levinson suggested that the appearance of this phrase in the list in Deut 13:7 reflects VTE's *aḫḫēšu mar'ē ummišu*.[51] As Levinson himself noted, however, the brother who is

---

Yahwistic king (Crouch, *War and Ethics*, 29–32); it also relates to the superlative, incomparable characterization of the deity as like a human king, but more ("most entailments of human kingship that are projected on to God convey God's superlative nature, combining the metaphor 'God is king' with the theological notion 'God is incomparable'"; Brettler, *God Is King*, 162–63).

[51] Levinson also suggests that the phrase "in/from your midst" (מקרבך/בקרבך) "corresponds precisely to Akkadian *ina birtūkunu* in the Zakutu treaty," but why this phrase need be sourced from an Assyrian treaty when it occurs more than a dozen times in—and throughout—Deuteronomy is unclear (Deut 13:2, 6, 12, 14, 15; 17:2, 7; 19:19, 20; 21:8, 9, 21; 22:24; 24:7) (B. M. Levinson, "Textual Criticism, Assyriology, and the History of Interpretation: Deuteronomy 13:7a as a Test Case in Method," *JBL* 120 [2001]: 239 n. 83). Both variants also appear elsewhere: מקרבך in Micah and Zephaniah

specified as the son of the same mother is attested in Northwest Semitic at Ugarit[52] as well as in a number of biblical passages, including Gen 27:29; 43:29; Judg 8:19; Pss 50:20; 69:9.[53] It seems unlikely, therefore, to have served as an effective signal to an Assyrian source—especially as it is substantially altered from its sense in VTE, where it refers to the brothers of Assurbanipal who might be threatened by disloyalty rather than the brother who might incite it. In the absence of other signals that would confirm to Deuteronomy's audience that this particular phrase ought to be taken as a deliberate and meaningful adaptation of an Akkadian phrase, either from VTE or from Akkadian phraseology more generally, it is difficult to envision how or why Deuteronomy's audience would have been inclined to do so. Indeed, given the use of such language in other, Hebrew contexts—combined with its fundamentally mundane character—it would have served as a very poor signal of Deuteronomy's relationship with Assyrian material.

The resemblance of the phrase דבר סרה in Deut 13:6 to Akkadian *dabābu surrātu* is more striking, though we should first recall the non-idiomatic use of these and similar words in Akkadian, which suggested that they reflected the use of everyday vocabulary rather than technical terminology for disloyalty. In Hebrew, דבר is by itself unremarkable. סרה is much less common, with a degree of uncertainty regarding its semantic domain reflected in the lexicons' differing divisions of its appearances under two entries. HALOT and Gesenius, for example, locate the majority under סרה II, derived from סרר "to be stubborn," and render סרה itself as "obstinacy" or "falsehood" (leaving only Isa 14:6 under סרה I "cessation," from סור).[54] DCH splits the difference between סרה I "rebellion," "falsehood" (from סרר I "to be rebellious") and סרה II "turning aside," "apostasy," "wrongdoing," "cessation," "deviation" (from סור I "to turn aside"), though in fact it actually replicates the majority of the biblical appearances of the term under all three of "rebellion," "falsehood," and "apostasy."[55] The thrust of not doing what one ought, especially in relation to some higher authority, is apparent throughout. The noun appears elsewhere in Deuteronomy in the legislation regarding witnesses (Deut 19:16, 18, 19).

---

and בקרבך in Exodus, Psalms, Joshua, and eight different prophetic books. It would make a poor signal to a foreign source.

[52] KTU 1.6 vi 10–11, 14–16; 1.14 i 8–9.

[53] Levinson, "Textual Criticism," 224–25.

[54] HALOT 2:769; Ges[18] 4:902 ("Widerspenstigkeit, Ungehorsam, Abfall (v. Jahwe)"; with דבר, "Falsches, Lüge sagen").

[55] DCH 6:196.

Both verbs are relatively common: סור especially so, but even סרר appears in more than a dozen texts, in both overtly political and non-political contexts, across a range of genres and periods. Perhaps the most notable for the present purposes is Deut 21:18, 20, in the law of the rebellious son. There are thus two other passages, within Deuteronomy, that might provide the most immediate context for Deuteronomy's audience's interpretation of the phrase in Deut 13:6.[56] Though attention to the phrase in Deut 13:6 has been focused on the noun, with enquiries as to "how the erstwhile Akkadian word *srh* managed to get into the Old Testament," the frequency of the verbal form also suggests that the phrase in Deut 13:6 cannot be understood simply as the limited transference of a self-contained foreign phrase from Akkadian into Hebrew, but must be understood as drawing on much more broadly Hebraic roots.[57] Contributing to the phrase's interpretation in Deut 13:6, it must of course be noted that this is the only instance in which the terms appear together; the appearance of a cognate phrase, *dabābu surrātu*, in VTE §57 attracted natural attention in the interpretation of the phrase in Deuteronomy. Again, however, the evidence to suggest that this constituted a stereotyped Akkadian phrase, recognizable as a technical means of referring to disloyalty, is very poor; it appears in the Assyrian treaties only at VTE §57 and neither there nor in the handful of other passages in which it occurs does it appear as part of a fixed formula. To see in the Hebrew דבר סרה an adaptation of an Akkadian *dabābu surrātu*, intended to carry the weight of Deuteronomy's allusion to an Assyrian treaty and loyalty oath tradition or text, is to ask a great deal of two isolated words. To recall Noble: "they are far more suggestive of the sort of random half-similarities which may arise between two texts simply by chance, than of a subtle author who is trying to intimate to his readers that he is covertly commenting upon another story that they know."[58]

---

[56] Even if Deut 13 and 28 are separated from the surrounding chapters, the appearance of this terminology elsewhere in Deuteronomy and elsewhere in the Hebrew Bible acts to dilute the impact of its appearance in Deut 13.

[57] Koch, *Vertrag*, 161 ("wie das ehedem akkadische Wort srh in das Alte Testament gelangt ist").

[58] P. R. Noble, "Esau, Tamar, and Joseph: Criteria for Identifying Inner-Biblical Allusions," *VT* 52 (2002): 227–28.

CONCLUSIONS

Insofar as we can, albeit approximately, correlate the expected knowledge of Deuteronomy's audience and the knowledge exhibited by other biblical texts, it is unlikely that Deuteronomy would have been able to expect its audience to be ignorant of treaty, loyalty oath, and curse traditions. The abundance of biblical material referencing treaty and loyalty oath concepts or deploying curses to make a point suggests that these were well known and familiar phenomena, and it is against this background that Deuteronomy would have been interpreted. In Hutcheon's terms, Deuteronomy's audience is a "differently knowing" audience, whose experience of Deuteronomy will have been shaped by its knowledge of much broader treaty, loyalty oath, and curse traditions than those manifest in Assyria alone.[59] Read in light of this wider knowledge base, there is nothing in Deuteronomy's rendering of this material that appears out of the ordinary: nothing that would have triggered the suspicion that this text intended to allude to some other source and nothing that might be considered distinctively Assyrian. There is, in sum, no reason to think that Deuteronomy's audience would have had any reason to understand this text in any context other than their own.

---

[59] Hutcheon, *Theory of Adaptation*, 125.

5

LANGUAGE, FUNCTION, AND COMPREHENSION

A successful case of subversion requires more than a single individual capable of reading and adapting a source; there must also be an audience sufficiently familiar with the source text as to recognize an adaptation of it.[1] To recall Hutton, "[t]he marking text's effectiveness requires the reader's sufficient competence to actualize the allusion to the earlier work."[2] The previous chapter considered the implications of a wider knowledge of treaties, loyalty oaths, and curses for the audience's interpretation of Deuteronomy as a new work. This chapter addresses the social role of treaties and loyalty oaths more broadly, considering the likely level of familiarity among Deuteronomy's audience of the Assyrian manifestation of this tradition—in the form of VTE or in the form of some other Assyrian-Judahite treaty or oath text—and asking whether Deuteronomy's audience would have been familiar enough with this tradition to recognize an allusion to it.

The nature and extent of Deuteronomy's audience's knowledge of Assyrian treaties, loyalty oaths, and curses naturally raises questions

---

[1] In theory, of course, it is possible to imagine a single scribe amusing himself with his ability to make clever allusions to other literary works, but it is difficult to interpret allusions of this sort as subversive, as there is no one whose opinions are intended to be changed. They are rather more in the nature of a private joke: entertaining, but inconsequential for the purpose of the new work.

[2] J. M. Hutton, "Isaiah 51:9–11 and the Rhetorical Appropriation and Subversion of Hostile Theologies," *JBL* 126 (2007): 277.

about the historical and social context of treaty and loyalty oath texts: about the physical forms that such texts might have taken, their presentation or distribution among oath-takers, and the languages involved in this process. For Deuteronomy to have functioned subversively its source material needed to be well known: "to serve as part of a shared community of knowledge, both for the interrelationships and interplay to be identifiable and for these in turn to have the required impact on their readership."[3] Especially critical in addressing this question, therefore, will be theories regarding the practical function of these texts, ideas and assumptions about the extent of bilingualism in Judah, and the likelihood that an Assyrian-Judahite treaty (on the model of VTE specifically or in the Assyrian tradition more generally) would have been translated from an Akkadian original into either Aramaic or Hebrew.

LOCATION, LOCATION, LOCATION

Whether a copy of an Assyrian-Judahite treaty in any language existed in Jerusalem remains unclear; until recently, no copies even of VTE were known outside of the Assyrian heartland.[4] Although the discovery of a copy of VTE at Tell Tayinat suggests that such documents could be preserved outside the Assyrian capital(s), two features of this new text should be particularly noted. First, the Tell Tayinat text is in Akkadian. Second, it was found not in a vassal state but in an Assyrian provincial territory, in "a carefully planned Assyrian administrative complex that replicated the various functional units of a typical royal citadel in the Assyrian heartland, albeit on a smaller scale."[5] There is still, in other words, only ambiguous evidence for the deposit of Assyrian vassal treaties in vassal capitals. It is thus perhaps unsurprising to see a recent trend towards hypotheses in which both the performance and the preservation of these types of texts are focused on the Assyrian core. Lauinger has suggested that any Assyrian-Judahite treaty would have been kept in Assyria, not in Judah, and would have been the focus of

---

[3] J. Sanders, *Adaptation and Appropriation* (The New Critical Idiom; Abingdon: Routledge, 97).

[4] On the Tell Tayinat text see J. Lauinger, "Some Preliminary Thoughts on the Tablet Collection in Building XVI from Tell Tayinat," *JCSMS* 6 (2011): 5–14 and T. P. Harrison and J. F. Osborne, "Building XVI and the Neo-Assyrian Sacred Precinct at Tell Tayinat," *JCS* 64 (2012): 125–43, with the *editio princeps* and commentary in J. Lauinger, "Esarhaddon's Succession Treaty at Tell Tayinat: Text and Commentary," *JCS* 64 (2012): 87–123.

[5] Harrison and Osborne, "Building XVI," 130.

oath-taking ceremonies there.[6] Sanders has suggested that the ritual performance of oath ceremonies might have occurred in connection with the annual delivery of tribute.[7] Even Berlejung, who supposes that there must have been a copy in Jerusalem, suggests that it would have been entrusted to the Assyrian *qīpu*, who was charged with its enforcement, rather than with the Judahite king.[8] Each of these scenarios renders the text's availability and familiarity to a Judahite scribe, especially one intent on subversive activity, more problematic than generally acknowledged.

Contributing to the suspicion that only a very limited number of people would have been privy to the details of this material are the identity and number of individuals who would have needed to be

---

[6] J. Lauinger, personal communication; cf. S. Z. Aster, "Transmission of Neo-Assyrian Claims to Empire to Judah in the Late Eighth Century B.C.E.," *HUCA* 78 (2007): 9–18, who argues for a progressive increase in the intensity of the southern Levant's exposure to Assyrian ideology over the course of the latter half of the eighth century. While the general trend he depicts is probably accurate, it is notable that the means of transmission he identifies are overwhelmingly focused on the communication of power rather than content (as Aster himself implicitly acknowledges in the numerous references to the "basic" content or messages thus conveyed). The points at which he perceives the possibility of the transmission of more specific details of "the motifs, images, and language in which this ideology was couched" rely on substantial Akkadian literacy and on the assumption that those in possession of such literacy would have been actively and extensively involved in the translation of Akkadian texts into Aramaic(!), for the sake of disseminating their detailed contents to the general public. Even if this did occur, the relationship of such translations to their source texts is problematic and, as will be discussed in greater detail below, likely to have diluted their distinctively Assyrian components considerably.

[7] S. L. Sanders, "Placing Scribal Culture in History: Deuteronomy and Late Iron-Age Text Production" (paper presented at the annual meeting of the Society of Biblical Literature, Baltimore, Md., 25 November 2013). Morrow has also suggested that diplomatic contacts, including delivery of tribute, would have provided the most likely context for the transmission of Assyrian ideology to vassals; he emphasizes, however, that this transmission would have been primarily oral and ideas-based, rather than literary and text-based (W. S. Morrow, "Tribute from Judah and the Transmission of Assyrian Propaganda," in *"My Spirit at Rest in the North Country" (Zechariah 6.8): Collected Communications to the XXth Congress of the International Organization for the Study of the Old Testament, Helsinki 2010* [ed. H. M. Niemann and M. Augustin; BEATAJ 57; Oxford: Peter Lang, 2011], 183–92).

[8] A. Berlejung, "The Assyrians in the West: Assyrianization, Colonialism, Indifference, or Development Policy?," in *Congress Volume Helsinki 2010* (ed. M. Nissinen; VTSup 148; Leiden: Brill, 2012), 23, 32.

intimately familiar with these texts. Liverani argued a number of years ago that VTE may not have been a widely used vassal treaty but a highly specific loyalty oath for Assurbanipal's Median bodyguards.[9] Although the discovery of a copy of VTE at Tell Tayinat precludes such an extremely limited use of the oath as Liverani envisions, it remains a pertinent emphasis that it and its analogues are unlikely to have been administered to large numbers of individuals. Practically speaking, only a relatively small number of individuals—the king and perhaps the most powerful of his court—would have been in the position to instigate disloyalty to the Assyrian empire in any meaningful fashion; only a very few individuals are therefore likely to have found themselves in the position of having to swear not to do so. In connection with this Radner argues that loyalty oaths would have been taken by individuals rather than collectives; in addition to the Assyrian *qīpu* in Jerusalem, only the king himself would have been party to the treaty.[10]

Though Sanders envisions a wider audience, seeing in the references to the speaking and writing of these texts the suggestion of large-scale public oath-taking ceremonies, he allows that such ceremonies would probably have occurred only intermittently.[11] The linguistic limitations of the overwhelming majority of the population also means that, in order for a larger audience of this kind to gain any comprehension of the treaty or loyalty oath's contents, these contents would have had to have been translated into an accessible language; one might also observe that the sheer size of the texts in question is unlikely to have been conducive to detailed retention by even the most attentive of audiences. Such occasional proclamation and the nature of the texts themselves thus raises significant doubts about the extent of even such a large audience's familiarity with the contents of the texts such that the members of the audience might be able to recognize it again elsewhere and out of context. Zehnder also suggests that these generalizing references to the whole population in Akkadian descriptions of the enactments of

---

[9] M. Liverani, "The Medes at Esarhaddon's Court," *JCS* 47 (1995): 57–62.

[10] K. Radner, "Assyrische *ṭuppi adê* als Vorbild für Deuteronomium 28,20–44?," in *Die deuteronomistischen Geschichtswerke: redaktions- und religionsgeschichtliche Perspektiven zur "Deuteronomismus"-Diskussion in Tora und Vorderen Propheten* (ed. M. Witte, et al.; BZAW 365; Berlin: de Gruyter, 2006), 351–378. Given the Assyrian habit of educating the children of vassal rulers in Assyria, it is tempting to imagine the king himself as one of the few Judahites with some skill in Akkadian and/or Aramaic.

[11] S. L. Sanders, *Textual Production and Religious Experience: The Transformation of Scribal Cultures in Judah and Babylon* (TSAJ; Tübingen: Mohr Siebeck, 2015) and personal communication; cf. D. Boyarin, *Sparks of the Logos: Essays in Rabbinic Hermeneutics* (Leiden: Brill, 2003), 59–88.

oaths/treaties are rhetorical devices, rather than a reflection of the text's real audience in practice.[12]

The evidence from Tell Tayinat on this particular point remains unclear; on the one hand, the copy found there opens with reference to the governor and to sixteen other officials, perhaps suggesting a number of oath-takers; on the other, all of these are anonymously identified by title rather than by name, and Lauinger suggests that it may be a deliberately vague text designed to cover all eventualities as individual personnel changed.[13] While rhetorically the entire population may be subordinate to the empire, in fact it is the actions of the elites, specifically the king, at stake. The practical implementation and dissemination of these texts would probably have reflected this.

The first obstacle to Deuteronomy's audience's knowledge of the contents of an Assyrian-Judahite treaty or loyalty oath, in sum, is the accessibility—or lack thereof—of the physical text itself, combined with the probably limited exposure of all but a few members of the population to its contents with any frequency. Exacerbating this situation is the issue of language.

Assyrian Power and Akkadian Comprehension

In a number of his discussions of language usage, Bourdieu raises the role of language in the formation and propagation of authority; he suggests that linguistic hegemony (the use of one particular language) may be employed as a tool of symbolic domination.[14] "Language," he writes, "is not only an instrument of communication or even of knowledge, but also an instrument of power. A person speaks not only to be understood but also to be believed, obeyed, respected, distinguished."[15] Although the universal applicability of this theory has been questioned, it raises for consideration several interesting issues

---

[12] M. P. Zehnder, "Building on Stone? Deuteronomy and Esarhaddon's Loyalty Oaths (Part 1): Some Preliminary Observations," *BBR* 19 (2009): 366–74.

[13] Lauinger, "Esarhaddon's Succession Treaty," 113.

[14] P. Bourdieu, "The Economics of Linguistic Exchanges" (transl. R. Nice), *SSI* 16 (1977): 645–68; idem, *Ce que parler veut dire* (Paris: Fayard, 1982), 35–36; idem, *Outline of a Theory of Practice* (transl. R. Nice; Cambridge Studies in Social Anthropology 16; Cambridge: Cambridge University Press, 1977), 150–51.

[15] Bourdieu, "Economics of Linguistic Exchanges," 648.

concerning linguistic usage in the ancient Near East and the implications of that usage for subversive acts.[16]

It is well-known that the Assyrian empire employed both Akkadian and Aramaic scribes for administrative purposes.[17] At the same time, however, the ideological priority of Akkadian is attested, not least by the adamant refusal of Sargon II to allow his administrators to communicate with him in Aramaic:

> [As to what you wrote]: "There are informers [... to the king] and coming to his presence; if it is acceptable to the king, let me write and send my messages to the king on Aram[aic] parchment sheets" — why would you not write and send me messages in Akkadian? Really, the message which you write in it must be drawn up in this very manner — this is a fixed regulation![18]

Though apparently not possible in practice, this suggests an ideological prioritization of Akkadian over Aramaic as the language of power in the Assyrian empire and suggests that, in instances where the demonstration

---

[16] See K. A. Woolard, "Language Variation and Cultural Hegemony: Toward an Integration of Sociolinguistic and Social Theory," *American Ethnologist* 12 (1985): 738–48.

[17] H. Tadmor, "On the Role of Aramaic in the Assyrian Empire," in *Near Eastern Studies Dedicated to H. I. H. Prince Takahito Mikasa on the Occasion of His Seventy-Fifth Birthday* (ed. M. Mori, H. Ogawa, and M. Yoshikawa; Bulletin of the Middle Eastern Culture Centre in Japan 5; Wiesbaden: Harrassowitz, 1991), 419–26; P. Garelli, "Importance et rôle des Araméens dans l'administration de l'empire assyrien," in *Mesopotamien und seine Nachbarn: Politische und kulturelle Wechselbeziehungen im alten Vorderasien vom 4. bis 1. Jahrtausend v. Chr.* (ed. H. J. Nissen and U. Renger; BBVO 1; Berlin: Reimer, 1982), 437–47; Z. Stefanovic, "Why the Aramaic Script Was Called 'Assyrian' in Hebrew, Greek, and Demotic," *Or* 62 (1993): 80–82; P. A. Beaulieu, "Official and Vernacular Languages: The Shifting Sands of Imperial and Cultural Identities in First Millennium B.C. Mesopotamia," in *Margins of Writing, Origins of Cultures: New Approaches to Writing and Reading in the Ancient Near East* (ed. S. L. Sanders; Chicago, Ill.: Oriental Institute, 2006), 187–216. Cf. SAA 16 63 12–20 (referring to activities in Guzana); SAA 16 99 8–11 (referring to a servant of Shalmaneser III's son).

[18] [šá taš-pu-ra um-ma L]Ú.EME.MEŠ i-ba-áš-ši [a-na LUGAL x x-k]a a-na pa-ni-šú il-lak-a-ni [um-ma] k[i]-[i IGI LUG]AL maḫ-ru ina ŠÀ si-ip-ri [KUR].ár-m[a-a-a lu-u]s-pi-ir-ma a-na LUGAL [l]u-še-bi-la mi-nam-ma ina ši-pir-ti ak-ka-da-at-tu la ta-šaṭ-ṭar-ma la tu-šeb-bi-la kit-ta ši-pir-tu šá ina ŠÀ-bi ta-šaṭ-ṭa-ru ki-i pi-i a-gan-ni-tim-ma i-da-at (SAA 17 2 13–21).

of Assyrian power was at stake, we should expect to find the use of Akkadian rather than the use of Aramaic.[19]

In the case of a treaty or oath document, this demonstration of power applies not only to a spoken form of the text but also to the written form of the text that is its physical representation. If the copies of VTE that have thus far been found are indicative, oath texts, and probably treaty texts, were preserved in two principle locations: libraries and temples.[20] In the latter in particular we are obliged to consider the role of the text not merely as a reference work but as a physical reminder of power, and in this role the use of Akkadian is both expected and affirmed by the existing evidence: despite the range of evidence for the use of Aramaic in the Assyrian imperial sphere, acts of symbolic domination occur overwhelmingly in Akkadian. All of the Assyrian treaty and oath texts yet known exist only in Akkadian; the sole possible exception is the Sefire material discussed in chapter four. In this quarter we might also note the royal palace reliefs preserved from the Assyrian capitals: despite being visual demonstrations of Assyrian power directed at visiting ambassadors and delegations from provincial territories or vassal states, the texts that accompany these images are invariably in Akkadian. Though visitors were probably guided through these images with the help of an *ad hoc* translator *cum* tour guide, the ultimate aim of the reliefs was achieved through their monumental nature and, perhaps, by their very inaccessibility to the non-Assyrian audience, insofar as the text's inaccessibility contributed to its aura of power.[21]

In these contexts the power of the object is its symbolic communicative value, rather than its linguistic communicative value; accordingly, the production of documents of Assyria's imperial power and authority—documents like loyalty oaths and vassal treaties—occurs in Akkadian, the language of power, as part of the expression of Assyrian domination. The point of such preservation is not that any

---

[19] Note that this should not be confused with attempts to force conquered peoples to adopt Akkadian in daily practice; the lack of a program of assyrianization, especially in the vassal states, speaks against any such attempt (Berlejung, "The Assyrians in the West").

[20] For discussion see Radner, "Assyrische *ṭuppi adê*"; Harrison and Osborne, "Building XVI"; Lauinger, "Preliminary Thoughts."

[21] J. M. Russell, "Sennacherib's 'Palace without Rival': A Programmatic Study of Texts and Images in a Late Assyrian Palace" (Ph.D. diss.; University of Pennsylvania, 1985), 273–80; cf. J. E. Reade, "Ideology and Propaganda in Assyrian Art," in *Power and Propaganda: A Symposium on Ancient Empires* (ed. M. T. Larsen; Mesopotamia 7; Copenhagen: Akademisk Forlag, 1979), 319–28.

individual to whom it applies can read it, but that he or she is appropriately in awe of what it represents. In the words of Machinist, "it was the very monumentality of the inscription ... which communicated the monumentality of power and sovereignty."[22] As expressions of power, any copies of treaty and loyalty oath texts held in vassal states are likely to have been preserved and presented in Akkadian.[23] We might, with Berlejung's suggestion in mind, thus envision the Jerusalem copy of an Assyrian-Judahite treaty on display in the reception area of the *qīpu's* residence, where it would serve as a physical reminder of Assyrian power on the king's and his courtiers' visits there.

The preservation and presentation of these texts in Akkadian raises, first, pressing questions regarding their accessibility to a would-be adaptor: that is, the ability of anyone in Judah to read one of these Akkadian texts well enough to be able to adapt it. A recent catalogue of all known cuneiform inscriptions from the southern Levant (Canaan, Palestine/Philistia, and the land of Israel) accounts fifteen from the (Neo-)Assyrian period: one each from Ashdod, Beer Sheva, Ben Shemen, Khirbit Kūsyi, Tell Qaqun, the Shephelah, and the Wingate Institute near Natanya; two each from Gezer and Tel Hadid; and four from Samaria.[24] With the exception of the votive cylinder from Beer Sheva and the fragment of a stone Lamaštu plaque found in the Shephelah, all of these are associated with coastal or northern sites, mostly in provincial territories, and are therefore of limited use for arguments in favor of cuneiform usage and literacy in Judah.[25] A few general observations on

---

[22] P. B. Machinist, "Final Response: On the Study of the Ancients, Language Writing, and the State," in *Margins of Writing, Origins of Cultures: New Approaches to Writing and Reading in the Ancient Near East* (ed. S. L. Sanders; Chicago, Ill.: Oriental Institute, 2006), 291–300.

[23] Cf. the Tell Tayinat tablets as a "display collection" (Lauinger, "Some Preliminary Thoughts," 10–12).

[24] W. Horowitz, T. Oshima, and S. L. Sanders, "A Bibliographical List of Cuneiform Inscriptions from Canaan, Palestine/Philistia, and the Land of Israel," *JAOS* 122 (2002): 753–66.

[25] The especially mixed material culture of the Beersheba and Arad valleys may also be worth mention with regard to the votive cylinder, as it seems to reflect the significant movement of people and/or objects across this southern region of Judah; the origin, destination, or owner of the votive cylinder is impossible to determine (on the diversity of the material culture of the Beersheba and Arad valleys see C. L. Crouch, *The Making of Israel: Cultural Diversity in the Southern Levant and the Formation of Ethnic Identity in Deuteronomy* [VTSup 162; Leiden: Brill, 2014], 61–70, with further references). With regard to the Lamaštu plaque, without further precision regarding the date of the object (it was not found in a stratified context) it is impossible to know

the nature of these texts may be instructive nevertheless. Four of the fifteen inscriptions are monumental stele, the type of inscription for which the prestige language would be expected regardless of the ability of a local audience to read it. Five are personal items—seals or private religious objects—that are likely to reflect the linguistic preferences of their individual owners and are of limited use in extrapolating wider linguistic abilities. The remaining five are administrative documents: two land sale contracts from Gezer, two administrative documents from Tell Hadid, and a judicial document from Samaria.[26] Samaria and Gezer are administrative centers of Assyrian provincial rule and therefore likely sites for native Akkadian speakers and scribes; Tell Hadid is likewise provincial and was probably inhabited by Mesopotamian deportees (as may have been Samaria and Gezer).[27] None of these, in other words, provides any evidence in favor of Akkadian literacy on the part of persons living in Judah; the majority of even these small numbers come from within the Assyrian provincial system, not from Assyria's vassal states. Combined with the lack of such documents from Jerusalem or its environs, this indicates that the suggestion that even a small handful of scribes in Judah would have been able to read a document in Akkadian to the degree that they might then adapt it for their own ends, is optimistic.[28] According to Morrow, "the idea that an educated elite of Judah would have been able to read cuneiform during the time period

---

whether its deposit in the Shephelah was during a period in which that region was under Judahite control or not.

[26] One of the fifteen is too fragmentary to identify.

[27] See N. Na'aman and R. Zadok, "Assyrian Deportations to the Province of Samerina in the Light of Two Cuneiform Tablets from Tel Hadid," *TA* 27 (2000): 159–88; R. Reich and B. Brandl, "Gezer under Assyrian Rule," *PEQ* 117 (1985): 41–54. It may be noted that the majority of the names in these various documents are also Akkadian, with some Aramaic and very few Hebrew-Canaanite, but given the propensity of individuals to adopt second or alternative names and the vagaries of generational shifts in name affiliations it is difficult to draw any decisive conclusions from this.

[28] Whether the administrative texts even indicate literacy on the part of the majority of the persons involved is equally debatable, given that the ability to "sign" a document need have no relation to this. One may also wish to note that even among educated members of the scribal classes *in Assyria* that there were those who could not read cuneiform Akkadian—no doubt in part due to the differentiation between spoken Assyrian and the written form of the language, Standard Babylonian (Beaulieu, "Official and Vernacular Languages," 191; A. R. Millard, "Assyrians and Arameans," *Iraq* 45 [1983]: 101–108).

under discussion is implausible."[29] Again: the purpose of the actual written document is as a monumental reminder of its contents in general, rather than the actual communication of its contents in specific.

Given the dual requirements for subversion—not only authorial skill but also audience knowledge—the concern raised by these considerations of language is the familiarity of Deuteronomy's audience with such expressions of power: if the Assyrian source material for Deuteronomy was in Akkadian, how likely is it that there was an audience able to access that text in enough detail that allusions to its specific and distinctive components might be recognized? Only very few individuals in Judah might have been able to access an Assyrian-Judahite treaty written in Akkadian; though perhaps a few more had some spoken competence, this still seems unlikely to have constituted a significant number of individuals. If an Assyrian-Judahite treaty or oath document was preserved in Jerusalem in Akkadian, therefore, it is extremely unlikely that there existed an audience sufficiently bilingual as to recognize any use made of it by the exceptional scribe who was able to read it. While literacy in Hebrew alone might not have been altogether uncommon (if not yet common, either), bilingualism—especially in Akkadian—would have been rare indeed.[30] While we might readily agree that the Covenant Code, in Hebrew, would have been accessible enough to a Hebrew-speaking (and -reading) audience as to render Deuteronomy recognizably subversive *vis-à-vis* that text, the subversion of an Akkadian oath or treaty text would require substantial linguistic skills for which there is limited evidence.

If the foregoing is even an approximately accurate assessment of the likely social and linguistic scenario involved in an Assyrian-Judahite treaty—combined with the growing suspicion that the primary locus for the performance of treaty and loyalty oath texts may not have been in Judah—the likelihood that the audience of a new text, based on an Akkadian original, would be familiar enough with an Akkadian source as to be able to recognize an adaptation of it is extremely slim.

Translation and Dissolution into Local Vernaculars

The lack of command of Akkadian by the general public in Judah, as well as the majority if not all of the elites, means that some level of

---

[29] Morrow, "Tribute from Judah," 183.

[30] C. A. Rollston, personal communication; cf. idem, *Writing and Literacy in the World of Ancient Israel: Epigraphic Evidence from the Iron Age* (SBLABS 11; Atlanta, Ga.: SBL, 2010), 89; W. S. Morrow, "Cuneiform Literacy and Deuteronomic Composition," *BO* 62 (2005): 203–14.

translational activity would probably have been necessary to convey the contents of a treaty or loyalty oath to the individuals or groups obliged to swear to it. Unsurprisingly, therefore, most scholars have assumed, explicitly or implicitly, that the author of Deuteronomy must have had access to a translated version of VTE (or its Assyrian-Judahite analogue).[31] However, the assumption that the author of Deuteronomy would have been working from either an Aramaic or a Hebrew version of an Assyrian-Judahite treaty or oath, and that its audience would have been familiar with such a text, is problematic for a number of reasons.

The first issue involved in imagining a translated treaty or loyalty oath as Deuteronomy's source concerns the nature of the translation itself. The preceding analysis of an oath or treaty's social role suggested that the written form of the text is likely to have remained in Akkadian, as an expression of power. How, then, might its contents have been conveyed to those about to acknowledge this power? Who needs to be able to access this material—a few elites, or the general public? In the former case, is it viable to envision a translation into Aramaic or, as in the latter, should we acknowledge a need to render the material into Hebrew?

Throughout the following the practicalities of such an undertaking should not be underestimated or forgotten. The largest of these texts, VTE, extends to hundreds of lines and, in its extant copies, represents some of the largest tablets ever discovered. Even the more abbreviated versions of treaties and loyalty oaths would have represented a significant investment of time and resources to translate formally. It may be the case that such formal translations were rarely if ever undertaken, with the limited number of individuals with an occasional need to consult these documents in detail reliant on occasional, *ad hoc* translations undertaken by the resident competent scribe—perhaps himself a representative of the Assyrian administration. For the vast majority of these texts' audiences, however, the objective was not the texts' conveyance of detailed knowledge of their contents but a message of power, achievable equally through generalized renderings of the thrust of their contents in the presence of representatives of that power and the reminder of that power in the monumental preservation of an Akkadian text. Whether even the king himself would have required a

---

[31] H. U. Steymans, *Deuteronomium 28 und die Adê zur Thronfolgeregelung Asarhaddons: Segen und Fluch im Alten Orient und in Israel* (OBO 145; Göttingen: Vandenhoeck & Ruprecht, 1995), 150–94, 380; cf. B. M. Levinson, "Textual Criticism, Assyriology, and the History of Interpretation: Deuteronomy 13:7a as a Test Case in Method," *JBL* 120 (2001): 236–37.

detailed translation of a treaty or loyalty oath may be questioned, given the intense repetitiveness of these texts; the point of the king's obligations could be readily paraphrased in far fewer words and with far less effort than that required of a formal translation. With this in mind, it may make more sense to envision the transmission of an Assyrian-Judahite treaty or loyalty oath in terms of oral translation, akin to the guided translations of the Assyrian royal palace reliefs. Such translations would have been performed as and when required, including the oath-taking ceremony itself, with subsequent reference access facilitated by an individual competent in Akkadian. There may, in other words, have been very little need for a written translation of this material.

Nevertheless, the working hypothesis of existing scholarship is that Deuteronomy is dealing with a written text in Aramaic, stored in the archives or libraries of Jerusalem. This, then, is the first possibility to consider in relation to Deuteronomy's subversive potential *vis-à-vis* a translation. In this scenario we must first note that the existence of an Aramaic translation of an Assyrian-Judahite treaty or loyalty oath only partially remedies the bilingualism obstacles already discussed with regard to Akkadian. Even if an Aramaic text existed in Jerusalem, in other words, we cannot be overly optimistic regarding the number of people who would have been able to access it in that form. Although the two languages are related, proficiency in Hebrew by no means amounted to proficiency in Aramaic; indeed, the incomprehensibility of Aramaic to most Hebrew speakers is presupposed by the political logic of 2 Kgs 18. Even that text attests to only three persons who claim (spoken) abilities in Aramaic: someone who appears to be a high-level administrator (אשר על הבית), a scribe (הספר), and a recorder (המזכיר). It is reasonably likely that the latter two would have had some abilities with written Aramaic, but the extent of this ability, and whether it extended beyond these two individuals, is unknown. If the translated text existed in Aramaic, in other words, we must reckon with a very small group of persons able to read it; a marginally larger group than that able to deal with an Akkadian text, but probably not by much.

That Aramaic was used alongside Akkadian for administrative purposes in the Assyrian empire is not in question; the extent to which this would have resulted in significant Aramaic literacy skills, however, especially among subject populations, is doubtful. Studies of bilingualism in the ancient world are invariably hampered by the range of materials available for study; the complexity of the relationship between written language and spoken language; and the variety of cultural, social, political, and economic factors that can affect the prestige, efficacy, or necessity of controlling multiple languages.[32] Given the relatively limited study of Akkadian and Aramaic bilingualism in monarchic Judah and the importance of these latter factors to the realities of bilingualism in any specific context, it is difficult to know which, if any, of the results achieved elsewhere with regard to other historical contexts might be relevant to the matter at hand; particularly worth bearing in mind is that the studies of bilingualism in the ancient world are invariably forced to rely on written texts, of which there is a relative dearth for the languages of the southern Levant when compared to, for example, ancient Greek or Latin. However, some observations from work elsewhere may provide useful fodder for consideration in the present context.

Discussing bilingualism in Roman Egypt, Fewster observes a number of interesting elements of the imperial system, starting from the fact that the Romans themselves did not bother with local languages, relying instead on provincial elites and officials to do the translational work for them.[33] This is a type of societal bilingualism in which the vast majority of individuals in a particular society are monolingual, with only a few bilingual individuals responsible for communication between these monolingual groups.[34] Fewster points to tax officials as a key locus

---

[32] For a range of attempts to overcome these difficulties with regard to ancient languages, see the essays in J. N. Adams, M. Janse, and S. Swain, *Bilingualism in Ancient Society* (Oxford: Oxford University Press, 2002). A sociolinguistic approach to modern bilingualism may be found in R. Appel and P. Muysken, *Language Contact and Bilingualism* (London: Edward Arnold, 1987).

[33] P. Fewster, "Bilingualism in Roman Egypt," in *Bilingualism in Ancient Society* (ed. J. N. Adams, M. Janse, and S. Swain; Oxford: Oxford University Press, 2002), 220–45.

[34] See Appel and Muysken, *Language Contact*, 1–2. Note also Janse's observation that the Greeks were similarly disinclined to learn local languages (M. Janse, "Aspects of Bilingualism in the History of the Greek Language," in *Bilingualism in Ancient Society* [ed. J. N. Adams, M. Janse, and S. Swain, Oxford: Oxford University Press, 2002], 334); while transposition of Greek and Roman imperial habits to their predecessors in the southern Levant can be no more than speculative, it does raise the question of whether (or the extent to which) the Assyrians would have troubled to learn local languages. The episode in 2 Kgs 18 implies that one member of the Assyrian entourage, at least, could speak Hebrew; for the suggestion that this is most likely to be a consequence of that individual's personal southern Levantine roots, see Tadmor, "On the Role of Aramaic," 425–26. Intriguingly, note Berlejung's observation that personal names indicate that most (though not all) of the individuals in charge of Assyrian administration in the West were Babylonian (Berlejung, "The Assyrians in the West," 39).

of this translation in Egypt, but argues that the textual witnesses indicate that even these individuals had limited competency in Greek beyond the specific terms and abbreviations necessary to their task: faced with literary or monumental works, these administrators would have been at a loss. Below these administrators, there was probably very little knowledge of the imperial administrative language, with the administrators' own preference for the local language creating little incentive for the wider population to learn Greek.[35] Indeed, the only part of the local Egyptian population that Fewster identifies as likely to have had more than a minimal command of Greek are the elites of the *metropoleis*, the native Greeks and Hellenized Egyptians left over from Greek rule.[36]

If some of these observations regarding the linguistic relationships between imperial rulers and the ruled are applicable to the southern Levantine context under Assyria, we might think of local administrators responsible for the collection and delivery of tribute payments as the most likely to have possessed some rudimentary Akkadian or Aramaic, but we ought not to think of these as possessing anything resembling a full command of either language. The Egyptian elites of the *metropoleis*, exposed to and motivated by the Greek of the *gymnasia*, have no equivalent in the southern Levant; it is difficult to imagine any substantial portion of the population with reason or motivation for learning Akkadian or Aramaic to any level of real oral command, let alone the requisite literary or scribal competence implied by the assumption of widespread recognition of allusions to a substantial written text like VTE or its analogues. The passing reference to linguistic diversity in Ezek 3:5–6 suggests that not even the figure of Ezekiel, who is generally agreed to be of the elite priestly class if not a priest himself— that is, the class whose work in the temple and association with the court might render it the most likely locus of literacy and linguistic skills—is expected to be able to understand or communicate with speakers of other languages (peoples of "unintelligible speech and difficult language," עמקי שפה וכבדי לשון).

In this respect it is also important to recognize that the ability to speak (some) Aramaic will not have been the same thing as the ability to read (some) Aramaic. This, in turn, will have also affected the extent of Deuteronomy's audience's familiarity with this material: those able to read and adapt an Aramaic text will be a smaller group than those able to catch the sense of an oral rendering. In this respect Taylor's discussion of bilingualism in late antique Syria and Mesopotamia is useful: he

---

[35] Fewster, "Bilingualism in Roman Egypt," 230–40.
[36] Ibid., 241–45.

reminds us that the Official or Imperial Aramaic that came into use as an administrative language from the late eighth and early seventh centuries BCE is "a High variety, which completely replaced other Aramaic dialects (the L varieties) as a written form—although they continued to be spoken and occasionally exercised some influence on Official Aramaic."[37] Over time, spoken Aramaic dialects came to vary both from each other and from the official, written form of Aramaic in morphology, phonology, vocabulary, and syntax; Taylor acknowledges that "it is hard for us to assess how mutually intelligible these regional dialects of Aramaic were."[38] This raises the point that, even if there were an Aramaic translation of an Assyrian-Judahite treaty, this was no guarantee that anyone other than someone trained specifically in Official/Imperial Aramaic would be able to understand such a translation. A vernacular, spoken Aramaic—itself unlikely to be widespread—will have been of limited use in dealing with official documentation of this type. Perversely, however, familiarity with a vernacular Aramaic translation, produced for oral performance, will have been hindered by the limited exposure to this material implied by an oral translational context.

The accessibility of an Aramaic translation of an Assyrian-Judahite treaty or loyalty oath to the audience of Deuteronomy is thus caught between a practical rock and a hard place. If the translation were oral, its

---

[37] D. G. K. Taylor, "Bilingualism and Diglossia in Late Antique Syria and Mesopotamia," in *Bilingualism in Ancient Society* (ed. J. N. Adams, M. Janse, and S. Swain; Oxford: Oxford University Press, 2002), 301. The "high" and "l(ow)" terminology he employs refers to the use of either two separate languages within a single society for different social contexts and with differing social status (one "high" status and one "low" status) or the use of two (or more) dialects to similar ends; see J. T. Irvine, "Status and Style in Language," *ARA* 14 (1985): 557–81; K. A. Woolard and B. B. Schieffelin, "Language Ideology," *ARA* 23 [1994]: 55–82 and the extensive literature reviewed there. Taylor recounts an episode from the Babylonian Talmud (Erubin 53b), in which the potential for unintelligibility amongst different dialects is highlighted: "Now, as for that Galilean who said: 'Who has ^{a}mar?' They said to him: 'Galilean fool! (Do you mean) an ass [h^amār] to ride on? Or wine [$hamar$] to drink? Wool ['^{a}mar] for clothing? Or a sheepskin ['$îmar$] for a covering?'" (Taylor, "Bilingualism and Diglossia," 303).

[38] Taylor, "Bilingualism and Diglossia," 302. Also, the extent to which someone "trained" in Official/Imperial Aramaic would be in control of the language beyond the specific context in which he needed to use it is doubtful; see Fewster, "Bilingualism in Roman Egypt," 220–45 and below. Recall also that not even all members of the Assyrian scribal class could work with cuneiform Akkadian, the result of a similar gulf between spoken and written forms of a language.

familiarity would have been limited both by linguistic obstacles as well as the occasional nature of the audience's exposure to it. If an Aramaic translation took written form, however, the number of individuals able to read the text is even smaller than that which might comprehend an oral version.

Only if the Assyrian-Judahite treaty or loyalty oath were rendered into Hebrew might we envision a reasonable audience of individuals able to familiarize themselves with such a text to the degree necessary to recognize allusions to it elsewhere, though if this took the form of an oral translation it would be similarly limited by its occasional repetition.[39]

In any of these scenarios, however, there is an additional and ultimately fatal impediment to the ability of Deuteronomy to draw on a translated source in the process of signaling its relationship to Assyrian ideology. While there is some evidence for the distribution of copies of VTE, at least, to oath-takers, all known copies and references to this text reflect its existence in Akkadian.[40] The case for the existence of a tradition of translating these texts into Aramaic or other local vernaculars relies heavily on the interpretation of the Sefire materials as Aramaic versions

---

[39] It might be suggested that Deuteronomy's use of Hebrew rather than Aramaic or Akkadian should be understood as an implicit "resistance" to language hegemony (see Woolard, "Language Variation," 740–45 and S. Gal, "Diversity and Contestation in Linguistic Ideologies: German Speakers in Hungary," *Language in Society* 22 [1993]: 337, who draws on idem, "Language and Political Economy," *ARA* 18 [1989]: 345–67; Woolard, "Language Variation"; and Bourdieu, "Economics of Linguistic Exchanges"; Sanders has explored this issue with regard to Hebrew specifically in *The Invention of Hebrew* [Traditions; Chicago, Ill.: University of Illinois, 2011]). It remains an inevitable fact, however, that the one language that no historical witness presumes the inhabitants of Judah to be able to speak (let alone read) is Akkadian; while at least a few of the administrators appear to be able to speak—and expect Assyrians to communicate with them in—Aramaic (2 Kgs 18), nowhere is the prospect of Judahites communicating in Akkadian raised. The point here is that the use of Hebrew may be understood as an expression of Israelite identity in Deuteronomy—in keeping with Deuteronomy's peculiar concerns—but it must be acknowledged that this would have derived in no small part from most Judahites' lack of control of any other language (on the complex relationship between language and peoplehood, see Woolard and Schieffelin, "Language Ideology," 60–63 and Gal, "Political Economy," 355–58, with further references).

[40] For discussion of the known copies, see Radner, "Assyrische *ṭuppi adê*"; Lauinger, "Esarhaddon's Succession Treaty"; cf. H. U. Steymans, "Die literarische und historische Bedeutung der Thronfolgevereidigungen Asarhaddons," in *Die deuteronomistischen Geschichtswerke: redaktions- und religionsgeschichtliche Perspektiven zur "Deuteronomismus"-Diskussion in Tora und Vorderen Propheten* (ed. M. Witte, et al.; BZAW 365; Berlin: de Gruyter, 2006), 331–49.

of Akkadian Assyrian treaties. As already noted above, this is a complicated issue. Most significantly, however, even if the Sefire treaties do represent a habit of translating Akkadian treaty and oath texts into Aramaic or other local language, the key translational feature of this material is the accumulation of native treaty and loyalty oath elements and the loss of Assyrian elements in the process.[41] The only evidence for the translation of Akkadian treaty and loyalty oath material thus very clearly indicates that the strategies involved in such a translation were profoundly target-oriented. This has implications for our understanding of the purpose of such translations; to recall Toury,

> the very extent to which features of a source text are retained in a particular translation thereof, or even regarded as requiring retention in the first place (which may at first sign seem to suggest operation in the interest of the *source* culture, if not the source *text* itself), is also determined on the target side, and according to its concerns.[42]

In contrast to the importance of adequacy in translations intended for subversion, the dominating feature of the Sefire (assumed) translations is their conformity to the norms of their target language. Acceptability overrides adequacy: "target norms [are] triggered and set into motion, thus relegating the source text and its unique web of relations based on SL [source language] features to a secondary position as a source of constraints."[43] If the Sefire material is a translation, it represents a process of translation in which the normalization of the target text into the target language and culture was far more important than the retention of the source language and culture of the source text: it does not represent characteristic elements of the Assyrian source material in the new text, but instead draws on the local manifestations of the treaty, loyalty oath, and curse traditions. Recall Toury's discussion of the train signage, mentioned in chapter two:

---

[41] Recall also the localization of god lists even in Akkadian versions of treaties (A. K. Grayson, "Akkadian Treaties of the Seventh Century B.C.," *JCS* 39 [1987]: 133–38, 139–47); this provokes questions about what the curse section of a Judahite-Assyrian treaty or loyalty oath might have looked like. If one wished to speculate, it could be suggested that the primary—or at least a prominent—appeal in such a text might have been to the Judahite god(s?); the use of such a text to subvert Assyrian ideology would have been problematic indeed.

[42] G. Toury, *Descriptive Translation Studies—and Beyond* (rev. ed.; Benjamins Translation Library 100; Amsterdam: John Benjamins, 2012), 6.

[43] Ibid., 79.

the replacement was indeed performed on the level of the textual repertoire: a habitual entity for another habitual entity of the same rank. It is not that no lower-rank coupled pairs could have been established in this case too … it is only that those pairs would be irrelevant for the mode of transition from one text to the other (i.e., the reconstructed translation process): they would have reflected the mere fact that similar (but not identical!) verbal formulations have been selected by members of different societies to indicate similar norms of behaviour under similar circumstances.[44]

If this type of translation even still qualifies as such, it reflects an "individual [who] did not start with a text in one language and then translate it into another, but had some essential information that he wished to communicate in two different languages."[45] The objective of such texts is not for one "translated" text to signal a relationship with the other, "original" text, in light of which its intended function should be interpreted; the two texts are intended to function effectively independently. Even if one—the "source"—is chronological and logically prior to the other—the "target"—this is immaterial to the point of the latter. Symmetry between such texts is not necessary and thus not prioritized.

In these circumstances the ability of a third work, based on the target text, to signal a relationship with the original source text becomes all but impossible: even a signal that exactly quoted the target text "translation" would struggle to signal to the original source text, insofar as the link to the source text (and its language and culture) has been already severed by the intermediary target text. In other words, the evidence that may exist in favor of imagining a Hebrew or Aramaic rendering of an Akkadian source text indicates that a new work, based on the Hebrew or Aramaic "translation," would have struggled to signal to the earlier Akkadian/Assyrian material in any recognizable way, because the mediating text—the Hebrew or Aramaic "translation"—will have already eliminated the distinctively Assyrian features of the original source in favor of the language and imagery of the local tradition. The audience's familiarity with the native tradition used by the translation will have dictated their understanding of the translated work and, in turn, dictated the interpretive possibilities available to any work based on such a translation.

In sum: the little direct evidence that remains from the ancient Near East suggests that an Aramaic or Hebrew rendering of an Assyrian-

---

[44] Ibid., 119.
[45] Taylor, "Bilingualism and Diglossia," 320–24.

Judahite treaty—the only versions which in written form might realistically be thought to have been accessible to even the elites of Jerusalem (and even the Aramaic is questionable on this point)—would have been unlikely to have retained its distinguishably Assyrian features through the process of its translation; rather, it would have employed the curse and loyalty traditions more familiar to its Hebrew-speaking audience in Judah. The "Assyrian" character of any curses rendered in this hypothetical translated document would have had limited Assyrian affinities: alluding to these curses would have been an ineffective means of referencing Assyria as the target of Deuteronomy's project.

CONCLUSIONS

Whichever linguistic scenario is preferred for the creation and transmission of an Assyrian-Judahite treaty text, deliberate subversion of Assyrian ideology as the reason for Deuteronomy's use of such a text is difficult to maintain. Proficiency in Akkadian would have been even less likely than proficiency in Aramaic, being an even more distant relative to Hebrew; its literary command would have also have been further hindered by its deliberately difficult script. To assume that a Hebrew-literate audience would have been capable of recognizing allusions to such a text is highly problematic. If a version of the treaty existed in Aramaic or Hebrew, it is unlikely to have preserved Assyrian features sufficiently for reference to it to have evoked specifically Assyrian ideology in the minds of its audience. These obstacles would have been equally, if not more, acute if this source material was conveyed to its audience orally: even if a non-literate audience had been privy to recitations of an Assyrian-Judahite treaty text, these are unlikely to have been so regular as to warrant an expectation on the part of Deuteronomy's author that this audience would have recognized this material—adapted, no less—elsewhere. If such performances were attended by only the king and a limited entourage, the audience capable of recognizing Deuteronomy's subversive allusions is rapidly shriveling towards non-existence.

In sum, the author of the Deuteronomy material cannot have expected his audience to recognize Deuteronomy's use of treaty and loyalty oath traditions as being specific to an Assyrian form of those traditions. Though recognizable to its audience as part of the treaty, loyalty oath, and curse tradition, as well as the wider context of ideas about loyalty to the sovereign and the consequences of sworn oaths, this audience is extremely unlikely to have (been able to) recognize(d) this material as specifically related to the concepts or text of an Assyrian-Judahite vassal treaty or loyalty oath, not least as any accessible rendering of that text would have lost most of its distinctively Assyrian features in the process. Once stripped of its specific association with Assyria, Deuteronomy loses its subversive power.

6
DEUTERONOMY'S RELATIONSHIP WITH ASSYRIA

Finally, a few observations regarding the wider book of Deuteronomy and its relationship with Assyria are worthwhile.[1] As already

---

[1] One of the more curious effects of the recognition of treaty and loyalty oath elements in Deut 13 and 28 has been the attempt, on the basis of these affinities, to extract these two chapters from the rest of the text. Once begun, these efforts have become entangled in arguments regarding the chapters' relationships with their respective surroundings, especially the relationship of the loyalty concerns in Deut 13 to the centralization agenda in Deut 12 and the redactional history of the blessings and curses, respectively, in Deut 28 (P. E. Dion, "Deuteronomy 13: The Suppression of Alien Religious Propaganda in Israel during the Late Monarchical Era," in *Law and Ideology in Monarchic Israel* [ed. B. Halpern and D. W. Hobson; JSOTSup 124; Sheffield: JSOT, 1991], 147–216; T. Veijola, *Das 5. Buch Mose: Deuteronomium. Kapitel 1,1–16,17* [ATD 8,1; Göttingen, 2004]; E. Otto, "Treueid und Gesetz: Die Ursprünge des Deuteronomiums im Horizont neuassyrischen Vertragsrechts," *ZABR* 2 [1996]: 47–52; idem, *Das Deuteronomium: Politische Theologie und Rechtsreform in Juda und Assyrien* [BZAW 284; Berlin: de Gruyter, 1999], 32–90; J. Pakkala, "Der literar- und religionsgeschichtliche Ort von Deuteronomium 13," in *Die deuteronomistischen Geschichtswerke: redaktions- und religionsgeschichtliche Perspektiven zur "Deuteronomismus"-Diskussion in Tora und Vorderen Propheten* [ed. M. Witte, et al.; BZAW 365; Berlin: de Gruyter, 2006], 125–37; C. Koch, *Vertrag, Treueid und Bund: Studien zur Rezeption des altorientalischen Vertragsrechts im Deuteronomium und zur Ausbildung der Bundestheologie im alten Testament* [BZAW 383; Berlin: de Gruyter, 2008], 106–70). The abandonment of the subversive hypothesis, therefore, has

established, the capacity of a new work to subvert an existing one relies on the author's ability to signal the identity of the source text, supported by sufficient detail about its relationship with that source as to clarify exactly how the new text is using, adapting, and subverting it. Given that Deuteronomy's identification of an Assyrian source as the framework for its own interpretation has been concluded extremely unlikely, at least with regard to the material in Deut 13 and 28, it is worth posing the question of how this relates to our understanding of other parts of the book, and whether there is anywhere else that Deuteronomy signals a relationship or particular concern with Assyria.[2] As with Deut 13 and 28, the necessities of subversion remain the same: in order to function as a subversive document, Deuteronomy will have been obliged to signal its source material to its audience in a way recognizable to that audience.

HIDDEN INTENTIONS

As far as explicit signaling is concerned, indications that Deuteronomy is meant to be read in relation to Assyrian imperial ideology are clearly absent; neither Assyria nor its cities nor its kings are mentioned in Deuteronomy. Nor is there anywhere an explicit mention of Assyrian ideology. With regard to this absence one might naturally hasten to suggest that, given the book's mutinously subversive intentions, this lack of clarity as to the book's target is a consequence of the danger of being explicit about such matters when under the gaze of imperial power. At least two things may be brought to bear on this suggestion. First, in the discussion of the definition of subversion in chapter one we noted that though the subversive intent of a text might be covert, it could only be so relative to the entity being subverted: the audience for the subversive effort must be able to recognize it in order for it to function as a subversive act. In other words, though Deuteronomy's subversive intent might need to be hidden from the Assyrians, it ought to be visible to

---

implications for any redactional argument that presupposes it, insofar as the separation of Deut 13 and 28 solely on the basis of their purportedly subversive content cannot be upheld. Here, however, as in the preceding, the strength of the argument disallows the elimination of potential signals through recourse to redaction.

   [2] The focus of attention in the following is the deuteronomic core, roughly defined as the legal material in Deut 12–26, a pared-down version of its hortatory introduction in Deut 6–11, and its warning conclusion in Deut 28. Most of the rest of the book is either recognized as deuteronomistic or later or as earlier material that has been appended to a deuteronomic core; by virtue of being all but universally agreed to derive from an exilic or post-exilic period, in other words, this material does not naturally impinge on discussions of Deuteronomy's relationship with Assyria.

Deuteronomy's audience. Second, and more concretely, the ability of an anti-imperial text to be quite explicit about its intention is actually witnessed by other biblical texts; here a useful comparison may be made between Deuteronomy's relationship with Assyrian source material and the relationship of Isa 10 to elements of Assyrian royal ideology.[3] The object of the Isaianic intent is explicitly declared to be the Assyrian king; the text's negative view of both him and his (attributed) perception of his place in the order of the universe is equally overt. Of particular interest in light of the preceding considerations of subversive signaling *vis-à-vis* texts and traditions is that in Isa 10 the interaction is not with a specific source text but with Assyrian ideology in a more general form; in light of this, the text has been obliged to be quite overt indeed as to its target. In Isa 10 the writer is critical of imperial power not through vague, easily misunderstood allusions to imprecise or non-distinctive ideas, but through explicit identification of the Assyrian king as its target and by explicitly negative evaluations of that king and his claims. Isaiah 10 thus suggests that the creation of explicitly subversive material was certainly possible.[4]

If, nevertheless, fear of discovery is allowed as an explanation for the absence of the overt identification of Assyria as Deuteronomy's object of interest, the subversive intent of Deuteronomy would need to have been "hidden" or "coded" such that the empire and its enforcers were unable

---

[3] Discussed most notably by P. B. Machinist, "Assyria and Its Image in the First Isaiah," *JAOS* 103 (1983): 719–37; cf. idem, "Final Response: On the Study of the Ancients, Language Writing, and the State," in *Margins of Writing, Origins of Cultures: New Approaches to Writing and Reading in the Ancient Near East* (ed. S. L. Sanders; Chicago, Ill.: Oriental Institute, 2006), 297–98.

[4] As this also suggests, the foregoing should not be taken as a rejection of the possibility or existence of anti-Assyrian (or anti-Babylonian, *et cetera*) material elsewhere in the Hebrew Bible. Where this subversive material is not explicit in its target, however, the principles used here to evaluate Deuteronomy also apply: the subversive text must indicate that which it intends to subvert—the text or tradition in relation to which it should be interpreted—in a way that is recognizable to its audience. In the current context it seems especially relevant to mention Nahum, whose polemic against Assyria is quite blatant; that this polemic uses allusions to Assyrian ideology has been argued by Johnston (G. H. Johnston, "Nahum's Rhetorical Allusions to Neo-Assyrian Treaty Curses," *BSac* 158 [2001]: 415–36). The content he identifies in this respect, however, is neither specific nor distinctive to Assyria; Nahum's subversive intent, in other words, works only because it is explicit in identifying its target (cf. the discussion of explicit announcements of works as adaptations, contrasted with the difficulties of using ideas and concepts as signals, in chapter one).

to recognize it while nevertheless remaining overt and recognizable to its native audience.[5] Given the possibility that Deuteronomy's targeting of Assyria might be thus hidden, we should take care to look for such activities in the deuteronomic text. The pervasiveness of the subversion hypothesis in the scholarly literature means that an exhaustive discussion of claims to have identified elements of Deuteronomy in relation to Assyrian practice is not possible. However, it is worth considering a few passages in particular: the law of the king, the law of centralization, the laws of warfare, and the laws involving foreigners. The text's overall lack of interest in outsiders will be discussed in the next section.

The law of the king in Deut 17:14–20 is universally acknowledged as a far more limited vision of kingship than that actually practiced during the monarchic period: the psalms, the prophets, and the stories about the kings in the narrative books make clear that the kings of both the northern and southern kingdoms were far more active than this law would suggest.[6] These limitations have naturally led to questions regarding the intent of the passage, with a notable propensity to locate

---

[5] On the concept of "hidden" transcripts of subversion, see J. Scott, *Domination and the Arts of Resistance: Hidden Transcripts* (New Haven, Conn.: Yale University Press, 1990); for critiques of Scott's approach, see S. Gal, "Language and the 'Arts of Resistance'," *CA* 10 (1995): 407–24; C. Tilly, "Domination, Resistance, Compliance, Discourse," *Sociological Forum* 6 (1991): 593–602). Unfortunately, the examples Scott compiles are overwhelmingly derived from oral and performative activities rather than from the written sphere, in which anonymity appears to be the primary mode of disguise; the limited literacy in Iron Age Judah, however, would have made the modern anonymity of the written form virtually impossible. The dynamic of power relations that Scott describes is also not especially well suited to the situation of Judah under Assyria (see chapter one). It has recently been suggested that Ezekiel is engaged in this type of covertly subversive polemic (C. A. Strine, *Sworn Enemies: The Divine Oath, the Book of Ezekiel, and the Polemics of Exile* [BZAW 436; Berlin: de Gruyter, 2013]). To succeed, however, Ezekiel must be understood as using specific elements of Babylonian ideology and mythology to signal his intended target to his audience.

[6] Detailed redactional analysis of this and the following passages are beyond the scope of the current discussion. Those interested in such matters may refer to C. L. Crouch, *The Making of Israel: Cultural Diversity in the Southern Levant and the Formation of Ethnic Identity in Deuteronomy* (VTSup 162; Leiden: Brill, 2014). Much of this chapter draws on the research and argumentation of the same volume; a much more extensive analysis of the function of the deuteronomic instructions in the context of the social, political, and economic conditions of the southern Levant and the ancient Near East than is possible here may be found in its pages.

the text in a post- and anti-monarchic context.[7] For the present purposes the interpretations of interest are those that view the limitations placed on the Israelite king—especially the emphasis that he must be an Israelite, not a foreigner—as expressions of anti-Assyrian sentiments. Thus Hamilton has argued that this prohibition constitutes "a refusal to submit to incorporation into the Assyrian provincial system," while Nicholson contended that "its author viewed entry into a client-state relationship with Assyria as effectively 'setting a foreigner' over the nation in the person of 'the Great King', the king of Assyria."[8]

This concern over the possibility of a non-native ruler does make sense in the context of imperial policies during the long seventh century, but the prohibition is not anti-Assyrian. Assyrian imperial policies reflect a progressive process of increasingly centralized control over the course of the empire's relationships with subordinate states: in cases of persistent rebellious activity, semi-autonomous governance by the local ruling house would be followed by the appointment of a local ruler of

---

[7] E. W. Nicholson, "*Traditum* and *traditio*: The Case of Deuteronomy 17:14–20," in *Scriptural Exegesis: The Shapes of Culture and the Religious Imagination: Essays in Honour of Michael Fishbane* (ed. D. A. Green and L. S. Lieber; Oxford: Oxford University Press, 2009), 46–61; cf. idem, *Deuteronomy and the Judaean Diaspora* (Oxford: Oxford University Press, 2014), 101–34; P. R. Davies, "Josiah and the Law Book," in *Good Kings and Bad Kings: The Kingdom of Judah in the Seventh Century B.C.E.* (ed. L. L. Grabbe; LHBOTS 393; London: T&T Clark, 2005), 65–77; J. Pakkala, "The Date of the Oldest Edition of Deuteronomy," *ZAW* 121 (2009): 388–401; M. Nevader, *Yahweh versus David: The Monarchic Debate of Deuteronomy and Ezekiel* (OTM; Oxford: Oxford University Press, 2014); N. Lohfink, "Distribution of the Functions of Power: The Laws Concerning Public Offices in Deuteronomy 16:18–18:22," in *A Song of Power and the Power of Song: Essays on the Book of Deuteronomy* (ed. D. L. Christensen; transl. R. Walls; SBTS 3; Winona Lake, Ind.: Eisenbrauns, 1993), 345–49; R. Achenbach, "Das sogenannte Königsgesetz in Deuteronomium 17,14–20," *ZABR* 15 (2009): 216–33; note also A. C. Hagedorn, *Between Moses and Plato: Individual and Society in Deuteronomy and Ancient Greek Law* (FRLANT 204; Göttingen: Vandenhoeck & Ruprecht, 2004), 140–46, 154–56, who reads these verses against a fifth century background. I have discussed reasons for understanding these verses as part of the deuteronomic negotiation of Israelite identity in the seventh century elsewhere and will not repeat those arguments here (Crouch, *Making of Israel*, 177–84).

[8] M. W. Hamilton, "The Past as Destiny: Historical Visions in Sam'al and Judah under Assyrian Hegemony," *HTR* 91 (1998): 241; for Nicholson this is part of his argument for an exilic dating of the text, in which the poor stature of the king is the highlight of Deuteronomy's "depoliticizing" of Israel (Nicholson, *Deuteronomy and the Judaean Diaspora*, 101–34 and idem, "»Do Not Dare to Set a Foreigner over You«: The King in Deuteronomy and »The Great King«," *ZAW* 118 [2006]: 46–61).

the Assyrians' own choosing and then, ultimately, an imperial governor.[9] Rebellion, in other words, led inexorably towards the loss of local autonomy. With this in mind, the warning against foreign rulers must be understood as a warning *against* rebellious political activities, not as incitement to them.[10] Though Dutcher-Walls focuses primarily on the internal political machinations that might have prompted the stipulations of this law, she has also suggested that it should be understood within the larger imperial framework as "a strategy of acquiescence to the domination of Assyria" rather than as a strategy of rebelliousness.[11]

The centralization of the Yahwistic cult in Deut 12 has also been interpreted as signaling a deliberate break from and contrast with Assyrian practices, especially in connection with interpretations of the "nationalist" reforms of Josiah as anti-Assyrian.[12] With this in mind

---

[9] See N. Na'aman, "Ekron under the Assyrian and Egyptian Empires," *BASOR* 332 (2003): 83 on the installation of new dynasties in Ekron and Gaza and the certain knowledge of the former, at least, in Judah; a similar process probably occurred in eighth-century Israel (M. Van De Mieroop, *A History of the Ancient Near East: ca. 3000–323 BC* [2d ed.; Oxford: Blackwell, 2007], 248–52).

[10] In making his case to the contrary, Hamilton fails to distinguish between provincial status, to which Judah was never converted under the Assyrians, and vassal status and, with regard to the latter, the multiple stages through which a vassal state might progress, depending on its degree of cooperation with Assyria. It cannot be a rejection of submission to Assyria but must be understood as a warning against (further) resistance. (Given the specific texts to which he appeals, one wonders whether he might have a better case for arguing that the parts of Deuteronomy with which his argument is concerned derive from an anti-Babylonian revision.)

[11] P. Dutcher-Walls, "The Circumscription of the King: Deuteronomy 17:16–17 in Its Ancient Social Context," *JBL* 121 (2002): 615.

[12] For a contextualization of this tendency in the relationship of biblical scholars to Assyriological discoveries see L. K. Handy, "Josiah in a New Light: Assyriology Touches the Reforming King," in *Orientalism, Assyriology and the Bible* (ed. S. W. Holloway; HBM 10; Sheffield: Sheffield Phoenix, 2007), 422–30. On the veracity and reliability of the 2 Kings account of this period, see among others, E. Ben Zvi, "Prelude to a Reconstruction of Historical Manassic Judah," *BN* 81 (1996): 31–44; F. Stavrakopoulou, *King Manasseh and Child Sacrifice: Biblical Distortions of Historical Realities* (BZAW 338; Berlin: de Gruyter, 2004); E. A. Knauf, "The Glorious Days of Manasseh," in *Good Kings and Bad Kings: The Kingdom of Judah in the Seventh Century B.C.E.* (ed. L. L. Grabbe; LHBOTS 393; London: T&T Clark, 2005), 164–88. Equally problematic is this reconstruction's characterization of Deuteronomy's interests in nationalist terms; it is only in the deuteronomistic material that the book begins to express a sentiment akin to a nationalist identity, in which control of a fixed geographical territory is an explicit element of the group's identity. For a lengthier

Altmann brings together a variety of chronologically and geographically disparate material to argue that cultic food consumption in Deuteronomy, including Deut 12, is an identity-formation activity formulated specifically as anti-Assyrian polemic, in connection with Assyrian banquet practices.[13] However, Altmann relies on a general ancient Near Eastern tradition of banquets while making claims regarding a specifically anti-Assyrian polemic. Without identifying the use of any more distinctive elements of Assyrian practice such general traditions make a poor signal to Assyrian practice in particular; the overall result is similar to that reached in the interpretation of Deut 13 and 28 in their ancient Near Eastern and Judahite contexts above.

A variant of arguments involving centralization concerns the language used to instruct the centralized cult itself, especially the phrase לשכן שמו, which has been traced to the Akkadian phrase *šuma šakānu*.[14] Morrow discusses this phrase in the context of its Akkadian usage and the usage of the native Hebrew equivalent, לשום שמו, arguing that the adoption of the Akkadian form should be interpreted, in light of post-colonial theories of hybridity, as a subversive neologism.[15] Morrow may, as far as he is willing to take this suggestion, be correct; the phrase certainly has an advantage over דבר סרה in being strange to the Hebrew lexicon, as well as being a much more widely used phrase in Akkadian. However, Morrow is rightly cautious: he notes at least six different meanings for the phrase—one or two of which would suit a subversive appropriation, but most of which would not—and is himself emphatic that the transference of the phrase probably did not involve any extensive knowledge of either Akkadian or its Mesopotamian context.

---

discussion of the appropriate terminology with which to discuss Deuteronomy's identity concerns see Crouch, *The Making of Israel*, 88–93, 107–12.

[13] P. Altmann, *Festive Meals in Ancient Israel: Deuteronomy's Identity Politics in Their Ancient Near Eastern Context* (BZAW 424; Berlin: de Gruyter, 2011). Note also that this, like most attempts to argue that specific elements of Deuteronomy intend to subvert Assyrian ideology, are usually based already on the presupposition that Deut 13 and 28 indicate a subversive deuteronomic project; Altmann works from Otto's *Das Deuteronomium* in particular (though note that there is a certain degree of inconsistency in this, insofar as Otto isolates Deut 13 and 28 from the rest of Deuteronomy whereas Altmann does not).

[14] Recently S. L. Richter, *The Deuteronomistic History and the Name Theology: lešakkēn šemô šām in the Bible and the Ancient Near East* (BZAW 318; Berlin: de Gruyter, 1999).

[15] W. S. Morrow, "'To Set the Name' in the Deuteronomic Centralization Formula: A Case of Cultural Hybridity," *JSS* (2010): 365–83.

While he is therefore right that "Jerusalem scribes could have learned about the equivilance [sic] of Assyrian *šakānu* and Hebrew *śwm/śym* on the basis of relatively little acquaintance with Akkadian," it is the context of the term's usage that renders it potentially subversive: it is only if the writer (and reader, though the importance of this is downplayed) knows that *šakānu* (may) be used in Akkadian as a way of talking about loyalty that its appropriation *vis-à-vis* YHWH may function subversively— otherwise it is little more than a loan word.[16] Recent discussions of the centralization legislation in comparison to Assyrian religious praxis have also raised significant doubts about proposals that contend that Yahwistic centralization ought somehow to be considered a challenge to a "centralized" Assyrian cult; thus Kratz concludes that "the idea of cultic centralization neither fits the rationality of neo-Assyrian politics nor any Judean anti-Assyrian political movement."[17]

---

[16] Ibid., 383.

[17] R. G. Kratz, "The Idea of Cultic Centralization and Its Supposed Ancient Near Eastern Analogies," in *One God—One Cult—One Nation: Archaeological and Biblical Perspectives* (ed. R. G. Kratz and H. Spieckermann in collaboration with B. Corzilius and T. Pilger; BZAW 405; Berlin: de Gruyter, 2010), 129; also H. Schaudig, "Cult Centralization in the Ancient Near East? Conceptions of the Ideal Capital in the Ancient Near East," in *One God—One Cult—One Nation: Archaeological and Biblical Perspectives* (ed. R. G. Kratz and H. Spieckermann in collaboration with B. Corzilius and T. Pilger; BZAW 405; Berlin: de Gruyter, 2010), 147–52; contra K. Schmid, *The Old Testament: A Literary History* (transl. L. M. Maloney; Minneapolis, Minn.: Fortress, 2012), 101 and Otto, *Das Deuteronomium*, 350–51, on the basis of S. M. Maul, "Die altorientalische Hauptstadt—Abbild und Nabel der Welt," in *Die Orientalische Stadt: Kontinuität, Wandel, Bruch* (ed. G. Wilhelm; CDOG 1; Saarbrücken: SDV Saarbrücker, 1997), 109–24. Note also that Maul grounds the connection between god and capital city in the mythology of the divine and human kings who fight against chaos; though well-attested elsewhere in the biblical material, this motif is entirely absent from Deuteronomy. On Assyrian religion in provincial and vassal territories see again A. Berlejung, "The Assyrians in the West: Assyrianization, Colonialism, Indifference, or Development Policy?," in *Congress Volume Helsinki 2010* (ed. M. Nissinen; VTSup 148; Leiden: Brill, 2012), 21–60; idem, "Shared Fates: Gaza and Ekron as Examples for the Assyrian Religious Policy in the West," in *Iconoclasm and Text Destruction in the Ancient Near East and Beyond* (ed. N. N. May; Oriental Institute Seminars 8; Chicago, Ill.: The Oriental Institute of the University of Chicago, 2012), 151–74; A. M. Bagg, "Palestine under Assyrian Rule: A New Look at the Assyrian Imperial Policy in the West," *JAOS* 133 (2013): 119–44; D. R. Miller, "The Shadow of the Overlord: Revisiting the Question of Neo-Assyrian Imposition on the Judaean Cult during the Eighth-Seventh Centuries BCE," in *From Babel to Babylon: Essays on Biblical History and Literature in Honor of Brian Peckham* (ed. J. R. Wood, J. E. Harvey, and M. Leuchter; LHBOTS 455; London: T&T Clark, 2006), 146–68; M. D. Cogan, *Imperialism and Religion: Assyria, Judah and Israel in the Eighth and Seventh Centuries B.C.E.* (SBLMS 19,

Also worth attention is the law concerning the appropriate conduct of siege warfare, which has been interpreted as a reaction to Assyrian siege practices (Deut 20:19–20). Among the more recent of such arguments are those of Wazana and Otto, the latter of whom links the prohibition of the destruction of fruit trees directly to the Assyrian habit.[18] Wright, however, has made the case that the law regarding the preservation of fruit trees in war cannot be construed as a rejection of Assyrian practice.[19] His examination of the witnesses to Assyrian military praxis suggests that the destruction of trees was used along with other "shock and awe" tactics (impalement, desecration of sacred space and property) as punitive measures, rather than as a way of exerting gradual pressure on a besieged town in the midst of the siege itself. Notable in the present context is his conclusion that the formulation of the law is not sufficiently distinctive of Assyrian practice as to indicate an intention to be understood in relation to it:

> If it were intended as a protest against this particular empire, one would expect it to have been formulated in a way that corresponds more closely to the Assyrian methods. In the inscriptions and reliefs, destruction of trees is a punitive measure and, rather than being isolated, is consistently part of a larger program of destruction and despoliation. One would expect these aspects to be integrated into the law if it were formulated specifically against the Assyrians. As it is, the reader has no reason to think specifically of these northern aggressors.[20]

In other words, the ability of this law to be understood by Deuteronomy's audience as anti-Assyrian depends on that audience

---

Missoula, Mont., Scholars Press, 1974); S. W. Holloway, *Aššur is King! Aššur is King!: Religion in the Exercise of Power in the Neo-Assyrian Empire* (CHANE 10, Leiden, Brill, 2001); contra J. W. McKay, *Religion in Judah under the Assyrians, 732–609 B.C.* (SBT 26, London, SCM, 1973) and H. Spieckermann, *Juda unter Assur in der Sargonidenzeit* (FRLANT 129, Göttingen, Vandenhoeck & Ruprecht, 1982).

[18] N. Wazana, "Are the Trees of the Field Human? A Biblical War Law (Deut. 20:19–20) and Assyrian Propaganda," *Treasures on Camels' Humps: Historical and Literary Studies from the Ancient Near East presented to Israel Eph'al* (ed. M. Cogan and D. Kahn; Jerusalem: Magnes, 2008), 275–95; E. Otto, *Krieg und Frieden in der Hebräischen Bibel und im Alten Orient: Aspekt für eine Friedensordnung in der Moderne* (TF 18; Berlin: Kohlhammer, 1999), 99–103.

[19] J. L. Wright, "Warfare and Wanton Destruction: A Reexamination of Deuteronomy 20: 19–20 in Relation to Ancient Siegecraft," *JBL* 127 (2008): 423–58.

[20] Ibid., 444–45.

recognizing in its description something distinctive and specific to Assyrian practice. In its absence, the law does not work as subversion.

INWARD ATTENTIONS

Compounding this picture, in which Deuteronomy has no recognizable interest in Assyrian practice or ideology, is the much more apparent interest of the book on issues confronting an Israel located in the southern Levant and absorbed with challenges largely internal to the community.[21] Though the final form of Deuteronomy has adjusted its outlook to deal with a global audience of non-Israelites, including Mesopotamians, the attention of the deuteronomic text is focused locally on the southern Levant and on the internal workings of the Israelite community, rather than on a global stage involving Mesopotamia and its inhabitants and Israel's relationship with those inhabitants.[22] There are a number of features of the text that reflect this inward focus and, in turn, reiterate the lack of interest in Assyria that has become increasingly apparent in the preceding analysis.

The most obvious sign of Deuteronomy's lack of interest in those from distant lands is the overwhelming attention of both the legislative and the hortatory material on the inner workings of the Israelite community, rather than on the relationship between that community and

---

[21] The nature of the entity to which Deuteronomy refers as "Israel" is complex and not fully agreed. There has been an unfortunate tendency in interpretations focused on the pre-exilic period to conflate the term with the population of Judah, often in connection with the interpretation of the book in nationalist terms. However, the political and territorial disinterest of the core deuteronomic material suggests that the terminology of nationalist identity is inappropriate. "Judah" and "Israel" are not, in this material, coterminous. With this in mind, the question here concerns the relationship between the idea(l) of "Israel" (as presented by the center core of Deuteronomy) and the Assyrian imperial political state (hence the title of this volume); the nature of the relationship between this idea(l)ized Israel and the geo-political state of Judah is another project.

[22] C. L. Crouch, "The Threat to Israel's Identity in Deuteronomy: Mesopotamian or Levantine?," *ZAW* 124 (2012): 541–54; also idem, *The Making of Israel*. There is a significant difference in the relative prominence of the non-Israelites who reside in the land and the non-Israelites who reside outside the land in the deuteronomic and deuteronomistic materials. Non-Israelites are explicitly mentioned in approximately half a dozen cases in the deuteronomic material, in all of which the non-Israelites in question are fellow-inhabitants of the land. By contrast, in the deuteronomistic and other post-deuteronomic material, non-Israelites appear in nearly fifty texts and, in nearly two-thirds of these, the non-Israelites in question are not inhabitants of the land but part of the wider global population.

external political entities. This focus is reflected most obviously in the language that the text uses to discuss the matters to which it attends: it speaks persistently in terms of relationships of Israelite "brothers" (אחים; Deut 13:7; 15:1–11, 12–18; 17:14–17; 18:15; 19:16–19; 20:5–9; 22:1–4; 23:8–9, 20–21; 24:7; 25:1–3, 5–8, 11–12) and of the threats that are "in your midst" or that must be purged "from your midst" (בקרבך, מקרבך; Deut 13:12; 17:2, 7; 19:19, 20; 21:8, 9, 21; 22:24; 24:7). The brother language appeals to the idea of Israel as a large extended family and draws on the affective power of such language in efforts to motivate certain kinds of behavior within the community. That this material is acutely focused on issues "in the midst" of Israel was noted perhaps most prominently by Stulman, using the terminology of "indigenous outsiders" and "bad insiders" to articulate the extent of the text's concern on problems within the community rather than problems presented by genuine outsiders to it.[23]

Reiterating this inward orientation is the limited role of the foreigner, who only appears four times in total: in passages concerning the sale of carrion (Deut 14:21), the remission of debts (Deut 15:2–3), the sort of king who is not allowed (Deut 17:15), and the permission of loans at interest (Deut 23:20–21).[24] The "Israel" with which Deuteronomy is

---

[23] L. Stulman, "Encroachment in Deuteronomy: An Analysis of the Social World of the D Code," *JBL* 109 (1990): 613–32; cf. C. A. Reeder, *The Enemy in the Household: Family Violence in Deuteronomy and Beyond* (Grand Rapids, Mich., Baker, 2012), 1–58. The rationale of this inward focus has been variously interpreted. Stulman, like most others, operates within a paradigm that assumes that pre-exilic Israelite identity phenomena constitute a response to the experience of Assyria; I have argued comprehensively against this assumption in Crouch, *The Making of Israel*. Nicholson has more recently focused on Deuteronomy's inward attentions to argue that the book is "depoliticizing" Israel in response to the destruction of the Judahite state by the Babylonians, but this depends on an unspoken conflation of ethnic and nationalist identities (Nicholson, *Deuteronomy and the Judaean Diaspora*). What Nicholson sees as depoliticization is a reflection of an ethnic, rather than nationalist, articulation of Israelite identity.

[24] It must be allowed that the three cases of economic legislation distinguish between the Israelite and the foreigner in such a way as to favor the Israelite and to do so in a way that was probably not apparent to the foreigner, for whom the laws prescribe what would otherwise constitute ordinary economic activity. These three laws might, therefore, be interpreted as legislating covertly anti-Assyrian practices. The difficulty consists of the identification of the foreigner in question: while the foreigner in the law of the king might be reasonably presumed to be Assyrian by virtue of the remit of the law, there is no similar reason to limit the definition of the foreigner in the economic legislation to Assyrians only. The exceedingly limited role of the foreigner overall also works against the interpretation of these three laws as

concerned, in other words, is not a collection of ardent nationalists, battling for political autonomy against the Assyrian empire, but a community that is in contention with itself over its own ethnic identity.

In sum, the search for a clue that might signal that the book's intended target is Assyrian comes up empty-handed. Deut 13 and 28 are in keeping with the rest of the deuteronomic material when they neglect to exhibit any significant or sustained interest in Assyrian affairs—cultural, political, or otherwise. The far more persistent focus of Deuteronomy's attentions is the local peoples and practices of the southern Levant. If anti-Assyrianism were the purpose of Deuteronomy's agenda, references to recognizably Assyrian ideas, concepts, people, or practices should surface with much greater frequency and clarity than actually occur.

Absent Pretentions

Worth final note is that Deuteronomy's lack of an anti-Assyrian agenda coheres with the general picture of seventh century Judah gleaned from other sources, in which the political reality of Assyrian power was tolerated without notable objection. The Assyrian inscriptions attest to Judah's timely delivery of the appropriate tribute and its involvement in the expeditions against Egypt; only Chronicles pretends that Judah was anything other than a docile vassal state during this period. There is a glaring absence of prophetic literature preserved from this period and a corresponding silence on the subject of Judah's foreign affairs. A text attempting to undermine Assyria not only makes no sense in this context, it goes against the grain of every other witness to Judah's political intentions during this period. The reign of Josiah, representing a period in which Assyrian power was still extant but already beginning to wane, is a frequent focal point for pre-exilic proposals regarding the date of Deuteronomy, yet it too fails to produce a coherent context for such subversion: the anti-Assyrianism purported to be rampant during this period is witnessed more in scholarly constructions than the relevant texts. If Deuteronomy does originate prior to the exile, there is very little of this period which might present a compelling context for subversive intent.

---

subversive; if such is their intent, they represent a remarkably minor theme in the book.

CONCLUSIONS

The preceding has sought to challenge the interpretation of Deuteronomy as intending to subvert Assyrian imperial power and ideology, either as formulated in a specific Assyrian treaty or loyalty oath or as formulated in the Assyrian tradition of treaties and loyalty oaths. It has approached the issue by understanding subversion as a form of adaptation, based on the importance, for the subverting text, of juxtaposing its message against the message of an older work or tradition, so that the differences between the new and the old might become apparent to the new work's audience.

In chapter one the mechanics of this type of relationship were examined in detail. The chapter argued that subversion, as a form of adaptation, requires that a new work signal its relationship with its source in a way that enables its audience to recognize and appreciate its use of the older tradition. This, in turn, is what allows the audience to recognize the points on which the new work diverges from—and, in the case of subversion, alters—the older tradition. Considering the means by which the new work might signal its source, the chapter suggested that this will depend on several factors: the nature of the source itself, its relationship to other possible sources, and authorial intention. The specificity required of a signal will correspond to the specificity with which the new work intends to indicate its source: does the work intend to signal a relationship with a single source text, or does it intend to signal a relationship with a source tradition? Also a factor is the source's relationship to other extant works: if the source is part of a(n even) wider tradition, the signals must be able to distinguish it from this tradition.

179

This led to the observation that the distinctiveness of the material chosen for the signal is an important factor in the signal's success: to indicate its source an adaptation should use material distinctive to it. The most straightforward means of signaling to a single source text is to use specific and distinctive words or phrases from the source, a fact which has been highlighted also in studies of allusion. If a work intends to signal to a tradition, the adaptation must use ideas or combinations of ideas specific to the tradition. It was noted, however, that signaling with ideas or concepts was much more difficult than signaling using words and phrases; to succeed, works that used concepts to signal their source had to rely especially heavily on both the distinctiveness of the concepts in question and on the compilation of several such concepts. Last but not least, then, frequency of shared material was also identified as a factor in a new work's ability to signal to its source. The difficulties of allusion through translation were also discussed, with the requirements of subversion deemed likely to affect translational activities by favoring those that adequately represented the source rather than assimilated to the accepted norms of the target language and culture.

Before moving on to an analysis of the texts, the role of the audience in this process was emphasized. In addition to the new work's technical skills in formulating its signals to its source, these signals must be recognizable to the new work's intended audience. If the audience is unable to recognize the signals for some reason, the new work will not be interpreted in relation to the source material but as a work *de novo*. An important aspect of subversion, therefore, is audience knowledge: in order to be able to recognize references to a source, the audience to whom the subversive signals are directed must know the source. In addition, the relationship of this source to the audience's wider knowledge will affect how the new work is read and will, in turn, affect the specificity of the work's signals if it intends to be read as an adaptation. In sum, the new work must anticipate the scope of its audience's knowledge in choosing its signals.

The discussion then turned to the texts. In chapter two, Deut 13 and 28 were compared to the specific source text of VTE to determine whether the material in the former should be understood as an attempt to signal a relationship with the latter. It made the case that, although some conceptual similarities exist between Deuteronomy and VTE, these similarities are not specific, distinctive, or frequent enough to act as an effective signal. They are, rather, the kind of similarities that arise when members of different societies use similar language to express similar norms in similar circumstances. Deuteronomy, therefore, should not be read as a subversive adaptation of VTE.

Having rejected the possibility that Deuteronomy intended to signal a subversive relationship with VTE, chapter three explored the possibility that it might be signaling a relationship with another Assyrian treaty or loyalty oath text or with Assyrian ideology as manifest in the Assyrian treaty, loyalty oath, and curse tradition more generally. Here some time was spent examining the wider ancient Near Eastern treaty, loyalty oath, and curse traditions of which the Assyrian material forms a part and in the context of which the Deuteronomy material would need to distinguish its specifically Assyrian source. Both the concept of loyalty to the sovereign and the use of curse material to enforce behavior were determined to be common ancient Near Eastern intellectual property; in order to be understood and interpreted in relation to the Assyrian form of this tradition, Deuteronomy would need to use distinctive elements of the Assyrian tradition. Bearing in mind that this form of signaling relies on ideas and concepts, which are not especially effective as signals, particular attention was paid to the distinctiveness and frequency of the proposed similarities between the Deuteronomy material and Assyrian treaties, loyalty oaths, and curses relative to the wider ancient Near Eastern tradition. An examination of the curse tradition represented by Deut 28 and the concept of loyalty to the sovereign used by Deut 13, however, indicated that there was nothing distinctively Assyrian about either of these as presented by Deuteronomy. Rather, they were quite at home in the wider ancient Near Eastern treaty, loyalty oath, and curse traditions. Deuteronomy's use of these common ancient Near Eastern treaty, loyalty oath, and curse traditions in general, however, cannot be used to support an interpretation of the text that requires it to be juxtaposed against the Assyrian traditions in particular. Without a specific connection between Deuteronomy and a recognizably Assyrian rendering of these traditions, Deuteronomy's use of treaty, loyalty oath, and curse material cannot signal an intention to be interpreted in relation to Assyria.

It was allowed, however that the exception to this rule would be if the Assyrian form of the treaty, loyalty oath, and curse traditions is the only form with which Deuteronomy's audience could be expected to have been familiar: if, for this audience, all treaties and loyalty oaths were Assyrian. Chapter four, therefore, undertook to determine whether this would have been the case. Evidence from numerous other biblical texts immediately eliminated the possibility that Deuteronomy's audience would have understood any treaty and loyalty oath material as Assyrian: there was abundant evidence to indicate familiarity with treaties, loyalty oaths, and curses that were not specifically Assyrian.

With this in mind, the chapter went on to evaluate the relationship of the material in Deuteronomy to this wider audience knowledge about treaties, loyalty, and curses. Recalling that in order for the audience to recognize a signal the material used for the signal needs to be distinctive—distinguishable from the audience's ordinary linguistic and conceptual *milieu*—the chapter considered whether Deut 13 and 28 contain distinctive material of this sort, which might have alerted its audience to an intention to be interpreted in relation to some other source. Observing that the overwhelming majority of the language and ideas of Deut 13 and 28 is common to other biblical traditions, the chapter concluded that Deuteronomy's audience would have been unlikely to have perceived any of its contents as a signal to an external source.

The focus on audience knowledge continued in chapter five. Recalling that the audience's ability to recognize a signal to a source depends on the audience's knowledge of that source, it was argued that the social and linguistic realities of Assyrian treaty and loyalty oath texts in Judah render it unlikely that Deuteronomy's audience would have been sufficiently familiar with the contents of any Assyrian source material as to recognize a signal to it. First it was noted that the existence of a copy of an Assyrian-Judahite loyalty oath or treaty in Judah is contested; the number of individuals for whom specific knowledge of the content of such a document would have been necessary is also likely to have been extremely limited.

Contributing to these constraints on the dissemination of the contents of an Assyrian-Judahite treaty or loyalty oath were a number of linguistic issues. All known copies of decisively Assyrian treaties and loyalty oaths are preserved in Akkadian; if a copy of an Assyrian-Judahite loyalty oath or treaty did exist in Judah, therefore, it is most likely that it was in Akkadian, contributing to its symbolic function as a sign of Assyrian power. As the extent of Akkadian bilingualism in Jerusalem is likely to have been very limited, however, familiarity with the specific contents of such a text would have been minimal. Allowing the possibility that a copy of the treaty or loyalty oath might have been made into Aramaic or into Hebrew, it was observed that the primary evidence for such a practice is the interpretation of the Sefire treaties as Aramaic translations of Assyrian treaty documents. The key feature of these texts, however, is that they use treaty, loyalty oath, and curse traditions that differ in significant ways from the manifestation of these traditions in the Akkadian texts; they are therefore most plausibly understood as local manifestations of these traditions. If translation into Aramaic or Hebrew is supposed to have occurred, therefore, the available data suggests that this would have been done according to local norms. An Aramaic or Hebrew version of an Assyrian-Judahite treaty, in other words, is unlikely to have retained the distinctive components of the Assyrian manifestation of the tradition. Even if Deuteronomy quoted this material directly, the material quoted would be Judahite: a poor signal of Assyria as the framework for Deuteronomy's interpretation.

Finally, chapter six made a brief foray into Deuteronomy's overall relationship with Assyria; it concluded that, outside of Deut 13 and 28, there are no distinctively Assyrian elements in the laws that might signal a specific concern with Assyria or Assyrians. Rather, the rest of the core of the book is focused on issues internal to the community and the population of the southern Levant. The fuller implications of this for the interpretation of the book remain to be worked out by future scholarship.

Interpretation in the latter half of the twentieth and the beginning of the twenty-first centuries has exhibited an almost overwhelmingly tendency to see Deuteronomy's similarities to the Assyrian treaties and loyalty oaths as a reflection of the book's subversive intention *vis-à-vis* Judah's Assyrian overlords, especially among scholars who entertain the possibility of the book's pre-exilic origins. It has been proposed, argued, and assumed to varying degrees that the object of the author's use of this tradition was to rewrite and thereby recast an instrument of foreign political domination as a document that declares the real power to be that of YHWH and the true allegiance of Israelites to be to their divine king, rather than an imperial Assyrian ruler. These interpretations, however, have failed to take into account what would be required for Deuteronomy to succeed in such an attempt. Its audience's awareness of treaties, loyalty oaths, and curses, beyond those employed by the Assyrian empire, meant that its inclusion of treaty, loyalty oath, and curse material would not have served to signal an intention to be interpreted in relation to the Assyrian use of such forms; something more specific would have been required. Rendering the effort an even greater challenge would have been the limited familiarity of Deuteronomy's audience with the aspects of the Assyrian tradition that made it distinctive and thereby recognizable amid this wider tradition. Fatally, examination of the contents of Deut 13 and 28 reveals a near total failure to employ material that might be traced to the Assyrians: it contains no more such material than that which might be expected of any Hebrew text. In the absence of the consistent and frequent use of distinctively Assyrian words, phrases, or ideas, which might have succeeded in signaling to Deuteronomy's audience a desire to be interpreted as an adaptation of Assyrian source material, these texts will have been understood and interpreted as a new work: one recognized as using existing native ideas and language to articulate its particular agenda, but an essentially new work. No more, no less.

CITED WORKS

Abu Assaf, A., P. Bordreuil, and A. R. Millard. *La statue de Tell Fekherye et sa bilingue assyro-araméene*. Paris: Editions Recherche sur les civilizations, 1982.

Achenbach, R. "Das sogenannte Königsgesetz in Deuteronomium 17,14–20." *ZABR* 15 (2009): 216–33.

Ackerman, S. "The Personal is Political: Covenantal and Affectionate Love (*'āhēb, 'ahăbâ*) in the Hebrew Bible." *VT* 52 (2002): 437–58.

Adam, K.-P. *Der Königliche Held: Die Entsprechung von kämpfendem Gott und kämpfendem König in Psalm 18*. WUANT 91. Neukirchen-Vluyn: Neukirchner Verlag, 2001.

Adams, J. N. "Bilingualism at Delos." Pages 103–27 in *Bilingualism in Ancient Society*. Edited by J. N. Adams, M. Janse, and S. Swain. Oxford: Oxford University Press, 2002.

Adams, J. N., and S. Swain. "Introduction." Pages 1–20 in *Bilingualism in Ancient Society*. Edited by J. N. Adams, M. Janse, and S. Swain. Oxford: Oxford University Press, 2002.

Adams, J. N., M. Janse, and S. Swain, eds. *Bilingualism in Ancient Society*. Oxford: Oxford University Press, 2002.

Aixelá, J. F. "Culture-specific Items in Translation." Pages 52–78 in *Translation, Power, Subversion*. Edited by R. Álvarez and M. C.-Á. Vidal. Topics in Translation 8. Philadelphia, Pa.: Multilingual Matters, 1996.

Altman, A. "What Kind of Treaty Tradition Do the Sefire Inscriptions Represent?" Pages 26–40 in *Treasures on Camels' Humps: Historical and Literary Studies from the Ancient Near East Presented to Israel Eph'al*. Edited by M. Cogan and D. Kahn. Jerusalem: Magnes, 2008.

Altmann, P. *Festive Meals in Ancient Israel: Deuteronomy's Identity Politics in Their Ancient Near Eastern Context*. BZAW 424. Berlin: de Gruyter, 2011.

Appel, R., and P. Muysken. *Language Contact and Bilingualism.* London: Edward Arnold, 1987.

Arneth, M. „*Sonne der Gerechtigkeit*": *Studien zur Solarisierung der Jahwe-Religion im Lichte von Psalm 72.* BZABR 1. Wiesbaden: Harrassowitz, 2000.

Assmann, J. "When Justice Fails: Jurisdiction and Imprecation in Ancient Egypt and the Near East." *JEA* 78 (1992): 149–62.

Aster, S. Z. "Transmission of Neo-Assyrian Claims to Empire to Judah in the Late Eighth Century B.C.E." *HUCA* 78 (2007): 1–44.

Bagg, A. M. "Palestine under Assyrian Rule: A New Look at the Assyrian Imperial Policy in the West." *JAOS* 133 (2013): 119–44.

Bar-Efrat, S. *Narrative Art in the Bible.* JSOTSup 70. Sheffield: Sheffield Academic, 1997.

Barré, M. L. "The First Pair of Deities in the Sefire I God-List." *JNES* 44 (1985): 205–10.

———. *The God-list in the Treaty between Hannibal and Philip V of Macedonia: A Study in Light of the Ancient Near Eastern Treaty Tradition.* Baltimore, Md.: Johns Hopkins University Press, 1983.

———. "The Meaning of *l' 'šybnw* in Amos 1:3–2:6." *JBL* 105 (1986): 611–31.

Bates, T. R. "Gramsci and the Theory of Hegemony." *JHI* 36 (1975): 351–66.

Beaulieu, P. A. "Official and Vernacular Languages: The Shifting Sands of Imperial and Cultural Identities in First Millennium B.C. Mesopotamia." Pages 187–216 in *Margins of Writing, Origins of Cultures: New Approaches to Writing and Reading in the Ancient Near East.* Edited by S. L. Sanders. Chicago, Ill.: Oriental Institute, 2006.

Beckman, G. *Hittite Diplomatic Texts.* 2d ed. SBLWAW 7. Atlanta, Ga.: Scholars Press, 1999.

Ben-Dov, J. "The Poor's Curse: Exodus XXII 20–26 and Curse Literature in the Ancient World." *VT* 56 (2006): 447–50.

Ben-Porat, Z. "The Poetics of Literary Allusion." *PTL: A Journal for Descriptive Poetics and Theory of Literature* 1 (1976): 105–28.

Ben Zvi, E. "Prelude to a Reconstruction of Historical Manassic Judah." *BN* 81 (1996): 31–44.

Berger, Y. "Ruth and Inner-Biblical Allusion: The Case of 1 Samuel 25." *JBL* 128 (2009): 253–72.

Berlejung, A. "The Assyrians in the West: Assyrianization, Colonialism, Indifference, or Development Policy?" Pages 21–60 in *Congress Volume Helsinki 2010.* Edited by M. Nissinen. VTSup 148. Leiden: Brill, 2012.

———. "Shared Fates: Gaza and Ekron as Examples for the Assyrian Religious Policy in the West." Pages 151–174 in *Iconoclasm and Text Destruction in the Ancient Near East and Beyond.* Edited by N. N. May. Oriental Institute Seminars 8. Chicago, Ill.: The Oriental Institute of the University of Chicago, 2012.

Berman, J. "CTH 133 and the Hittite Provenance of Deuteronomy 13." *JBL* 131 (2011): 25–44.

———. "Historicism and Its Limits: A Response to Bernard M. Levinson and Jeffrey Stackert." *JAJ* 4 (2013): 297–309.

Bienkowski, P., and E. Van der Steen. "Tribes, Trade, and Towns: A New Framework for the Late Iron Age in Southern Jordan and the Negev." *BASOR* 323 (2001): 21–47.

Borger, R. *Beiträge zum Inschriftenwerk Assurbanipals: Die Prismenklassen A, B, C = K, D, E, F, G, H, J und T sowie andere Inschriften, mit einem Beitrag von Andreas Fuchs.* Weisbaden: Harrassowitz, 1996.

Bourdieu, P. *Ce que parler veut dire.* Paris: Fayard, 1982.

———. "The Economics of Linguistic Exchanges." Translated by R. Nice. *SSI* 16 (1977): 645–68.

———. *Outline of a Theory of Practice.* Cambridge Studies in Social Anthropology 16. Translated by R. Nice. Cambridge: Cambridge University Press, 1977.

Boyarin, D. *Sparks of the Logos: Essays in Rabbinic Hermeneutics.* Leiden: Brill, 2003.

Brettler, M. Z. *God Is King: Understanding an Israelite Metaphor.* JSOTSup 76. Sheffield: Sheffield Academic, 1989.

Bridge, E. J. "Loyalty, Dependency and Status with YHWH: The Use of '*bd* in the Psalms." *VT* 59 (2009): 360–78.

Cathcart, K. J. "Treaty-curses and the Book of Nahum." *CBQ* 34 (1973): 179–187.

Cinderella. Directed by C. Geronimi, W. Jackson, and H. Luske. Walt Disney Productions, 1950.

Clines, D. J. A., ed. *The Dictionary of Classical Hebrew.* 9 vols. Sheffield: Sheffield Phoenix, 1993–2014.

Cogan, M. D. *Imperialism and Religion: Assyria, Judah and Israel in the Eighth and Seventh Centuries B.C.E.* SBLMS 19. Missoula, Mont.: Scholars Press, 1974.

———. "Judah under Assyrian Hegemony: A Reexamination of Imperialism and Religion." *JBL* 112 (1993): 403–14.

Crouch, C. L. "Ezekiel's Oracles against the Nations in Light of a Royal Ideology of Warfare." *JBL* 130 (2011): 473–92.

———. "Ištar and the Motif of the Cosmological Warrior: Assurbanipal's Adaptation of *Enuma Elish.*" Pages 129–141 in *"Thus Speaks Ishtar of Arbela": Prophecy in Israel, Assyria, and Egypt in the Neo-Assyrian Period.* Edited by R. P. Gordon and H. M. Barstad. Winona Lake, Ind.: Eisenbrauns, 2013.

———. *The Making of Israel: Cultural Diversity in the Southern Levant and the Formation of Ethnic Identity in Deuteronomy.* VTSup 162. Leiden: Brill, 2014.

———. "The Threat to Israel's Identity in Deuteronomy: Mesopotamian or Levantine?" *ZAW* 124 (2012): 541–54.

———. *War and Ethics in the Ancient Near East: Military Violence in Light of Cosmology and History.* BZAW 407. Berlin: de Gruyter, 2009.

Davies, P. R. "Josiah and the Law Book." Pages 65–77 in *Good Kings and Bad Kings: The Kingdom of Judah in the Seventh Century B.C.E.* Edited by L. L. Grabbe. LHBOTS 393. London, T&T Clark, 2005.

Day, J. *Yahweh and the Gods and Goddesses of Canaan.* JSOTSup 265. Sheffield: Sheffield Academic Press, 2002.

Delcor, M. "Les attaches litteraires, l'origine et la signification de l'expression biblique 'Prendre a temoin le ciel et la terre'." *VT* 16 (1966): 8–25.

Dietrich, M. *The Neo-Babylonian Correspondence of Sargon and Sennacherib.* SAA 17. Helsinki: Helsinki University Press, 2003.

Dietrich, M., O. Loretz, and J. Sanmartín. *Die keilalphabetischen Texte aus Ugarit, Ras Ibn Hani und anderen Orten (Dritte, erweiterte Auflage) / The Cuneiform Alphabetic Texts from Ugarit, Ras Ibn Hani and Other Places (KTU: Third, Enlarged Edition).* Münster: Ugarit-Verlag, 2013.

Dion, P. E. "Deuteronomy 13: The Suppression of Alien Religious Propaganda in Israel during the Late Monarchical Era." Pages 147–216 in *Law and Ideology in Monarchic Israel.* Edited by B. Halpern and D. W. Hobson. JSOTSup 124. Sheffield: JSOT, 1991.

———. Review of A. Lemaire and J.-M. Durand, *Les inscriptions araméennes de Sfiré et l'Assyrie de Shamshi-ilu. JBL* 105 (1986): 510–12.

Donner, H., and W. Röllig, eds. *Kanaanäische und aramäische Inschriften.* Vol. 1. 5th ed. Wiesbaden: Harrassowitz, 2002.

Dutcher-Walls, P. "The Circumscription of the King: Deuteronomy 17:16–17 in Its Ancient Social Context." *JBL* 121 (2002): 601–16.

Eph'al, I. *The Ancient Arabs: Nomads on the Borders of the Fertile Crescent 9th–5th Centuries B.C.* Jerusalem: Magnes, 1982.

Fales, F. M. "Le double bilinguism de la statue de Tell Fekherye." *Syria* 60 (1983): 233–50.

———. "On Pax Assyriaca in the Eighth-Seventh Centuries BCE and Its Implications." Pages 17–35 in *Swords into Plowshares: Isaiah's Vision of Peace in Biblical and Modern International Relations.* Edited by R. Cohen and R. Westbrook. Basingstoke: Palgrave Macmillan, 2008.

Faust, A., and E. Weiss. "Judah, Philistia, and the Mediterranean World: Reconstructing the Economic System of the Seventh Century BCE." *BASOR* 338 (2005): 71–92.

Fewster, P. "Bilingualism in Roman Egypt." Pages 220–45 in *Bilingualism in Ancient Society.* Edited by J. N. Adams, M. Janse, and S. Swain. Oxford: Oxford University Press, 2002.

Finkelstein, I. "The Archaeology of the Days of Manasseh." Pages 169–87 in *Scripture and Other Artifacts: Essays on the Bible and Archaeology in Honor of Philip J. King.* Edited by M. D. Coogan, J. C. Exum, and L. E. Stager. Louisville, Ky.: Westminster John Knox, 1994.

———. "Horvat Qitmīt and the Southern Trade in the Late Iron Age II." *ZDPV* 108 (1992): 156–70.

Finkelstein, I., and N. Na'aman. "The Judahite Shephelah in the Late 8th and Early 7th Centuries BCE." *TA* 31 (2004): 60–79.

Fishbane, M. *Biblical Interpretation in Ancient Israel.* Oxford: Oxford University Press, 1985.

Fitzmyer, J. A. *The Aramaic Inscriptions of Sefire.* Rev. ed. BibOr 19A. Rome: Pontifical Biblical Institute, 1995.

Flynn, S. W. *YHWH is King: The Development of Divine Kingship in Ancient Israel.* VTSup 159. Leiden: Brill, 2013.

Fuchs, A. "Der Turtān Šamšī-ilu und die große Zeit der assyrischen Großen (830–746)." *WO* 38 (2008): 61–145.

Frankena, R. "The Vassal-Treaties of Esarhaddon and the Dating of Deuteronomy." *OTS* 14 (1965): 122–54.

Gal, S. "Diversity and Contestation in Linguistic Ideologies: German Speakers in Hungary." *Language in Society* 22 (1993): 337–59.

———. "Language and the 'Arts of Resistance'." *CA* 10 (1995): 407–24.

———. "Language and Political Economy." *ARA* 18 (1989): 345–67.

Garelli, P. "Importance et rôle des Araméens dans l'administration de l'empire assyrien." Pages 437–47 in *Mesopotamien und seine Nachbarn: Politische und kulturelle Wechselbeziehungen im alten Vorderasien vom 4. bis 1. Jahrtausend v. Chr.* Edited by H. J. Nissen and U. Renger. BBVO 1. Berlin: Reimer, 1982.

Gaster, T. H. *Thespis: Ritual, Myth and Drama in the Ancient Near East.* Garden City, N.Y.: Doubleday, 1961.

Gelb, I. J. Review of D. J. Wiseman, "The Vassal Treaties of Esarhaddon." *BO* 19 (1962): 159–62.

Gerstenberger, E. S. "'World Dominion' in Yahweh Kingship Psalms: Down to the Roots of Globalizing Concepts and Strategies." *HBT* 23 (2001): 192–210.

Ginsberg, H. L. "Reflexes of Sargon in Isaiah after 715 B.C.E." *JAOS* 88 (1968): 47–53.

Grayson, A. K. "Akkadian Treaties of the Seventh Century B.C." *JCS* 39 (1987): 127–60.

Grayson, A. K., and J. Novotny. *The Royal Inscriptions of Sennacherib, King of Assyria (704–681 BC), Part 1.* RINAP 3/1. Winona Lake, Ind.: Eisenbrauns, 2012.

Greenfield, J. C. "Some Aspects of the Treaty Terminology of the Bible." Pages 117–19 in vol. 1 of *Fourth World Congress of Jewish Studies: Papers.* Jerusalem: World Union of Jewish Studies, 1967.

Greenfield, J. C., and A. Shaffer. "Notes on the Akkadian-Aramaic Bilingual Statue from Tell Fekherye." *Iraq* 45 (1983): 109–16.

Gropp, D. M., and T. J. Lewis. "Notes on Some Problems in the Aramaic Text of the Hadd-Yith'i Bilingual." *BASOR* 259 (1985): 45–61.

Hackett, J. A., and J. Huehnergard. "On Breaking Teeth." *HTR* 77 (1984): 259–75.

Hagedorn, A. C. *Between Moses and Plato: Individual and Society in Deuteronomy and Ancient Greek Law.* FRLANT 204. Göttingen: Vandenhoeck & Ruprecht, 2004.

Hallo, W. W., and K. L. Younger, Jr., eds. *Canonical Compositions from the Biblical World.* Vol. 1 of *Context of Scripture.* Leiden: Brill, 1997.

———. *Monumental Inscriptions from the Biblical World.* Vol. 2 of *Context of Scripture.* Leiden: Brill, 2000.

Halpern, B. "Jerusalem and the Lineages in the Seventh Century BCE: Kinship and the Rise of Individual Moral Liability." Pages 11–107 in *Law and Ideology in Monarchic Israel.* Edited by B. Halpern and D. W. Hobson. JSOTSup 124. Sheffield: JSOT, 1991.

Hamilton, M. W. "The Past as Destiny: Historical Visions in Sam'al and Judah under Assyrian Hegemony." *HTR* 91 (1998): 215–50.

Hamori, E. "Echoes of Gilgamesh in the Jacob Story." *JBL* 130 (2011): 625–42.

Handy, L. K. "Josiah in a New Light: Assyriology Touches the Reforming King." Pages 415–35 in *Orientalism, Assyriology and the Bible.* Edited by S. W. Holloway. HBM 10. Sheffield: Sheffield Phoenix, 2007.

Harrison, T. P., and J. F. Osborne. "Building XVI and the Neo-Assyrian Sacred Precinct at Tell Tayinat." *JCS* 64 (2012): 125–43.

Hawkins, J. D. "The Hittite Name of Til-Barsip: Evidence from a New Hieroglyphic Fragment from Tell Ahmar." *Anatolian Studies* 33 (1983): 131–36.

Hays, C. B. *Death in the Iron Age II and in First Isaiah.* FAT 79. Tübingen: Mohr Siebeck, 2011.

Hays, R. B. *Echoes of Scripture in the Letters of Paul.* New Haven, Conn.: Yale University Press, 1989.

Henry V. Directed by K. Branagh. Renaissance Films, 1989.

Henry V. Directed by L. Olivier. Two Cities Films, 1944.

Hillers, D. R. "A Difficult Curse in Aqht (19 [1 Aqht] 3.152–154)." Pages 107–109 in *Biblical and Related Studies Presented to Samuel Iwry.* Edited by A. Kort and S. Morschauser. Winona Lake, Ind.: Eisenbrauns, 1985.

———. *Treaty-Curses and the Old Testament Prophets.* BibOr 16. Rome: Pontifical Biblical Institute, 1964.

Holladay, Jr., J. S. "Assyrian Statecraft and the Prophets of Israel." *HTR* 63 (1970): 29–51.

Holloway, S. W. *Aššur is King! Aššur is King!: Religion in the Exercise of Power in the Neo-Assyrian Empire.* CHANE 10. Leiden: Brill, 2001.

———. "Distaff, Crutch or Chain Gang: The Curse of the House of Joab in 2 Samuel III 29." *VT* 37 (1987): 370–75.

Horowitz, W., T. Oshima, and S. L. Sanders. "A Bibliographical List of Cuneiform Inscriptions from Canaan, Palestine/Philistia, and the Land of Israel." *JAOS* 122 (2002): 753–66.

Huffmon, H. B. "The Treaty Background of Hebrew Yāda'." *BASOR* 181 (1966): 31–37.

Huffmon, H. B., and S. B. Parker. "A Further Note on the Treaty Background of Hebrew Yāda'." *BASOR* 184 (1966): 36–38.

Hutcheon, L. *A Theory of Adaptation.* New York, N.Y.: Routledge, 2006.

Hutton, J. M. "Isaiah 51:9–11 and the Rhetorical Appropriation and Subversion of Hostile Theologies." *JBL* 126 (2007): 271–303.

Ikeda, Y. "Looking from Til Barsip on the Euphrates: Assyria and West in Ninth and Eighth Centuries BCE." Pages 271–311 in *Priests and Officials in the Ancient Near East: Papers of the Second Colloquium on the Ancient Near East— The City and Its Life, Held at the Middle Eastern Culture Center in Japan (Mitaka, Tokyo) March 22–24, 1996.* Edited by K. Watanabe. Heidelberg: Universitätsverlag C. Winter, 1999.

Irvine, J. T. "Status and Style in Language." *ARA* 14 (1985): 557–81.

Janse, M. "Aspects of Bilingualism in the History of the Greek Language." Pages 332–90 in *Bilingualism in Ancient Society.* Edited by J. N. Adams, M. Janse, and S. Swain. Oxford: Oxford University Press, 2002.

Johnston, G. H. "Nahum's Rhetorical Allusions to Neo-Assyrian Treaty Curses." *BSac* 158 (2001): 415–36.

Kim, U. Y. *Identity and Loyalty in the David Story: A Postcolonial Reading.* HBM 22. Sheffield: Sheffield Phoenix, 2008.

Kitchen, K. A., and P. J. N. Lawrence. *Part 1: The Texts.* Vol. 1 of *Treaty, Law and Covenant in the Ancient Near East.* Wiesbaden: Harrassowitz, 2012.

———. *Part 2: Text, Notes and Chromograms.* Vol. 2 of *Treaty, Law and Covenant in the Ancient Near East.* Wiesbaden: Harrassowitz, 2012.

———. *Part 3: Overall Historical Survey.* Vol. 3 of *Treaty, Law and Covenant in the Ancient Near East.* Wiesbaden: Harrassowitz, 2012.

Kitz, A. M. "Curses and Cursing in the Ancient Near East." *Religion Compass* 1 (2007): 615–27.

———. "An Oath, Its Curse and Anointing Ritual." *Journal of the American Oriental Society* 124 (2004): 315–21.

Knauf, E. A. "The Glorious Days of Manasseh." Pages 164–88 in *Good Kings and Bad Kings: The Kingdom of Judah in the Seventh Century B.C.E.* Edited by L. L. Grabbe. LHBOTS 393. London: T&T Clark, 2005.

Koch, C. *Vertrag, Treueid und Bund: Studien zur Rezeption des altorientalischen Vertragsrechts im Deuteronomium und zur Ausbildung der Bundestheologie im alten Testament.* BZAW 383. Berlin: de Gruyter, 2008.

Koehler L., and W. Baumgartner, eds. *The Hebrew and Aramaic Lexicon of the Old Testament.* Translated by M. E. J. Richardson. 5 vols. Leiden: Brill, 1994–2000.

Kratz, R. G. "The Idea of Cultic Centralization and Its Supposed Ancient Near Eastern Analogies." Pages 121–44 in *One God—One Cult—One Nation: Archaeological and Biblical Perspectives.* Edited by R. G. Kratz and H. Spieckermann in collaboration with B. Corzilius and T. Pilger. BZAW 405. Berlin, de Gruyter, 2010.

Langslow, D. R. "Approaching Bilingualism in Corpus Languages." Pages 23–51 in *Bilingualism in Ancient Society.* Edited by J. N. Adams, M. Janse, and S. Swain. Oxford: Oxford University Press, 2002.

Lauinger, J. "Esarhaddon's Succession Treaty at Tell Tayinat: Text and Commentary." *JCS* 64 (2012): 87–123.

———. "Some Preliminary Thoughts on the Tablet Collection in Building XVI from Tell Tayinat." *JCSMS* 6 (2011): 5–14.

Layton, S. C., and D. Pardee. "Literary Sources for the History of Palestine and Syria: Old Aramaic Inscriptions." *BA* 51 (1988): 172–89.

Lears, T. J. J. "The Concept of Cultural Hegemony: Problems and Possibilities." *AHR* 90 (1985): 567–93.

Leichty, E. *The Royal Inscriptions of Esarhaddon, King of Assyria (680–669 BC).* RINAP 4. Winona Lake, Ind.: Eisenbrauns, 2011.

Lemaire, A. "Une inscription araméenne du VIIe siècle avant J.-C. trouvée à Bukân." *Studia Iranica* 27 (1998): 15–30.

Lemaire, A., and J.-M. Durand. *Les inscriptions araméennes de Sefiré et l'Assyrie de Shamshi-ilu.* Hautes études orientales 20. Paris: Librairie Droz, 1984.

Lemche, N. P. "Kings and Clients: On Loyalty between Ruler and the Ruled in Ancient Israel." *Sem* 66 (1994): 119–32.

Leonard, J. "Identifying Inner-Biblical Allusions: Psalm 78 as a Test Case." *JBL* 127 (2008): 241–365.

Lernau, H., and O. Lernau. "Fish Bone Remains." Pages 155–61 in *Excavations in the South of the Temple Mount: The Ophel of Biblical Jerusalem*. Edited by E. Mazar and B. Mazar. Qedem 29. Jerusalem: Institute of Archaeology, Hebrew University of Jerusalem, 1989.

———. "Fish Remains." Pages 131–48 in *Stratigraphical, Environmental, and Other Reports*. Vol. 3 of *Excavations at the City of David 1978–1985 Directed by Yigal Shiloh*. Edited by A. De Groot and D. T. Ariel. Qedem 33. Jerusalem: Hebrew University of Jerusalem, 1992.

Levinson, B. M. "'But You Shall Surely Kill Him!': The Text-Critical and Neo-Assyrian Evidence for MT Deuteronomy 13:10." Pages 37–63 in *Bundesdokument und Gesetz: Studien zum Deuteronomium*. Edited by G. Braulik. HBS 4. Freiburg: Herder, 1995.

———. *Deuteronomy and the Hermeneutics of Legal Innovation*. Oxford: Oxford University Press, 1997.

———. "Esarhaddon's Succession Treaty as the Source for the Canon Formula in Deuteronomy 13:1." *JAOS* 130 (2010): 337–48.

———. "The Neo-Assyrian Origins of the Canon Formula in Deuteronomy 13:1." Pages 25–45 in *Scriptural Exegesis: The Shapes of Culture and the Religious Imagination: Essays in Honour of Michael Fishbane*. Edited by D. A. Green and L. S. Lieber. Oxford: Oxford University Press, 2009.

———. *"The Right Chorale": Studies in Biblical Law and Interpretation*. Winona Lake, Ind.: Eisenbrauns, 2011.

———. "Textual Criticism, Assyriology, and the History of Interpretation: Deuteronomy 13:7a as a Test Case in Method." *JBL* 120 (2001): 211–243.

Levinson, B. M., and J. Stackert. "Between the Covenant Code and Esarhaddon's Succession Treaty: Deuteronomy 13 and the Composition of Deuteronomy." *JAJ* 3 (2012): 123–40.

———. "The Limitations of »Resonance«: A Response to Joshua Berman on Historical and Comparative Method." *JAJ* 4 (2013): 310–33.

Lewis, T. J. "The Identity and Function of El/Baal Berith." *JBL* 115 (1996): 401–23.

Liverani, M. "Distribution of the Functions of Power: The Laws Concerning Public Offices in Deuteronomy 16:18–18:22." Pages 345–49 in *A Song of Power and the Power of Song: Essays on the Book of Deuteronomy*. Edited by D. L. Christensen. Translated by R. Walls. SBTS 3. Winona Lake, Ind.: Eisenbrauns, 1993.

———. "The Medes at Esarhaddon's Court." *JCS* 47 (1995): 57–62.

Livingstone, A. *Court Poetry and Literary Miscellanea*. SAA 3. Helsinki: Helsinki University Press, 1989.

Luuko, M., and G. Van Buylaere. *The Political Correspondence of Esarhaddon*. SAA 16. Helsinki: Helsinki University Press, 2002.

Machinist, P. B. "Assyria and Its Image in the First Isaiah." *JAOS* 103 (1983): 719–37.

―――. "Final Response: On the Study of the Ancients, Language Writing, and the State." Pages 291–300 in *Margins of Writing, Origins of Cultures: New Approaches to Writing and Reading in the Ancient Near East*. Edited by S. L. Sanders. Chicago, Ill.: Oriental Institute, 2006.

Magnetti, D. L. "The Function of the Oath in the Ancient Near Eastern International Treaty." *American Journal of International Law* 72 (1978): 815–29.

Malbran-Labat, F. Review of A. Lemaire and J.-M. Durand, *Les inscriptions araméennes de Sfiré et l'Assyrie de Shamshi-ilu*. RHR 204 (1987): 84–86.

Margalit, B. *The Ugaritic Poem of AQHT*. BZAW 182. Berlin: de Gruyter, 1989.

Marzouk, S. A. "Not a Lion but a Dragon: The Monstrification of Egypt in the Book of Ezekiel." Ph.D. diss. Princeton Theological Seminary, 2012.

Master, D. "Trade and Politics: Ashkelon's Balancing Act in the Seventh Century B.C.E." *BASOR* 330 (2003): 47–64.

Mattila, R. "Šamši-ilū." Page 1226 in *The Prosopography of the Neo-Assyrian Empire, Volume 3, Part II: Š–Z*. Edited by H. D. Baker. Helsinki: Neo-Assyrian Text Corpus Project, 2011.

Maul, S. M. "Die altorientalische Hauptstadt—Abbild und Nabel der Welt." Pages 109-24 in *Die Orientalische Stadt: Kontinuität, Wandel, Bruch*. Edited by G. Wilhelm. Colloquien der Deutschen Orient-Gesellschaft 1. Saarbrücken: SDV Saarbrücker, 1997.

Mayes, A. D. H. *Deuteronomy*. NCB. London: Marshall, Morgan & Scott, 1981.

McCarthy, D. J. *Treaty and Covenant: A Study in Form in the Ancient Oriental Documents and in the Old Testament*. AnBib 21A. Rome: Pontifical Biblical Institute, 1978.

McKay, J. W. *Religion in Judah under the Assyrians, 732–609 B.C.* SBT 26. London: SCM, 1973.

Mienes, H. K. "Molluscs." Pages 122–30 in *Stratigraphical, Environmental, and Other Reports*. Vol. 3 of *Excavations at the City of David 1978–1985 Directed by Yigal Shiloh*. Edited by A. De Groot and D. T. Ariel. Qedem 33. Jerusalem: Hebrew University of Jerusalem, 1992.

Millard, A. R. "Assyrians and Arameans." *Iraq* 45 (1983): 101–108.

Millard, A. R., and P. Bordreuil. "A Statue from Syria with Assyrian and Aramaic Inscriptions." *BA* 45 (1982): 135–41.

Miller, D. R. "The Shadow of the Overlord: Revisiting the Question of Neo-Assyrian Imposition on the Judaean Cult during the Eighth-Seventh Centuries BCE." Pages 146–68 in *From Babel to Babylon: Essays on Biblical History and Literature in Honor of Brian Peckham*. Edited by J. R. Wood, J. E. Harvey, and M. Leuchter. LHBOTS 455. London: T&T Clark, 2006.

Mitchell, T. C. "Judah until the Fall of Jerusalem (*c.* 700–586 B.C.)." Pages 371–409 in *The Cambridge Ancient History III, Part 2: The Assyrian and Babylonian Empires and Other States of the Near East, from the Eighth to the Sixth Centuries B.C.* Edited by J. Boardman. Cambridge: Cambridge University Press, 1991.

Moran, W. L. "The Ancient Near Eastern Background of the Love of God in Deuteronomy." *CBQ* 25 (1963): 77–87.

Morrow, W. S. "Cuneiform Literacy and Deuteronomic Composition." *BO* 62 (2005): 203–14.

———. "Mesopotamian Scribal Techniques and Deuteronomic Composition: Notes on Deuteronomy and the Hermeneutics of Legal Innovation." *ZABR* 6 (2000): 302–13.

———. "The Sefire Treaty Stipulations and the Mesopotamian Treaty Tradition." Pages 83–99 in *The World of the Aramaeans III: Studies in Language and Literature in Honour of Paul-Eugène Dion*. Edited by P. M. M. Daviau, J. W. Wevers, and M. Weigl. JSOTSup 326. Sheffield: Sheffield Academic, 2001.

———. "'To Set the Name' in the Deuteronomic Centralization Formula: A Case of Cultural Hybridity." *JSS* (2010): 365–83.

———. "Tribute from Judah and the Transmission of Assyrian Propaganda." Pages 183–192 in *"My Spirit at Rest in the North Country" (Zechariah 6.8): Collected Communications to the XXth Congress of the International Organization for the Study of the Old Testament, Helsinki 2010*. Edited by H. M. Niemann and M. Augustin. BEATAJ 57. Oxford: Peter Lang, 2011.

Moss, C. R., and J. Stackert. "The Devastation of Darkness: Disability in Exodus 10:21–23, 27, and Intensification in the Plagues." *JR* 92 (2012): 362–72.

Na'aman, N. "An Assyrian Residence at Ramat Raḥel?" *TA* 28 (2001): 260–80.

———. "Ekron under the Assyrian and Egyptian Empires." *BASOR* 332 (2003): 81–91.

———. "Province System and Settlement Pattern in Southern Syria and Palestine in the Neo-Assyrian Period." Pages 103–115 in *Neo-Assyrian Geography*. Edited by M. Liverani. Quaderni di geografia storica 5. Rome: University of Rome, 1995.

Na'aman, N., and Y. Thareani-Sussely. "Dating the Appearance of Imitations of Assyrian Ware in Southern Palestine." *TA* 33 (2006): 61–82.

Na'aman, N., and R. Zadok. "Assyrian Deportations to the Province of Samerina in the Light of Two Cuneiform Tablets from Tel Hadid." *TA* 27 (2000): 159–88.

Nelson, R. D. *Deuteronomy*. OTL. London: Westminster John Knox, 2004.

Nevader, M. *Yahweh versus David: The Monarchic Debate of Deuteronomy and Ezekiel*. OTM. Oxford: Oxford University Press, 2014.

Nicholson, E. W. *Deuteronomy and the Judaean Diaspora*. Oxford: Oxford University Press, 2014.

———. "»Do Not Dare to Set a Foreigner over You«: The King in Deuteronomy and »The Great King«." *ZAW* 118 (2006): 46–61.

———. *God and His People: Covenant and Theology in the Old Testament*. Oxford: Oxford University Press, 2002.

———. "*Traditum* and *traditio*: The Case of Deuteronomy 17:14–20." Pages 46–61 in *Scriptural Exegesis: The Shapes of Culture and the Religious Imagination: Essays in Honour of Michael Fishbane*. Edited by D. A. Green and L. S. Lieber. Oxford: Oxford University Press, 2009.

Nida, E. *Toward a Science of Translating: With Special Reference to Principles and Procedures Involved in Bible Translating*. Leiden: Brill, 1964.

Nielsen, E. *Deuteronomium*. HAT I/6. Tübingen: Mohr Siebeck, 1995.

Noble, P. R. "Esau, Tamar, and Joseph: Criteria for Identifying Inner-Biblical Allusions." *VT* 52 (2002): 219–52.

O'Connell, R. H. "Isaiah XIV 4b–23: Ironic Reversal through Concentric Structure and Mythic Allusion." *VT* 38 (1988): 407–18.

Oded, B. *War, Peace and Empire: Justifications for War in the Assyrian Royal Inscriptions.* Wiesbaden: Ludwig Reichert, 1992.

OED Online. Oxford University Press, 2014. Online: http://www.oed.com/.

Ollenberger, B. C. *Zion the City of the Great King: A Theological Symbol of the Jerusalem Cult.* JSOTSup 41. Sheffield: Sheffield Academic, 1987.

Olyan, S. *Disability in the Hebrew Bible: Interpreting Mental and Physical Differences.* Cambridge: Cambridge University Press, 2008.

Otto, E. *Das Deuteronomium: Politische Theologie und Rechtsreform in Juda und Assyrien.* BZAW 284. Berlin: de Gruyter, 1999.

———. *Krieg und Frieden in der Hebräischen Bibel und im Alten Orient: Aspekt für eine Friedensordnung in der Moderne.* TF 18. Berlin: Kohlhammer, 1999.

———. "Treueid und Gesetz: Die Ursprünge des Deuteronomiums im Horizont neuassyrischen Vertragsrechts." *ZABR* 2 (1996): 1–52.

Pakkala, J. "The Date of the Oldest Edition of Deuteronomy." *ZAW* 121 (2009): 388–401.

———. "The Dating of Deuteronomy: A Response to Nathan MacDonald." *ZAW* 123 (2011): 431–36.

———. "Die Entwicklung der Gotteskonzeptionen in den deuteronomistischen Redaktionen von polytheistischen zu monotheistischen Vorstellungen." Pages 239–48 in *Die deuteronomistischen Geschichtswerke: redaktions- und religionsgeschichtliche Perspektiven zur "Deuteronomismus"-Diskussion in Tora und Vorderen Propheten.* Edited by M. Witte, K. Schmid, D. Prechel, and J. C. Gertz. BZAW 365. Berlin: de Gruyter, 2006.

———. "Der literar- und religionsgeschichtliche Ort von Deuteronomium 13." Pages 125–37 in *Die deuteronomistischen Geschichtswerke: redaktions- und religionsgeschichtliche Perspektiven zur "Deuteronomismus"-Diskussion in Tora und Vorderen Propheten.* Edited by M. Witte, K. Schmid, D. Prechel, and J. C. Gertz. BZAW 365. Berlin: de Gruyter, 2006.

Pardee, D. Review of J. C. L. Gibson, *Textbook of Syrian Semitic Inscriptions, Vol. 2, Aramaic Inscriptions, Including Inscriptions in the Dialect of Zenjirli. JNES* 37 (1978): 195–97.

Parker, B. J. "At the Edge of Empire: Conceptualizing Assyria's Anatolian Frontier ca. 700 BC." *JAA* 21 (2002): 371–95.

Parpola, S. "Assyria's Expansion in the 8th and 7th Centuries and Its Long-Term Repercussions in the West." Pages 99–111 in *Symbiosis, Symbolism, and the Power of the Past: Canaan, Ancient Israel, and Their Neighbors—From the Late Bronze Age through Roman Palaestina.* Edited by W. G. Dever and S. Gitin. Winona Lake, Ind.: Eisenbrauns, 2003.

———. "Neo-Assyrian Treaties from the Royal Archives of Nineveh." *JCS* 39 (1987): 161–89.

Parpola, S., and K. Watanabe. *Neo-Assyrian Treaties and Loyalty Oaths*. SAA 2. Helsinki: Helsinki University Press, 1988.

Podany, A. H. *Brotherhood of Kings: How International Relations Shaped the Ancient Near East*. Oxford: Oxford University Press, 2010.

Postgate, J. N. "The Land of Assur and the Yoke of Assur." *World Archaeology* 23 (1992): 247–63.

Radner, K. "Assyrische *ṭuppi adê* als Vorbild für Deuteronomium 28,20–44?" Pages 351–78 in *Die deuteronomistischen Geschichtswerke: redaktions- und religionsgeschichtliche Perspektiven zur "Deuteronomismus"-Diskussion in Tora und Vorderen Propheten*. Edited by M. Witte, K. Schmid, D. Prechel, and J. C. Gertz. BZAW 365. Berlin: de Gruyter, 2006.

Ramos, M. "Malediction and Oath: The Curses of the Sefire Treaties and Deuteronomy 28." Paper presented at the annual meeting of the Society of Biblical Literature. Baltimore, Md., 23 November 2013.

Reade, J. E. "Ideology and Propaganda in Assyrian Art." Pages 319–28 in *Power and Propaganda: A Symposium on Ancient Empires*. Edited by M. T. Larsen. Mesopotamia. Copenhagen: Akademisk Forlag, 1979.

Reeder, C. A. *The Enemy in the Household: Family Violence in Deuteronomy and Beyond*. Grand Rapids, Mich.: Baker, 2012.

Reich, R., and B. Brandl. "Gezer under Assyrian Rule." *PEQ* 117 (1985): 41–54.

Renfroe, F. "*QR–MYM*'s Comeuppance." *UF* 18 (1986): 455–57.

Richter, S. L. *The Deuteronomistic History and the Name Theology: lᵉšakkēn šᵉmô šām in the Bible and the Ancient Near East*. BZAW 318. Berlin: de Gruyter, 1999.

Rimbach, J. "Bears or Bees? Sefire I A 31 and Daniel 7." *JBL* 97 (1978): 565–66.

Rollston, C. A. *Writing and Literacy in the World of Ancient Israel: Epigraphic Evidence from the Iron Age*. SBLABS 11. Atlanta, Ga.: Society of Biblical Literature, 2010.

Roth, M. T. *Law Collections from Mesopotamia and Asia Minor*. 2d ed. SBLWAW 6. Atlanta, Ga.: Scholars Press, 1997.

———, ed. *The Assyrian Dictionary*. 21 vols. Chicago, Ill.: The Oriental Institute of the University of Chicago, 1956–2010.

Russell, J. M. "Sennacherib's 'Palace without Rival': A Programmatic Study of Texts and Images in a Late Assyrian Palace." Ph.D. diss. University of Pennsylvania, 1985.

Rütersworden, U. "Dtn 13 in neueren Deuteronomiumforschung." Pages 185-203 in *Congress Volume: Basel 2001*. Edited by A. Lemaire. VTSup 92. Leiden: Brill, 2002.

Rüterswörden, U., R. Meyer, and H. Donner, eds. *Wilhelm Gesenius' Hebräisches und aramäisches Handwörterbuch über das Alte Testament*. 7 vols. 18th ed. London: Springer, 1987–2012.

Rutherford, I. "Interference or Translation? Some Patterns in Lycian-Greek Bilingualism." Pages 197–219 in *Bilingualism in Ancient Society*. Edited by J. N. Adams, M. Janse, and S. Swain. Oxford: Oxford University Press, 2002.

Sakenfeld, K. D. *Faithfulness in Action: Loyalty in Biblical Perspective*. OBT 16. Philadelphia, Penn.: Fortress. 1985.

——. "Loyalty and Love: The Language of Human Interconnections in the Hebrew Bible." *MQR* 22 (1983): 190–204.

Sanders, J. *Adaptation and Appropriation*. The New Critical Idiom. Abingdon: Routledge, 2006.

Sanders, S. L. *The Invention of Hebrew*. Traditions. Chicago, Ill.: University of Illinois, 2011.

——. "Placing Scribal Culture in History: Deuteronomy and Late Iron-Age Text Production." Paper presented at the annual meeting of the Society of Biblical Literature. Baltimore, Md., 25 November 2013.

——. *Textual Production and Religious Experience: The Transformation of Scribal Cultures in Judah and Babylon*. TSAJ. Tübingen: Mohr Siebeck, 2015.

Schaudig, H. "Cult Centralization in the Ancient Near East? Conceptions of the Ideal Capital in the Ancient Near East." Pages 145–68 in *One God—One Cult—One Nation: Archaeological and Biblical Perspectives*. Edited by R. G. Kratz and H. Spieckermann in collaboration with B. Corzilius and T. Pilger. BZAW 405. Berlin: de Gruyter, 2010.

Schmid, K. *The Old Testament: A Literary History*. Translated by L. M. Maloney. Minneapolis, Minn.: Fortress, 2012.

Scott, J. *Domination and the Arts of Resistance: Hidden Transcripts*. New Haven, Conn.: Yale University Press, 1990.

Shakespeare, W. *King Henry V*. Edited by T. W. Craik. The Arden Shakespeare (Third Series). London: Arden Shakespeare, 2001.

Sherlock. Directed by M. Gatiss and S. Moffat. Hartswood Films and BBC Wales, 2010–.

Singer-Avitz, L. "Beersheba: A Gateway Community in Southern Arabian Long-Distance Trade in the Eighth Century B.C.E." *TA* 26 (1999): 3–75.

——. "On Pottery in Assyrian Style: A Rejoinder." *TA* 34 (2007): 182–203.

Smith, M. S. *God in Translation: Deities in Cross-Cultural Discourse in the Biblical World*. Grand Rapids, Mich.: Eerdmans, 2010.

——. "The Near Eastern Background of Solar Language for Yahweh." *JBL* 109 (1990): 29–39.

——. "When the Heavens Darkened: Yahweh, El, and the Divine Astral Family in Iron Age II Judah." Pages 265–77 in *Symbiosis, Symbolism, and the Power of the Past: Canaan, Ancient Israel, and Their Neighbors—From the Late Bronze Age through Roman Palaestina*. Edited by W. G. Dever and S. Gitin. Winona Lake, Ind.: Eisenbrauns, 2003.

Smith, M. S., and S. B. Parker. *Ugaritic Narrative Poetry*. SBLWAW 9. Atlanta, Ga.: Scholars Press, 1997.

Smoak, J. D. "Building Houses and Planting Vineyards: The Early Inner-Biblical Discourse on an Ancient Israelite Wartime Curse." *JBL* 127 (2008): 19–35.

Sommer, B. D. "Exegesis, Allusion and Intertextuality in the Hebrew Bible: A Response to Lyle Eslinger." *VT* 46 (1996): 479–89.

——. *A Prophet Reads Scripture: Allusion in Isaiah 40–66*. Contraversions. Stanford, Ca.: Stanford University Press, 1998.

Spieckermann, H. *Juda unter Assur in der Sargonidenzeit.* FRLANT 129. Göttingen: Vandenhoeck & Ruprecht, 1982.

Stackert, J. "Why Does Deuteronomy Legislate Cities of Refuge? Asylum in the Covenant Collection (Exodus 21:12–14) and Deuteronomy (19:1–13)." *JBL* 125 (2006): 23–49.

Stähli, H. P. *Solare Elemente im Jahweglauben des Alten Testaments.* OBO 66. Göttingen: Vandenhoeck & Ruprecht, 1985.

Stavrakopoulou, F. "Gog's Grave and the Use and Abuse of Corpses in Ezekiel 39:11–20." *JBL* 129 (2010): 67–85.

———. *King Manasseh and Child Sacrifice: Biblical Distortions of Historical Realities.* BZAW 338. Berlin: de Gruyter, 2004.

Stefanovic, Z. "Why the Aramaic Script Was Called 'Assyrian' in Hebrew, Greek, and Demotic." *Or* 62 (1993) 80–82.

Steymans, H. U. "Eine assyrische Vorlage für Deuteronomium 28:20–44." Pages 119–41 in *Bundesdokument und Gesetz: Studien zum Deuteronomium.* Edited by G. Braulik. HBS 4. Freiburg: Herder, 1995.

———. *Deuteronomium 28 und die Adê zur Thronfolgeregelung Asarhaddons: Segen und Fluch im Alten Orient und in Israel.* OBO 145. Göttingen: Vandenhoeck & Ruprecht, 1995.

———. "Die literarische und historische Bedeutung der Thronfolgevereidigungen Asarhaddons." Pages 331–349 in *Die deuteronomistischen Geschichtswerke: redaktions- und religionsgeschichtliche Perspektiven zur "Deuteronomismus"-Diskussion in Tora und Vorderen Propheten.* Edited by M. Witte, K. Schmid, D. Prechel, and J. C. Gertz. BZAW 365. Berlin: de Gruyter, 2006.

Strine, C. A. *Sworn Enemies: The Divine Oath, the Book of Ezekiel, and the Polemics of Exile.* BZAW 436. Berlin: de Gruyter, 2013.

Strine, C. A., and C. L. Crouch. "Yahweh's Battle against Chaos in Ezekiel: The Transformation of Judahite Mythology for a New Situation." *JBL* 132 (2013): 883–903.

Stulman, L. "Encroachment in Deuteronomy: An Analysis of the Social World of the D Code." *JBL* 109 (1990): 613–32.

Sweeney, M. A. *Isaiah 1–39: With An Introduction to Prophetic Literature.* FOTL 16. Grand Rapids, Mich.: Eerdmans, 1996.

Tadmor, H. "On the Role of Aramaic in the Assyrian Empire." Pages 419–26 in *Near Eastern Studies Dedicated to H. I. H. Prince Takahito Mikasa on the Occasion of His Seventy-Fifth Birthday.* Bulletin of the Middle Eastern Culture Centre in Japan 5. Edited by M. Mori, H. Ogawa, and M. Yoshikawa. Wiesbaden: Harrassowitz, 1991.

Tadmor, H., and S. Yamada. *The Royal Inscriptions of Tiglath-pileser III (744–727 BC) and Shalmaneser V (726–722 BC).* RINAP 1. Winona Lake, Ind.: Eisenbrauns, 2011.

Taggar-Cohen, A. "Biblical *Covenant* and Hittite *išḫiul* Reexamined." *VT* 61 (2011): 461–88.

———. "Political Loyalty in the Biblical Account of 1 Samuel xx–xxii in the Light of Hittite Texts." *VT* 55 (2005): 251–68.

Tawil, H. "A Curse Concerning Crop-Consuming Insects in the Sefîre Treaty and in Akkadian: A New Interpretation." *BASOR* 225 (1977): 59–62.

Taylor, D. G. K. "Bilingualism and Diglossia in Late Antique Syria and Mesopotamia." Pages 298–331 in *Bilingualism in Ancient Society*. Edited by J. N. Adams, M. Janse, and S. Swain. Oxford: Oxford University Press, 2002.

Taylor, J. G. "A Response to Steve A. Wiggins, 'Yahweh: The God of the Sun?'" *JSOT* 71 (1996): 107–19.

———. *Yahweh and the Sun: Biblical and Archaeological Evidence for Sun Worship in Ancient Israel*. JSOTSup 111. Sheffield: JSOT, 1993.

Thareani-Sussely, Y. "The 'Archaeology of the Days of Manasseh' Reconsidered in the Light of Evidence from the Beersheba Valley." *PEQ* 139 (2007): 69–77.

Thompson, R. J. *Terror of the Radiance: Aššur Covenant to YHWH Covenant*. OBO 258. Göttingen: Vandenhoeck & Ruprecht, 2013.

Tigay, J. H. "Psalm 7:5 and Ancient Near Eastern Treaties." *JBL* 89 (1970): 178–86.

Tilly, C. "Domination, Resistance, Compliance, Discourse." *Sociological Forum* 6 (1991): 593–602.

Toury, G. *Descriptive Translation Studies—and Beyond*. Rev. ed. Benjamins Translation Library 100. Amsterdam: John Benjamins, 2012.

———. "The Nature and Role of Norms in Literary Translation." Pages 51–62 in *In Search of a Theory of Literary Translation*. Tel Aviv: Porter Institute for Poetics and Semiotics, 1980.

Tsevat, M. "The Neo-Assyrian and Neo-Babylonian Vassal Oaths and the Prophet Ezekiel." *JBL* 78 (1959): 199–204.

Van De Mieroop, M. *A History of the Ancient Near East: ca. 3000–323 BC*. 2d ed. Oxford: Blackwell, 2007.

Veijola, T. *Das 5. Buch Mose: Deuteronomium: Kapitel 1,1–16,17*. Das Alte Testament Deutsch 8,1. Göttingen: Vandenhoeck & Ruprecht, 2004.

Von Soden, W. "Das Nordsyrische Ktk/Kiski und der Turtan Šamšī-ilu: Erwängungen zu einem neuen Buch." *Studi epigraphici e linguistici sul Vincino Oriente antico* 2 (1985): 133–41.

Wazana, N. "Are the Trees of the Field Human? A Biblical War Law (Deut. 20:19–20) and Assyrian Propaganda." Pages 275–95 in *Treasures on Camels' Humps: Historical and Literary Studies from the Ancient Near East presented to Israel Eph'al*. Edited by M. Cogan and D. Kahn. Jerusalem: Magnes, 2008.

Weeks, N. *Admonition and Curse: The Ancient Near Eastern Treaty/Covenant Form as a Problem in Inter-Cultural Relationships*. JSOTSup 407. London: T&T Clark, 2004.

Weinfeld, M. "Ancient Near Eastern Patterns in Prophetic Literature." *VT* 27 (1977): 178–95.

———. *Deuteronomy 1–11: A New Translation with Introduction and Commentary*. AB 5. London: Doubleday, 1991.

———. *Deuteronomy and the Deuteronomic School*. Winona Lake, Ind.: Eisenbrauns, 1992.

———. "The Loyalty Oath in the Ancient Near East." *UF* 8 (1976): 379–414.

———. "Traces of Assyrian Treaty Formulae in Deuteronomy." *Bib* 46 (1965): 417–27.

Weiss, E., and M. E. Kislev. "Plant Remains as Indicators of Economic Activity: A Case Study from Iron Age Ashkelon." *JAS* 31 (2004): 1–13.

Wiggins, S. A. "A Rejoinder to J. Glen Taylor." *JSOT* 73 (1997): 109–12.

———. "Yahweh: The God of the Sun?" *JSOT* 71 (1996): 89–106.

William Shakespeare's Romeo + Juliet. Directed by B. Luhrmann. Bazmark Films and Twentieth Century Fox, 1996.

Williamson, H. G. M. "Marginalia in Micah." *VT* 47 (1997): 360–72.

Wiseman, D. J. "The Vassal Treaties of Esarhaddon." *Iraq* 20 (1958): 1–99.

Wittstruck, T. "The Influence of Treaty Curse Imagery on the Beast Imagery of Daniel 7." *JBL* 97 (1978): 100–102.

Woolard, K. A. "Language Variation and Cultural Hegemony: Toward an Integration of Sociolinguistic and Social Theory." *American Ethnologist* 12 (1985): 738–48.

Woolard, K. A., and B. B. Schieffelin. "Language Ideology." *ARA* 23 (1994): 55–82.

Wright, D. P. *Ritual in Narrative: The Dynamics of Feasting, Mourning, and Retaliation Rites in the Ugaritic Tale of Aqhat.* Winona Lake, Ind.: Eisenbrauns, 2001.

Wright, J. L. "Warfare and Wanton Destruction: A Reexamination of Deuteronomy 20: 19–20 in Relation to Ancient Siegecraft." *JBL* 127 (2008): 423–58.

Zehnder, M. P. "Building on Stone? Deuteronomy and Esarhaddon's Loyalty Oaths (Part 1): Some Preliminary Observations." *BBR* 19 (2009): 341–74.

———. "Building on Stone? Deuteronomy and Esarhaddon's Loyalty Oaths (Part 2): Some Additional Observations." *BBR* 19 (2009): 511–35.

Zertal, A. "The Province of Samaria (Assyrian *Samerina*) in the Late Iron Age (Iron Age III)." Pages 377–412 in *Judah and the Judeans in the Neo-Babylonian Period.* Edited by O. Lipschits and J. Blenkinsopp. Winona Lake, Ind.: Eisenbrauns, 2003.

AUTHOR INDEX

BIBLICAL INDEX

ANCIENT TEXTS INDEX

SUBJECT INDEX

CPSIA information can be obtained
at www.ICGtesting.com
Printed in the USA
FFOW03n0919011214
9118FF